The Writings of Frithjof Schuon
Series

World Wisdom
The Library of Perennial Philosophy

The Library of Perennial Philosophy is dedicated to the exposition of the timeless Truth underlying the diverse religions. This Truth, often referred to as the *Sophia Perennis*—or Perennial Wisdom—finds its expression in the revealed Scriptures as well as the writings of the great sages and the artistic creations of the traditional worlds.

Sufism: Veil and Quintessence appears as one of our selections in the Writings of Frithjof Schuon series.

The Writings of Frithjof Schuon

The Writings of Frithjof Schuon form the foundation of our library because he is the preeminent exponent of the Perennial Philosophy. His work illuminates this perspective in both an essential and comprehensive manner like none other.

Books by Frithjof Schuon

The Transcendent Unity of Religions
Spiritual Perspectives and Human Facts
Gnosis: Divine Wisdom
Language of the Self
Stations of Wisdom
Understanding Islam
Light on the Ancient Worlds
In the Tracks of Buddhism
Treasures of Buddhism
Logic and Transcendence
Esoterism as Principle and as Way
Castes and Races
Sufism: Veil and Quintessence
From the Divine to the Human
Christianity/Islam: Essays on Esoteric Ecumenicism
Survey of Metaphysics and Esoterism
In the Face of the Absolute
The Feathered Sun: Plains Indians in Art and Philosophy
To Have a Center
Roots of the Human Condition
Images of Primordial and Mystic Beauty: Paintings by Frithjof Schuon
Echoes of Perennial Wisdom
The Play of Masks
Road to the Heart: Poems
The Transfiguration of Man
The Eye of the Heart
Songs for a Spiritual Traveler: Selected Poems
Form and Substance in the Religions
Adastra & Stella Maris: Poems by Frithjof Schuon
Autumn Leaves & The Ring: Poems by Frithjof Schuon
Songs without Names: Volumes I-VI
Songs without Names: Volumes VII-XII
World Wheel: Volumes I-III
World Wheel: Volumes IV-VII

Edited Writings of Frithjof Schuon

The Essential Writings of Frithjof Schuon, ed. Seyyed Hossein Nasr
The Fullness of God: Frithjof Schuon on Christianity,
ed. James S. Cutsinger
Prayer Fashions Man: Frithjof Schuon on the Spiritual Life,
ed. James S. Cutsinger
Art from the Sacred to the Profane: East and West,
ed. Catherine Schuon

Sufism: Veil and Quintessence

A New Translation with Selected Letters

by

Frithjof Schuon

Includes Other Previously
Unpublished Writings

Edited by James S. Cutsinger

Foreword by Seyyed Hossein Nasr

World Wisdom

Sufism: Veil and Quintessence
A New Translation with Selected Letters
© 2006 World Wisdom, Inc.

Translated by Mark Perry, Jean-Pierre Lafouge,
and James S. Cutsinger

Published in French as
Le Soufisme: voile et quintessence
Dervy-Livres, 1980.

Library of Congress Cataloging-in-Publication Data

Schuon, Frithjof, 1907-1998.
[Soufisme. English]
Sufism : veil and quintessence : a new translation with selected letters / by Frithjof
Schuon ; edited by James S. Cutsinger ; foreword by Seyyed Hossein Nasr.
p. cm.
"Includes other previously unpublished writings."
Includes bibliographical references and index.
ISBN-13: 978-1-933316-28-4 (pbk. : alk. paper)
ISBN-10: 1-933316-28-4 (pbk. : alk. paper) 1. Sufism--Doctrines. I. Cutsinger, James
S., 1953- II. Title.
BP189.3.S3913 2006
297.4--dc22

2006035233

Cover Art: Detail of a Timurid Koran cover, Istanbul, 15th century

Printed on acid-free paper in Canada.

For information address World Wisdom, Inc.
P. O. Box 2682, Bloomington, Indiana 47402-2682

www.worldwisdom.com

CONTENTS

FOREWORD

Before mentioning a few points about the content of this important book, it is of interest to give an account of an incident which deals with its title. The titles of Frithjof Schuon's books are themselves of significance for the understanding of his message and teachings. Many of his books have general titles with a metaphysical or religious connotation of a universal order such as *The Transcendent Unity of Religions*, *Spiritual Perspectives and Human Facts*, *Stations of Wisdom*, and *Esoterism as Principle and as Way*. Others mention a particular tradition or a distinct symbol belonging to an identifiable religion such as *Understanding Islam*, *Treasures of Buddhism*, *Christianity/Islam*, and *The Feathered Sun*. The first work of Schuon belonging to this second category was *Understanding Islam*, his most widely read book. Being aware of the importance that he placed on the titles of his books, we asked him, upon the appearance of the original French version of this work as *Comprendre l'islam*, why the title of the book did not contain the word Sufism, seeing that he lived the life of Sufism every day and that this work was concerned to a large extent with Sufism. He responded that he wanted to deal with Sufism as the esoteric dimension of Islam and not as a separate reality as many in the West have thought. This decision is also to be seen in two collections of his essays in English, in whose publication we were very much involved, writing forewords to both. Following his specific instructions, one came to be entitled *Dimensions of Islam* and the second *Islam and the Perennial Philosophy*, although both of these books deal very much with Sufism, especially the second.

It took over thirty years from the date of the publication of his first book in French for Schuon to use the term Sufism in the title of one of his books, that is, the present work. When we turned to him again and asked why it was that he had now changed his view and decided to use the word Sufism as part of the title of his new book, he said that through all these years he had established the truth that Sufism was the inner dimension of Islam, and now he could deal with Sufism itself and the intricate factors that were involved in the formulation, exposition, and practice within this tradition. Hence the title of this book which itself is drawn from classical Sufi terminology.

In Sufism one speaks often of the shell or husk (*al-qishr*) of religion associated with exoterism and the kernel or marrow (*al-lubb*), which alludes to esoterism. Sufis have also spoken of the veil (*al-hijāb*) which at once veils and reveals the inner essence or meaning of various aspects and dimensions of all reality including, of course, religion. Moreover, in the Sufi tradition many masters have spoken of levels of inner meaning, hence the terms *lubb al-lubāb*, kernel of the kernel, *sirr*, inner secret, *sirr al-asrār*, secret of secrets, etc. Making use of this symbolism in the title of the present work, Schuon penetrates, in this remarkable book, into the various levels of the inner reality within Sufism and the veils that hide the quintessential meaning from more outward dimensions of Sufism which are themselves inward in relation to the most outward forms of the Islamic tradition.

Schuon had an incredible mastery of not only the metaphysical realities of Sufism and its spiritual practices as well as the treasures that can be attained through walking upon the Sufi path, but also of the Sufi tradition as it has manifested itself in Islamic history. Having been exposed to the writings of Guénon, whose knowledge of the historical manifestations of Sufism were almost completely confined to the Arab world, and having received a Shadhili initiation in the Maliki ambience of North Africa in a totally Arab ambience and furthermore being himself knowledgeable in Arabic, Schuon was primarily concerned, in his earlier days, with the manifestations of Sufism in the Arab world and with such authorities as Ibn Arabi.

When we first met him in 1957 in Lausanne, he had little knowledge of the manifestations of Sufism in the Persian world or of Shiite esoterism. But in long conversations that we carried out with him on these subjects, he showed great interest in the manifestations of Sufism in the Persian world. He also wanted to go beyond the limiting of Sufism to Ibn Arabian teachings as had become common among so many of the so-called Guénonians. The discovery of other pearls of Sufism and Islamic esoterism in general was therefore warmly embraced by Schuon. We translated some Persian Sufi poems for him such as the quatrain by Jami that is found in *Understanding Islam.* Henceforth, he began to read much Persian Sufi poetry in translation, especially Rumi, and the fruit of this study is reflected in *Sufism: Veil and Quintessence.*

Schuon was also very much interested in Sayyiduna Ali and his wife Fatimah, who was the daughter of the Prophet of Islam, and through these figures he began to show some interest in Shiism, especially its mystical and esoteric aspects. In the 1960s he said to us that he wanted to write a book on Ali and Fatimah, the second Mary as she is called in Islam, and asked us to send him all pertinent works in European languages on these two figures. Although there are numerous treatises on them in Arabic, Persian, Urdu, and other Islamic languages, the dearth of material on these seminal figures in European languages is truly astonishing considering their religious and spiritual preeminence. We sent him a few works that were worthy of his attention, but he decided against carrying out the project of writing such a book. Instead he wrote a number of essays and paragraphs within essays that reflect this interest. This knowledge of Shiite *gnosis* and esoterism is also reflected, albeit indirectly, in this book.

With the vast knowledge that Schuon had of Sufism on all levels, in this work he has analyzed linguistic characteristics, ethnic and psychological types, confessional attitudes, cultural determinants, and many other factors that in one way or another have acted as a veil vis-à-vis the quintessential truth of Sufism that Schuon has unveiled and summarized in the last two chapters.

This book also includes a chapter that at first seems to have little to do with Sufism, but if studied in depth reveals why he included it in this book. It is entitled "Tracing the Notion of Philosophy". In this seminal essay he departs from the total dismissal of philosophy by Guénon, and explains how traditional philosophy is wed to the metaphysics and *gnosis* that are at the heart of the doctrine of every integral esoteric tradition, including of course Sufism. Schuon told us that several French philosophers, some well known, had turned to the traditional worldview upon reading this essay.

Sufi literature is a vast ocean including not only exposition of doctrine—at the heart of which stands metaphysics and *gnosis*—but also spiritual ethics, a sacred cosmology and anthropology, symbolic narratives, aphorisms, letters of spiritual advice, and some of the greatest mystical poetry the world has ever witnessed. Until the twentieth century the languages of this literature were naturally the Islamic languages, especially Arabic and Persian. During the past century, however, some European languages, especially French and English, have also gradually become first-hand languages for the exposition of the truths of Sufism. This book has a place of honor in this genre of literature. It is not only a book about Sufism, but also a Sufi book.

Moreover, it is a unique work in that it peals away, layer by layer, contingent elements and draws aside the many veils that have, under particular circumstances, conditioned and colored the exposition and practice of Sufism and also hidden its essence to one degree or another, leaving the reader at last with a vision of the naked truth of quintessential Sufism.

We must all be grateful to Professor James Cutsinger for the new edition of this work, which includes his own helpful editorial notes, and to which have been added many valuable unpublished letters and texts, not included in the original edition, and also to World Wisdom for publishing the work and making it available once again.

Seyyed Hossein Nasr
Bethesda, Maryland
July 2006

EDITOR'S PREFACE

We are pleased to present this new edition of Frithjof Schuon's *Sufism: Veil and Quintessence.*

Widely regarded as one of the greatest spiritual writers of the twentieth century, Frithjof Schuon (1907-1998) was an authority on an extraordinary range of religious and philosophical topics, and his books have been praised by scholars and spiritual teachers from many different traditions. He was also the leading representative of the perennialist school of comparative religious thought. Deeply rooted in the *sophia perennis, philosophia perennis,* or *religio perennis*—that is, the perennial wisdom, perennial philosophy, or perennial religion, as he variously called it—Schuon's perspective embodies the timeless and universal principles underlying the doctrines, symbols, sacred art, and spiritual practices of the world's religions.

Sufism: Veil and Quintessence, Schuon's thirteenth major work, was published in Paris in 1980 by Dervy-Livres under the title *Le Soufisme: voile et quintessence;* an English translation by William Stoddart appeared with World Wisdom Books in 1981. The present edition is based on a fully revised translation of the original French.

Among the special features of this new edition is an appendix containing previously unpublished selections from the author's letters and other private writings. Throughout his life Schuon carried on an extensive correspondence, much of it in response to questions posed by the many inquirers and visitors, from a variety of religious backgrounds, who looked to him for advice; over a thousand of his letters have been preserved. He also composed nearly twelve hundred short spiritual texts for close friends and associates, compiled in his later years as "The Book of Keys". These and other private writings often contained the seeds of ideas that were later developed into published articles and chapters, and it is hoped that the selections included here will afford the reader a glimpse into a new and very rich dimension of this perennial philosopher's message.

The breadth of Schuon's erudition can be somewhat daunting, especially for those not accustomed to reading philosophical and religious works. The pages of his books contain numerous allusions to traditional theological doctrines, important philosophers or spiritual authorities, and the sacred Scriptures of the world's religions, but a citation or other reference is not often provided. A series of editor's notes, organized by chapter and tagged to the relevant page numbers, has therefore been added to this new edition. Dates are provided for historical figures together with brief explanations regarding the significance of their teachings for Schuon, and citations are given for his frequent quotations from the Bible, Koran, and other sacred texts. The Authorized Version of the Bible has been used throughout; since the author made his own translations from the Koran, we have chosen to render his French for these passages directly into English, though the Pickthall interpretation of the Arabic has been given a certain preference when Koranic quotations appear in our editorial notes.

It is customary for Schuon to employ a number of technical terms in his writings, drawn from a multitude of traditions and involving several languages, including Arabic, Latin, Greek, and Sanskrit. A glossary has therefore been provided as well; here one will find foreign terms and phrases appearing both in Schuon's text and in our notes, together with translations and definitions. ·

James S. Cutsinger

PREFACE

"Veil" (*hijāb*) and "quintessence" (*lubāb*): two words that indicate an opposition in the symbolic and doctrinal order and refer respectively to the outward and inward or to contingency and necessity. In taking note of a "veil" in Sufism, we do not have in mind the completely general sense that applies to every expression of the transcendent, but a sense that is specific to historical Sufism because of its close connection with a sectarian psychology and an ardent temperament. Nor in this case is the term "esoterism" entirely unambiguous; it must be interpreted at various degrees or from different points of view. In order to give an account of quintessential Sufism that is free from all restrictions, we believe it is necessary to speak first of all about certain veilings, which all too often prevent one from approaching the subject impartially and perceiving its true nature.

When one speaks of a doctrinal "quintessence", this can be either of two things: first, the loftiest and subtlest part of a doctrine, and it is in this sense that Sufis distinguish between the "husk" (*qishr*) and the "marrow" (*lubb*); and second, an integral doctrine considered in view of its fundamental and necessary nature, hence in a way that disregards all outward trappings and superstructure. To give an account of Sufism, it would in fact be possible to limit oneself to dealing with the mystery of the "unicity of the Real" (*wahdat al-Wujūd*) or to providing a "survey" of the characteristic and therefore indispensable elements of the doctrine as a whole; it goes without saying that the two points of view are interdependent in principle, for to seek out the essential in itself, hence in simplicity, prompts one to look for it also in complexity, and conversely. The present book does not separate these two intentions.

Some have thought to serve the reputation of Sufism or safeguard its mystery by declaring that it is not a system like the philosophies, but presents itself on the contrary as a collection of formulations and symbolisms that have freely sprung forth from the Intellect and inspiration. Leaving aside the fact that the one does not preclude the other, we do not see how there could possibly be anything pejorative in the notion of a system: every cosmos, from the order of the stars to the smallest crystal, is a system in the sense that it reflects the homogeneity of the principial order; the universe is woven of necessity and liberty, of mathematical rigor and musical play, of geometry and poetry. It would do an injustice to Sufism to assert that it is in no way capable of systematic formulation or that it is not, like every other integral doctrine, a crystal that captures the divine Light, refracting it in accordance with a language that is at once particular and universal.

Furthermore, doctrinal expressions are not meant to be exhaustive, their function being simply to provide points of reference for a complex truth and for the sake of the Inexpressible. This is what modern critics have never understood, they who reproach the ancient doctrines for being both dogmatic and insufficient, whereas in reality a theoretical expression can only be an "allusive indication" (*ishārah*), the implications of which are limitless; and they are limitless to the very degree the thesis is fundamental. For it is not a question of inventing truth, but of remembering it.

Objectivity is the essence of intelligence, but intelligence is often far from being conformed to its essence. In fact objectivity may be seen as the quasi-moral quality—or condition—of intelligence, which becomes mere cleverness or ingenuity as soon as it is separated from this condition. Ingenuity may be self-interested, serving some thesis or other; but objectivity by definition cannot adopt an arbitrary stance; and it has no need to do so since no secondary paradox can impair the essential truth it takes into account. Man may have his attachments, and his instinct of self-preservation may lead him into error; this is why in many instances to be objective is to die a little: "There is no right superior to that of truth." The present book contains criticisms that at first sight are not at all in the interest of its fundamental thesis, but this thesis has nothing to fear from secondary observations that seem to detract from it, for a spirituality cannot be substantially at the mercy of human imperfections. "If thou wouldst reach the kernel," said Eckhart, "thou must break the shell."

There is a "contingent" Islam just as there is an "absolute" Islam. In order to separate the second from certain debatable elements that pertain only to the human clothing of the Message and not to the Message in itself, we are obliged to give an account of the first as well, especially since esoterism is at stake; but it is obviously "absolute" Islam that matters to us, and it is of this we shall speak, starting with the chapter on quintessential esoterism. The distinction between a dimension that is "absolute" and another that is "relative" is clearly valid for every religion, but it is only Islam we intend to treat in this book. In any event only pure Revelation can be the vehicle of eso-terism *de jure*: "by right" and not only "in fact".

*
*   *

The intrinsic orthodoxy of Islam results from its Message: God (*Allāh*), the Prophet (*Muhammad*), Prayer (*Salāt*), Almsgiving (*Zakāt*), the Fast (*Siyām*), the Pilgrimage (*Hajj*), to which the Holy War (*Jihād*) may be added. God: the Absolute is real; that is, He is Reality (*Haqq*), Neces-sary Being (*al-Wujūd al-Mutlaq*), hence That which cannot not be, whereas things can either be or not be; being unique He excludes all that is not He; being total He includes all that is possible or existent; there is nothing "alongside" Him and nothing "outside" Him. The Prophet: this thesis states the very principle of Revelation, its modes, and its rhythms; if there is a God and if there are men, there must necessarily be Messengers of God as well. Prayer: likewise, if there is a God and if there are men, there is necessarily a dialogue; it is given by this very confrontation. Almsgiving: this principle results from the fact that man is not alone, that he lives in society and must know and feel that "the other" is also "I", whence the necessity for charity at all levels. The Fast: this principle is founded on the necessity of sacrifice; whoever receives must also give, and furthermore the body is not everything any more than is the world; the spirit can ennoble matter, but matter is nonetheless fallen. The Pilgrimage: this is the principle of return to the source, the primordial sanctuary, hence also to the heart. Holy War: this results from the right, and possibly the duty, to defend the Truth; esoterically, or even morally, it becomes the struggle against passional and mental darkness; it is necessary to overcome the innate worship of the world and the ego in order to be integrated into the reign of Peace (*dār al-Salām*).

All these principles, which confer on Islam its undeniable char-acter and universality, are to be found in ourselves; their outward manifestations derive all their meaning—metaphysically and contem-platively—from their archetypes, which are at once transcendent and immanent.

Frithjof Schuon in 1989

Ellipsis and Hyperbolism in Arab Rhetoric

The Arab style favors synthetic and indirect figures of speech: ellipsis, synecdoche, and metonymy are common, as are metaphor, hyperbole, and tautology. The Semite tends to distinguish between an "essence" and a "form" and does not hesitate to sacrifice the homogeneity of the latter for the veracity of the former, so that in Semitic texts of a religious or poetic nature one must always perceive the intention behind the expression and not misconstrue it because of some formal incoherence; and it is not only the spiritual intention that must be discovered, but also the emotion that determines its outpouring and verbal concretization. Thus hyperbole often conveys an emotion provoked by a direct perception of the spiritual reality to be defined; what counts above all, however, is the use of hyperbole to indicate a precise though implicit relationship, a use that gives the proposition all its meaning and by this very fact compensates or abolishes any appearance of absurdity when it is taken literally.

It is true that Arab stylists demand both logical clarity and dialectical effectiveness, the first pertaining to formal rectitude (*fasāhah*) and the second to a rhetoric that is mindful of content (*balāghah*); but this does not at all conflict with the Semitic tendency toward indirect expression, since for the Arabs a thing is clear if in their opinion it is well said; the frequent use of "disguise" (*kināyah*) shows on the contrary that for the Arab it is natural to "embellish" an expression by making it less direct and, from his point of view, all the more rich. Nevertheless, there are as it were two poles in the Arab style, one fully corresponding to what we have just described and the other of a more abstract or logician-like character; these two poles are crystallized respectively in the schools of Kufa and Basra, the first based on scriptural paradigms and thus possessing an illustrative and empirical character and the second inspired by a more principial or theoretical conception of language; this second form of rhetoric predominates in theological, scientific, and philosophical writings, including the strictly doctrinal treatises of the Sufis.

But what concerns us here is the Arabic language in its most spontaneous expression, with its metaphorical and readily hyperbolic style, a style inspired by the *Sunnah* and, consciously or not, by

1

ancient poetry. Since one cannot help taking into account the ethnic or psychological conditioning of a language—apart from its strictly spiritual foundation—we should not pass over in silence the noble impulsiveness, and the resulting superficial rashness, characteristic of the Arabs of old, who would draw the sword "for a yea or a nay"; this is so true that the Koran had to state specifically that God does not hold believers responsible for their unconsidered oaths. At the level of language, the vice of an impulsive hyperbolism—especially in spiritual contexts—would be seriously disconcerting if allowance were not made for an explosive temperament, noble in its very sincerity.

We have already mentioned the frequently indirect character of Arab rhetoric, and it would be fitting for us to dwell on this a little longer. The Gospel injunction not to cast pearls before swine nor to give what is holy unto dogs, apart from its obvious and universal significance, indicates at the same time—and as if by accident—a specifically Semitic trait: direct and naked truth is at once too precious and too dangerous, it intoxicates and kills, and it runs the risk of being profaned and inciting revolt; it is like wine, which must be sealed and which in fact Islam prohibits, or like woman, who must be covered and whom in fact Islam veils. The spiritual style of the Semites is often full of reservations and indirect figures of speech; it is like a subtle play of veilings and unveilings; the inspired word is an inviolable bride, and the aspirant must be worthy of her even at the level of mere language.[1] Esoteric precaution has thus affected all Arab rhetoric and has established a kind of modesty or discretion on the plane of verbal manifestation as well as a particular aesthetic: in other words there is also present an element of play or art, of musical calligraphy, if one prefers. Language appears to the Arab almost as an end in itself, an autonomous substance, which pre-exists in relation to its contents; like universal Existence, which is its prototype, language encloses us ontologically in the truth whether we wish it or not: before all words

---

[1] This mentality, or this principle, evokes the initiatic symbolism of Perseus and Andromeda, hence also the victory over Medusa. The symbolism of the truth-bride is also found in the Song of Songs and again, from an iconographic point of view, in the "black Virgins": "I am black, but beautiful," says the Shulamite as well. Blackness is the secret, supra-formal character of *gnosis*, although in certain cases—applied for example to the city of Jerusalem—it may have the negative meaning of distress.

its all-embracing meaning is "Be!" (*Kun*); it is divine in its essence. "In the beginning was the Word."

Veiling and bursting forth are as it were the two complementary poles of the Arab mentality in particular and the Muslim mentality in general. The Muslim spirit is rooted in certitude of the Absolute and oriented toward this certitude and its object; but this awareness of the highest and most uncompromising Truth has as its human complement an emotionalism that is all the more fulgurating, though it is compensated for by a profound generosity; and here we have in mind not so much the Bedouin temperament in itself as its development by way of Islam; what this means is that the two opposite and complementary characteristics just mentioned pertain to the genius of Islam as well as pertaining—even more profoundly—to the positive mentality of the Arab race. The ternary "Truth-Victory-Generosity" describes the very soul of the Prophet, in which the genius of Islam and the Arab race are combined: consciousness of the Absolute has as its dynamic repercussion the holy war, for the Absolute excludes all that is not it, being in this respect like a devouring fire; but at the same time the Absolute is the Infinite, which is maternal and encompasses everything, and in this respect consciousness of the One engenders appeasing and charitable attitudes, such as almsgiving and forgiveness.

*

*   *

Arab hyperbole, as we have said, has the function of indirectly throwing into relief a particular relationship, one which is not expressed but which must be perceived by means of the apparent absurdity of the image. For example, a *hadīth* relates that a woman entered Paradise in advance of the elect for the simple reason that she had brought up her children well; this means that the fact of having brought up her children with perfect abnegation and with the best possible result manifests the sanctity of the mother. As for being in advance of the elect—a seemingly contradictory image—this is a metaphor; spatial advance represents here an advantage of easiness, not of distance or movement, which means that there are simple souls who enter Paradise relatively easily or in other words without having to undergo the great trials of the heroes of spirituality. Needless to say the *hadīth* makes no allusion to the degrees of Paradise; it has no other intention than to emphasize the ease attributed to humble but steadfast qualities, which presuppose moreover a completely religious environment. Its teaching is as follows: the believer who fulfills to perfection the duties corresponding to his state of life without concerning himself with anything else except religion and these duties, however humble they may be, will go to Paradise if he perseveres to the end; but this does not amount to an "easy way out", for each person has his own nature, vocation, duty, and destiny.[2]

In a similar manner, when the Prophet said that "those who receive the severest punishment on the Day of Resurrection will be those who imitate what God has created" or "who make representations of (living) things", and that God will then order them to give life to the images, which they will be incapable of doing, the fact of fashioning images implies the intention of equaling the Creator, hence of denying His uniqueness and transcendence; if the punishment is the severest possible—though in this case the severity seems exaggerated and even absurd—this is because the plastic arts are identified in the psychology of the nomadic and monotheistic Semites with a kind of luciferianism or idolatry, hence with the greatest of sins or sin as such.

When certain *ahādīth* tell us of a woman who was damned because she allowed her cat to die of hunger or of a prostitute who was saved because she gave a drink of water to a dog, the meaning is that man is saved or damned by virtue of his essence even if it is veiled by characteristics which are opposed to it, but which are peripheral and therefore accidental. Here the act is not the efficient cause, but the sign of a fundamental cause that resides in the very nature of the individual; the act is the criterion-manifestation of a fundamental and decisive quality, so much so that there is no reason to be surprised if an apparently trifling act should have an effect that is quasi-absolute or incommensurate with its cause.

An example of hyperbolism that simultaneously veils and unveils a hidden relationship—a relationship outside of which the state-

---

[2] This is one of the meanings of this verse, which appears several times in the Koran: "No soul shall bear the burden of another."

ment remains unintelligible—is provided by this saying of Junayd: "A moment of forgetfulness of the Lord ruins a thousand years of service (to God)." Here again forgetfulness of God is identified with sin as such, and it is precisely the nearly insane exaggeration of the image that proves it. Here virtue or merit—the only virtue or the only merit—is remembrance of God; Junayd in other words wishes to emphasize that this remembrance is the quintessence of every virtue and by this fact constitutes the entire reason for the human state. The same remark can be applied to this other saying of the same saint: "A thousand years of obedience cannot annul a moment of disobedience toward God,"[3] with the sole difference that here it is obedience that is identified with virtue as such; and the same remark also applies *mutatis mutandis* to the following passage from Samarqandi: "Even if a man has performed the prayer of the inhabitants of Heaven and earth . . . if I (*Allāh*) were to find that in his heart there still remains an atom of love for the world, whether a desire to please the eyes or ears of someone else or a worldly ambition . . . I would uproot his love for Me from his heart . . . until he forgot Me."[4] Here again the exaggeration serves to indicate a particular relationship that gives the whole meaning to the saying, namely, that hypocrisy, like the Christian notion of pride, sums up every possible vice of the spirit; being the very quality of evil, no quantity of good can annul it.[5] It is true that its opposite, sincerity, the

[3] "I am a slave and have no liberty; I shall go wherever God orders me to go, whether to Paradise or to hell." This saying of Junayd shows that he looks on obedience as the most perfect conformity to the Will—or Nature—of God or that he considers perfection under the aspect of obedience; but here again a spiritual sublimity entails a logical or rhetorical defect, for apart from the fact that the Koran does not ordain that any believer should go to hell, a pious man who thinks like Junayd obviously cannot be damned since he is obedient to God.

[4] Quite apart from the literal meaning, one might wonder whether it is permissible or opportune to express oneself as if God were speaking.

[5] Let us note that the reference to the "heart" indicates that what is in question is the essence of the individual, although the idea of "atom" weakens this meaning; here there are two "absolutizations" that contradict each other within the surge of spiritual emotion, which all told mixes together two different propositions. What is only an "atom" cannot be situated in the "heart"; what is situated in our essence cannot be reduced to an infinitesimal quantity, morally or spiritually speaking.

fundamental quality of goodness, can similarly conquer every quantitative evil; but the presence of sincerity excludes hypocrisy precisely, and thus this remedy is not accessible to the hypocrite. Taken literally all these sayings are contrary to Koranic doctrine, according to which divine punishment is proportionate to human transgression, whereas divine reward immensely surpasses our merit; the legitimacy of these sayings—in any case quite relative—therefore resides in their intention alone, namely, in the emphasis they place on the "sin against the Holy Spirit", whatever may be the angle of vision; this emphasis is clearly their entire excuse and reason for being, but it cannot be a total justification. In taking account of the spirituality of a Junayd and a Samarqandi, we may perhaps deduce from their verbal excesses what their "station" (*maqām*) was: a reduction of all temporal awareness to an instant of eternity made of pure adequation to the Real, hence free from all "association" (of other realities with God: *shirk*), from every "covering" (or "stifling" of the Truth: *kufr*), from every hypocrisy (*nifāq*): this is practically the meaning of the expression "son of the present moment" (*ibn al-waqt*), which is applied to the Sufis.

Be that as it may, if the sayings quoted and others of the same kind can be justified by their intentions, or rather can justify their authors, they remain subject to caution in other respects, first of all with regard to intelligibility—a spiritual saying has the right to be unintelligible on condition that it is not absurd—and then with regard to the esoteric perspective, which cannot coincide purely and simply with an ascetical-mystical perspective. We shall return to this question, which is of capital importance, in the next chapter.[6]

*

*   *

The effort to depict the plenitude and limitlessness of Paradise has given rise to quantitative metaphors, which can be accepted without question only if one is either naive or on the contrary particularly

---

[6] One will no doubt encounter inevitable repetitions and perhaps also apparent contradictions in the present book, the latter owing to our twofold obligation to criticize and to justify in a domain where the line of demarcation between the permissible and the abusive is unclear.

perspicacious, or else simply resigned to the feebleness of human understanding and earthly language. The first key to this symbolism is that quantity assumes therein a qualitative role, and the very excessiveness of the image invites us to go to the root of things; but side by side with the quantitative images there are other hyperboles as well, whose intention may be divined by examining the nature of things. For example: according to tradition, the houris wear seventy dresses, but at the same time they are transparent and one can see the marrow flowing in their bones—"like liquid and luminous honey," we are told; the dresses symbolize the beauties of veiling, hence the formal or "liturgical" aspects of beauty, whereas the marrow represents the uncreated essence, which is none other than an aspect of the divine Substance or a kind of emanation from a beatific divine Quality. What this means is that God makes Himself perceptible through everything in Paradise; but the connection between the relativity of the created and the absoluteness of the Essence requires an indefinite play of veiling and unveiling, of formal coagulation and compensatory transparency.

When one reads that in Paradise the least of the blessed enjoys such and such marvels or delights, that he has so many wives, servants, and so on, one may wonder what those who would appreciate or bear so oppressive a luxury are doing in Paradise; now as a matter of principle Islam always includes at its base the most earthly of possibilities—this is a "card in its hand" that it never neglects—and thus it places itself at the standpoint not so much of coarseness as of mercy, even at the risk of appearing "earthy" or trivial; it requires *a priori* neither detachment from the world nor refinement of taste, but only faith in God and the putting into practice of divine Laws, a practice implying in any case the fundamental virtues; and it is faith and practice that will transmute the soul of the believer, detach him from the world, and refine his tastes. On the one hand Islam means to capture the most naive and unpolished of mentalities; but on the other hand it also takes into account—in the *ahādīth*—the most diverse mentalities, so much so that there are sayings addressed to a given character and not another.

What we have said about the paradisiacal hyperboles applies as well, in an inverse sense, to infernal imagery; the historical experience of both East and West superabundantly proves that a great deal is necessary to dissuade the sinner from sinning; it is true that the most terrible descriptions of hell may remain ineffective for the most hardened criminals, but when these descriptions are effective they too are a part of mercy since they prevent some souls from becoming lost. But in the eschatological metaphors it is not a question solely of baits and bugbears: the delights and torments are respectively the cosmic equivalents of virtues and vices, merits and demerits, and they disclose their true nature in light of the divine standard. It is true that this consideration removes us somewhat from questions of rhetoric, but it is necessary here, and it seems useful to us at this point to make the following remark: paradisiacal or infernal images are always symbolic paraphrases of realities indescribable in sensory terms, whence their excessive character; it would therefore be futile to complain—solely from this point of view—about all that is humanly unimaginable or unintelligible, even absurd, in the images of Paradise, for example. The fact that earthly man, enclosed in the prison of his five senses, cannot imagine anything other than what they offer him does not at all mean that he would not be infinitely happier outside this happy prison and within vaster and more profound perceptions.

Furthermore, to speak as if Paradise adapted itself to the believer's every mood is a way of saying that the believer adapts himself perfectly to the possibilities of Paradise; to use excessive language is thus to say in earthly terms that the blessed possess not just five senses, but innumerable senses opening onto Felicity, analogically and metaphorically speaking; it means at the same time that the blessed are by nature profoundly satisfied with all that the paradisiacal state offers them. When the Prophet promises a Bedouin who loves horses a winged horse in Paradise, this does not mean that the paradisiacal possibilities will fulfill all possible desires, but that they will realize every possibility of happiness for the believing man; the adjective "believing" is essential, for true faith excludes precisely—and *a fortiori* before God—a desire for just anything. Without faith, no Paradise; with faith, no senseless or harmful desires; and let us recall that every pleasure we can describe as "normal" is a kind of reverberation and therefore an anticipation—quite imperfect, no doubt—of a celestial joy, as the Koran declares: "Each time a fruit (of Paradise) is offered to them, they will say: This is what was offered us aforetime (on earth); for it is something similar that will be given them" (*Sūrah* "The Cow" [2]:25). Finally, this should be considered: the Oriental starts from the idea that in this world below man is easily deprived of what he desires and separated from what he loves; to conclude that in Paradise we instantly obtain whatever we desire is but a short step, and this step has in fact been taken with an impeccable and somewhat expeditious logic;[7] the minimization by the Sufis of what might seem a "celestial nightmare" is the result of this two-edged logic, all the more so in that the Koran itself teaches that the "divine Contentment" (*Ridwān*) granted the believer is "greater" than the "Garden".

*
* *

Before going further let us return for a moment to the question of emotionalism or impulsiveness, which is inseparable from the psychological aspect of hyperbolism: when reading traditional writings—not forgetting profane literature, such as the "Thousand and One Nights" and poetry—one is struck by the ease with which old-fashioned Orientals weep, tear their garments, utter a great cry, fall down in a swoon if not dead, all this while under the sway of some visual, auditive, or mental excitement; this temperament obliges us to recognize the appropriateness of an exoterism that is in some respects pedantic and formalistic, but well suited to curb a thoughtless exuberance.

Metaphorically speaking, the Bedouin is a man who kills a fly on his wife's cheek with a tremendous blow, forgetting that in so doing he is striking his wife; despite its appearance of commonplace humor this image has the advantage of characterizing the temperament in question in a straightforward way. Example: according to some holy man, it is better to be seated in a miserable spot on earth while remembering God than to be seated under a tree in Paradise without remembering Him; the intention of this saying is impeccable and transparent, but the literal sense nevertheless ruins the Koranic idea of Paradise and the elect. Another example: in his book on marriage, Ghazzali mentions a bachelor who, dying of the plague, asks for a wife "in order to appear before God according to the *Sunnah*, that is, married"; the absurd serves here to create the sublime.

---

[7] On the basis of the Koranic promise that the blessed "shall have what they desire"; this leaves open the question of what desires are still possible in Paradise, hence of the very nature of the blessed themselves.

9

If it is true that a given religion creates or predisposes a man to given sentimental tendencies, it is even truer that Revelation must take account of pre-existing tendencies of this kind and must more or less come to meet them: to offer images to souls at their own level and to transmute these souls without their being aware of it is the very definition of *upāya*, the "provisional means" or "saving mirage" of Buddhism. The Bedouin is so made that in his heart of hearts he wants to be chief, governor, or king; he is violent, generous, and insatiable, his imagination opening not only onto riches and pleasures, but also onto power and glory;[8] hence it is necessary to present him with a Paradise that is able to attract him.

Be that as it may, it is quite obvious that pious exaggeration, even pious absurdity, is not the exclusive property of any race or of any religion: it is encountered notably—always as an inevitable excess or "lesser evil"—in the Christian ambience as well, as when a devout man, because of "humility" or "charity", accuses himself of sins he has not committed or accuses himself of being the greatest sinner or the vilest of men, or when he acts foolishly in order to be despised, without concerning himself with the effects of his attitudes on the souls of others, and so on.

From another point of view, one must guard against seeing in a certain kind of modern rationality a total superiority; contemporary man, in spite of his being marked by certain experiences resulting from the senescence of humanity, is spiritually soft and ineffective and intellectually prone to all possible betrayals, which will seem to him to be summits of intelligence, whereas in reality they are far more absurd than the excesses of simplicity and emotionalism of traditional man. In a general way the man of the "last days" is a blunted creature, and the best proof of this is that the only "dynamism" of which he is still capable is that which tends downward and which is no more than a passivity taking advantage of cosmic gravity; it is the agitation of a man who lets himself be carried away by a torrent and who imagines he is creating this torrent himself by his agitation.

---

[8] Let us note in this regard the relative frequency in Arab texts of allusions to a society at once patriarchal, chivalrous, and mercantile: the notions of "ransom", "redemption", "debt", "hostage", "intercession", and others of the kind seem to be landmarks of this psychology.

*

*   *

A few words on Arab tautology are called for here since we have spoken of hyperbole and disparity. As a first example we shall adduce the following Koranic passage: "Shall I take (other) gods besides Him? If the All-Merciful should wish me any harm, their intercession would avail me naught, nor would they save me. Then truly I would be in manifest error" (*Sūrah* "Yā Sīn" [36]:23, 24). The last phrase does not serve to explain what is already obvious, namely, that one must not accept false gods; it serves to emphasize that this error is not subtle or secret, hence possibly benefiting from extenuating circumstances, but that it is on the contrary unpardonable, since the truth of the One God imposes itself—as Saint Thomas would say—by the superabundance of its clarity; in reality what is in question here is the metaphysical self-evidence of the Absolute, a self-evidence that is subjectively innate and pre-rational and objectively recognizable in the profound nature of things.[9]

Another example is provided us by a nearby Koranic passage (verse 46 of the same *Sūrah*): "And when it is said unto them: Give in alms a part of what God hath provided you, those who disbelieve say unto those who believe: Should we feed someone whom God would feed, if He so willed? Ye are in manifest error." Here again the final proposition emphasizes the evident nature of the idea expressed in what went before: it means that the state of obscuration of unbelievers is such that charity, which nevertheless is within human nature and thus pertains to the primordial norm (*fitrah*), appears to them as a patent error, which shows precisely the measure of their perversion. Unbelievers cannot reconcile divine Omnipotence with human freedom, and in this they are "hypocrites" (*munāfiqūn*), for everyday experience proves that man is free; and what proves it above all is the distinction made by every man between the state of a creature who is free and that of one who is not, a spontaneous distinction constituting

---

[9] In our day there is much talk about "sincere" atheism; however, apart from the fact that sincerity neither prevents error from being error nor adds any value to it whatsoever, there is always in this system of sincerity—or "sincerist" narcissism—a point that constitutes total sin and seals off entry to Truth and Mercy.

the very notion of freedom; the fact that the freedom of creatures is determined by "divine choice" or that it merely reflects divine Freedom or All-Possibility within contingency in no way invalidates the concrete reality of our free will, without which there could be no question of the moral notions of merit and demerit.

*

*   *

Two examples of doctrinal enunciation that make use of contradiction are the following Koranic expressions: "He punisheth whom He will, and He pardoneth whom He will" (a recurring idea expressed in different ways), and "I seek refuge in the Lord of Daybreak from the evil of that which He created" (*Sūrah* "The Daybreak" [113]:1-2); the first of these expressions seems to imply that God is arbitrary since He apparently acts without motive, and the second that He is evil since He causes evil. The key to the correct interpretation is provided us by the very definition of God as it results from the "most beautiful Names" (*al-asmā' al-husnā*) and above all from the Names of Mercy, which appear at the head of every *Sūrah*; the question that arises is thus the following: how can God punish since "He does what He wills", and how can He cause or create evil when He is the All-Merciful (*Rahmān, Rahīm*), the Holy (*Quddūs*), and the Just (*'Adl*)? The answer will be: to assert that God punishes and forgives according to His good pleasure does not mean that He is arbitrary, but that this "good pleasure" represents motives that escape our limited understanding;[10] and to say that God creates evil does not mean that He wills it as evil, but that He produces it indirectly as a fragment—or as an infinitesimal constitutive element—of a "greater good", the extent of which compensates and absorbs that of evil.

    This truth perhaps requires some further precisions, which we shall provide here even though they go beyond the framework of our general subject and though we have already provided them on

---

[10] The story of Moses accompanying a mysterious and paradoxical master (*Sūrah* "The Cave" [18]:66-83) furnishes the classic paradigm of this problem, at least on the human level; and what is true for the master in question is true all the more for God.

12

other occasions and may need to return to them in the course of the present book: every evil is by definition a "part", never a "totality"; and negations or fragmentary privations, which are the various forms of evil, are inevitable since the world, not being God and unable to be Him, is of necessity situated outside of God. But with regard to their cosmic function as necessary elements of a total good, evils are in a certain way integrated into this good, and this point of view makes it possible to affirm that metaphysically there is no evil; the notion of evil presupposes in fact a fragmentary vision of things, characteristic of creatures, who are themselves fragments; man is a "fragmentary totality".[11]

As we have seen, evil is in the world because the world is not God; now from a certain point of view—of which the Vedantists are especially aware—the world is "none other than God"; *Māyā* is *Ātmā*, *Samsāra* is *Nirvāna*; from this point of view evil does not exist, and this is precisely the point of view of the macrocosmic totality.[12] This is suggested in the Koran by means of the following antinomy: on the one hand it declares that good is "from God" and evil is "from yourselves", and on the other hand that "all is from God" (*Sūrah* "Women" [4]:78, 79), the first idea having to be understood on the basis of the second, which is more universal, hence more real; it is the difference between fragmentary vision and total truth. The fact that the two maxims nearly follow each other—the more universal coming first—proves moreover the lack of concern in sacred dialectic for surface contradictions and the importance attached to penetration and synthesis.[13]

---

[11] To solve the rational problem of the incompatibility between the existence of evil and the goodness of God, curiously feeble arguments have sometimes been used, as for example in maintaining that evil arises from the stipulations of some law as a simple contrast and in a completely extrinsic manner—just as a shadow is cast by an object— or that it arises by contrast with our conventional attitudes, and so on, as if God would condemn the entire man for such fundamentally unreal transgressions.

[12] This is also the legitimate aspect of pantheism; pantheism is illegitimate when it is given an exclusive and unconditional application, one that is valid from every point of view and that makes things appear as "parts" of God, *quod absit*; the error is in the philosophy, not in the term.

[13] See likewise this antinomy: "This is but a reminder unto the worlds for whomsoever among you willeth to follow the straight path. But ye will it not unless God so willeth, Lord of the Worlds" (*Sūrah* "The Overthrowing" [81]:27-29).

13

And this brings us back to our more general subject, the question of antinomic expressions in the Koran; an example that has become classic is found in the following verse: "Nothing is like unto Him (God), and He it is that hears, that sees" (*Sūrah* "Counsel" [42]:11). The flagrant contradiction between the first assertion and the second—the second drawing a comparison, precisely, and thereby proving that an analogy between things and God does exist—has the function of showing that this evident analogy, without which not a single thing would be possible, in no way implies an imaginable resemblance and does not abolish in the least the absolute transcendence of the divine Principle.

*

* *

The Western reader is frequently shocked—and one cannot blame him—by the juxtaposition of terms having no obvious connection, as for example when the Prophet "seeks refuge in God from hunger and betrayal"; now in both cases—hunger and betrayal—it is a question of earthly insecurity, purely physical in the first instance and social and moral in the second. This way of suggesting something precise by means of certain of its aspects—which appear incongruous in the absence of their common denominator—is not exclusively Arab, but is also found in the Bible and in the majority of sacred Books, perhaps even in all; in any case there is in language the possibility of indirect suggestion, which is parallel to the purely descriptive role of the words and which gives rise to the most diverse modalities and combinations.

A feature of Islam that is particularly disconcerting for Westerners is what might be called its "belittling of the human"; this feature is explained by a concern for relating every greatness to God alone[14] and forestalling the emergence of a "humanism", hence a way of seeing things that leads to a cult of titanesque and luciferian man. Apparent tautologies in the Koran that seem to belittle the Prophets must be

---

[14] As is declared in one of the most famous *ahādīth*: "There is no power and no strength but in God."

interpreted as a function of this concern; if a given "Messenger" is called "one of the just",[15] this is because no other aspect is of interest in the Islamic perspective. That which goes beyond "justice" or "piety"—and which for this reason cannot be an example for simple believers—is on the one hand a mystery with which the common religion does not have to concern itself and on the other hand a quality whose glory belongs to God alone. A factor that must be kept in view is that in the Koran it is God and not man who speaks, and one of the reasons for the existence of certain disconcerting expressions is precisely to recall the smallness of the human—not for its own sake, but in the interest of man and in connection with the doctrine of Unity.[16]

*

* *

The use of antinomy is doubtless not of the same order as the use of hyperbole; it is nonetheless related to hyperbolic exaggeration in the sense that it indicates, like hyperbolism, an implicit relationship that gives the surface contradiction all its meaning.[17] In both of these cases, as in that of tautology, it is thus a question of a language at once abrupt and indirect, manifesting on the one hand sacred emotion and modesty with regard to precious truths and on the other the dazzling supra-rationality of the divine order.

---

[15] The word *sālih*, translated here as "just", includes the ideas of norm, equilibrium, betterment, appeasement, and return to original perfection: this is everything that Islam "officially" requires of "Messengers".

[16] The Islamic morality of smallness, obedience, and servitude has little chance of being understood in an age of false liberty and revolt. Certainly one has every right to rebel against purely human oppressions; but this contingent question apart, one does not have the choice of wishing for anything other than to resign oneself to the divine mold, which is Origin, Archetype, Norm, and Goal and which alone gives peace of heart by allowing us to be truly what we are. It is in this acceptance of our absolute destiny that true freedom is realized, but this can only be "in Him" and "through Him" and over and above all our worldly alternatives.

[17] It goes without saying that antinomism is not part of the ordinary dialectic of logicians; moreover, rhetoric and dialectic merge into each another at the level of sacred or sapiential expression.

If the logical coherence of the literal wording is not a criterion or guarantee of truth or sanctity, neither is the obscure and more or less paradoxical character of a language—at least within certain limits—a sign of error or weakness; apart from the fact that sacred language may in some respects be a "shock therapy" rather than a neutral communication,[18] it inevitably contains infinitely more than ordinary language, whence a rhetorical use of key words that does not necessarily conform to logic pure and simple; and what is true of sacred language properly so-called may also be the case for the spiritual language inspired by it. Certainly logical expression, or the homogeneous and consistent surface of language, may convey the highest truth and therefore also sanctity, and it would be absurd to maintain the contrary;[19] but consciousness of the Absolute may also fracture, so to speak, the outward form of language, and in this case—though in this case only—it must be admitted that truth justifies its expression and indeed proves it by the perfume of the expression itself. One should not assert, however—and this is an altogether different question—that the spiritual worth of a man is always the guarantee of his dialectical powers, given the possible tyranny of his surroundings or of conventions he may not be conscious of and for which *a fortiori* he is not responsible, unless he makes himself their spokesman by affinity or vocation, if only with a superficial layer of his being.

---

[18] In the formulas of Zen, the element "shock" has precedence over the element "information" proper to language, which is possible because shock informs in its turn and in its way.

[19] Witness the *Bhagavad Gītā*, whose language appears as a perfectly simple and homogeneous surface.

The Exo-Esoteric Symbiosis

When speaking of spirituality one calls to mind *ipso facto* the sources of knowledge, which in this case are revelation, inspiration, intellection, and—secondarily—reflection; it is necessary to know exactly what is meant by these terms.

Inspiration, like revelation, is a divine dictation, with the difference that in the case of revelation the Spirit dictates a lawgiving and obligatory Message of overriding force whereas in inspiration the Message, whatever its value, has no dogmatic import, but plays an illustrative role within the framework of the fundamental Message.

Reflection, like intellection, is an activity of the intelligence, with the difference that in the case of intellection this activity springs from the immanent divine spark that is the Intellect whereas in reflection the activity starts from the reason, which is capable only of logic and not intellective intuition. The *conditio sine qua non* of reflection is that a man reasons from facts that are at once necessary and sufficient and does so with a view to a conclusion,[1] this conclusion being the reason for the existence of the mental operation.

From the point of view of knowledge properly so called, reasoning is like the groping of a blind man, with the difference that—by removing obstacles—it may bring about flashes of insight; it is blind and groping because of its indirect and discursive nature, but not necessarily so in its function, for it may be no more than the description—or verbalization—of a vision one possesses *a priori*, and in this case it is not the mind that is groping, but the language. If we compare reasoning to groping it is in the sense that it is not a vision, and not in order to deny its capacity for adequation and exploration; it is a means of knowledge, but this means is mediate and fragmentary like the sense of touch, which enables a blind man to find his way and even to feel the heat of the sun, but not to see.[2]

---

[1] It is precisely the absence of such facts that makes modern science aberrant from the speculative point of view and hypertrophied from the practical point of view; likewise for philosophy: criticism, existentialism, and evolutionism have their respective points of departure in the absence of a datum that in itself is as self-evident as it is essential.

[2] It is said that angels do not possess reason since they have a vision of causes and consequences, which obviously does not signify an infirmity.

As for intellection, on the one hand it necessarily expresses itself by means of reason, and on the other hand it can make use of reason as a support for actualization. These two factors enable theologians to reduce intellection to reasoning; that is, they deny it—while nonetheless seeing in rationality an element that is more or less problematic, if not contrary to faith—without seeking or being able to account for the fact that faith is itself an indirect and in a way anticipated mode of intellection.

If on the one hand reasoning can provoke—but not pro-duce—intellection and if on the other hand intellection is necessarily expressed by reasoning, a third combination is also possible, but it is abnormal and improper: namely, the temptation to support a real intellection by aberrant reasoning either because the intellection does not operate in all domains on account of some blind spot in the mind or character or because religious emotionalism leads thought toward opportunistic solutions, faith being inclined to assume, even if only subconsciously, that "the end justifies the means".

In any case it is impossible to deny that Sufis sometimes write "philosophically"—rather than from "inspiration"—especially since the philosopher, far from being by definition a rationalist, is simply a man who reflects on the meaning and causes of phenomena or on the combinations of things, which after all is entirely normal for a creature endowed with intelligence but not omniscience. On the other hand Sufis reason "theologically" insofar as they seek—to the detriment of their esoterism—to combine an anthropomorphist, moralistic, and sentimental monotheism with metaphysics and *gnosis;* but this particularity plays no role from the point of view of speculative ratio-nality, for in this regard there is no strict line of demarcation between philosophy and theology.

*
* *

Another mode of knowledge, if one may put it this way, is the inter-pretation of sacred Scriptures; one knows that in a Semitic context scriptural interpretation, with its play of associations of ideas springing from words or images, often takes the place of thinking. Hermeneutics pertains to inspiration as a prerogative of sanctity, but without being able to dispense with the concurrence of reasoning or *a fortiori* intellection, which it is sometimes difficult to separate in practice from inspiration; in any case inspired interpretation is distinguished by the fact that the reference points of spiritual or mental activity are passages or words from Scripture and not in the first place ideas or intuitions. The fact that the boundary between the supernatural and the natural is not always precise explains the diversity and inequality of Sufic, Shiite, and Rabbinical speculations; one has the impression with many of these speculations that it is not a question of liberating oneself from cosmic *Māyā*, but on the contrary of entrenching oneself more deeply in it, of plunging into a religious mythology with piety and ingenuity but without the desire to escape from it. Thus the notion of esoterism is rather precarious in the Semitic monotheistic world, although it is precisely in this world that it is the most necessary;[3] indeed all too often it conveys either an exoterism that is simultaneously severe and refined or else an esoterism that is both fragmentary and vulgarized, hence exoterized. "If thou wouldst reach the kernel, thou must break the shell": this maxim, which is as dangerous as it is true, runs the risk of remaining a dead letter in an esoterism conventionally entrenched in dogmatic theology and denominational "mythology". We shall no doubt be told that exoterism is the necessary starting point for the corresponding esoterism, which is true insofar as it is a question of a symbolism that is pure, hence open to the universal, and not of an exclusivist particularism;[4] obviously one must take into account the need for circumspection, which in a religious context may distort the dialectic of sapience, and this argument can carry much weight.

Sufism seems to derive its originality, both positive and problematical, from the fact that it mixes—metaphorically speaking—the spirit of the Psalms with that of the *Upanishads*, as if David had chanted the *Brahmasūtra* or Badarayana had implored the God of Israel. Needless to say this often gives rise to a harmonious, profound, and powerful combination, in Ibn Ata Allah for example; as for the

---

[3] In the Hindu context, Shankarian *Vedānta* is not properly speaking an esoterism since the Ramanujian perspective, which corresponds to exoterism, does not act as a cover for it, but leads an independent existence.

[4] For all the more reason religious fanaticism cannot be a starting point for *gnosis*, a truth that Omar Khayyam expressed in his own way.

drawbacks of this amalgam—which in fact is not an amalgam since it is spontaneous—one must always take the eschatological idealism into account, an idealism that can greatly compensate for pious inconsistencies even as the ardor of faith can compensate for many human imperfections.

Christ said two things that are equally plausible but at first sight seem contradictory: on the one hand he prescribed obedience to the scribes and Pharisees, since they "sit in Moses' seat", and on the other he described many of their commandments as "human"; what this means is that tradition includes—or may include—elements which, without departing from "orthodoxy", are unnecessary luxuries, to say the least, and which are sometimes harmful to the moral or spiritual essentiality of the divine Message. These distorting and alienating elements—"human" without being "heterodox"—also exist *de facto* in esoterism, always by virtue of a "human margin" that Heaven concedes to our freedom; it is not of course a question here of elements that enter directly into the elaboration of sanctity, but of those luxuriant speculations that produce vertigo rather than light.

*

*   *

Like the Semites, the Aryans constitute above all a linguistic group, which implies that they also constitute, though more vaguely, a psychological group and even a racial group, at least originally; on the other hand this homogeneity is quite relative since the Aryans form but a fragment in a much vaster collectivity, namely, the white race.[5] Psychologically, there are "introverted" and contemplative Aryans, the Hindus, and "extroverted" and enterprising Aryans, the Europeans— "East and West", with the obvious reservation that the characteristics of the one are also to be found in the other. In the case of Semites, who on the whole are more contemplative than Europeans and less contemplative than Hindus, there are also two principal groups, Jews

---

[5] This race also includes the Hamites and Dravidians, but these groups have far less historical and spiritual importance than the Aryans and Semites, at least in a direct sense.

and Arabs: the soul of the first is richer but more turned in on itself whereas that of the second is poorer but more expansive, more gifted from the point of view of radiance and universality.[6]

For the Semite, everything begins with Revelation and therefore with faith and submission; man is *a priori* a believer and consequently a servant: intelligence itself takes on the color of obedience. For the Aryan by contrast—and we are not thinking of the Semiticized Aryan[7]—it is intellection that has the first word even if it springs forth as the result of a Revelation; Revelation is not a commandment that seems to create intelligence *ex nihilo* while at the same time enslaving it, but appears instead as the objectification of the one Intellect, which is at once transcendent and immanent. Intellectual certainty has priority here over a submissive faith; the *Veda* does not give orders to the intelligence, but awakens it and reminds it of what it is.

Grosso modo Aryans—except in cases of intellectual obscuration where they have retained only their mythology and ritualism—are above all metaphysicians and therefore logicians whereas Semites, unless they have become idolaters and magicians, are *a priori* mystics and moralists, each of the two mentalities or capacities repeating itself within the framework of the other in keeping with the Taoist diagram of the *yin-yang*. Or again, Aryans are objectivists, for good or ill, while Semites are subjectivists; deviated objectivism gives rise to rationalism and scientism whereas excessive subjectivism engenders all the illogicalities and pious absurdities of which a sentimental, zealous, and conventional fideism is capable. It is the difference between intellectualism and voluntarism; the first tends to reduce the volitive

---

[6] In this comparison we are thinking of orthodox Jews—those who have remained Orientals even in the West—and not of the totally Europeanized Jews, who combine certain Semitic characteristics with Western extroversion. Moreover, Judaism had a certain radiation in the Roman period, but after that it was only indirectly and through Christianity and Islam that the essential monotheistic Message spread, of which Judaism, after Abraham and with Moses, was the first crystallization.

[7] It would be a mistake to argue that al-Ghazzali was a Persian and therefore an Aryan, for the Persians were Arabized by Islam whether they were Shiite or Sunni; and it goes without saying that a Hellenized Arab is more "Aryan" than an Arabized Persian, schematically speaking. An Iranian or Indian can be Arabized *a priori* and Hellenized *a posteriori*, and as a result an Aryanized Semite can be superimposed on a Semiticized Aryan within the same person.

element to the intelligence or to integrate it therein, and the second on the contrary tends to subordinate the intellectual element to the will; this may be said while still taking into account the fluctuations necessarily contained in the concrete reality of things. It is sometimes necessary to express oneself in a schematic fashion for the sake of clarity if one is to express oneself at all.

*

*   *

The Arabs of old were both skeptical and superstitious; if they were rationalists, it was because of worldliness and not because of a shadow of intellectuality; they did not think of putting their rationality, however acute, into the service of a truth that was in practice distant and unverifiable and that seemed in addition to go against their interests; on the contrary they put it into the service of effectiveness, on the plane of magical idolatry as well as on that of commercial enterprises. In order to pull them out of their indifferentism it was necessary to cause a chord to vibrate in them other than this completely "horizontal" sagacity; to make them accept a "vertical" truth it was necessary to impose on them a simple and enthralling faith while discrediting a rationality compromised by its pagan character; the man who is converted must "burn what he has worshipped".

The lasting result of this change is that the pious Muslim is mistrustful of the need for explanations in matters of faith; rationality appears to him as a pagan memory and an invitation to doubt and insubordination, hence unbelief; even so fideism developed its own rationality—dogmatic theology (*kalām*) and the science of the divine Law (*fiqh*)—though al-Ghazzali nonetheless thinks that on the Day of Resurrection the Imams of primitive Islam will be opposed to the doctors of the Law, the former having sought only to "please God"; he believes that learned theology is there only to prevent innovations (*bida*) and that true knowledge of God is at the antipodes of *kalām*. All this enables us to explain the paradox of an esoterism founded less on an intellectuality conscious of its nature and rights than on a voluntaristic, individualistic, and sentimental fideism that prolongs exoterism, radicalizing or refining it in a certain way, but only insufficiently perceiving its relativity. Nonetheless we have here the two essential aspects of plenary esoterism: on the one hand a penetration of the symbols of exoterism and on the other hand an affirmation on the contrary of the independence—and pre-excellence—of essence in relation to forms or substance in relation to accidents, that is, the formulations precisely of the common religion.[8] With regard to this "non-conformist" aspect of esoterism, we would say by way of illustration that the abrogations of Koranic verses and the matrimonial exceptions in the life of the Prophet are there to indicate respectively the relativity of the formal Revelation and that of social morality, which amounts to saying that these abrogations and exceptions pertain to the esoteric perspective, leaving aside their immediate and practical significance.[9]

As for the affinity—in some respects paradoxical and yet fundamental—between Islam and *gnosis*, it is necessary to understand that Islam has the greatest respect for intelligence, this being consistent with the Koran and the *Sunnah* and contrary to what takes place in Christianity—contrary also to the wishes of certain Muslim fideists; but here it is a question of intelligence in itself (*ʿaql*)—which includes the Intellect as well as the reason, or conversely—and not the Intellect alone, which the believer may accept or not depending on his degree of understanding. Intelligence for the Muslim is the faculty that allows us to distinguish between what pleases God and leads to salvation and what displeases God and leads to perdition, or between good and evil, true and false, the real and the illusory, whether in the most elementary or the very highest sense.[10]

---

[8] Abu Hurairah: "I kept precious in my memory two stores of knowledge I received from the Messenger of God; I passed on one of them, but if I passed on the other you would cut my throat." One finds a completely analogous passage in the Gospel of Saint Thomas. As the Taoists say, "Only error is transmitted, not the truth."

[9] This is not unconnected with the mysterious passage that relates the meeting between Moses and al-Khidr, the latter representing—like Melchizedek—supraformal, universal, and primordial spirituality (*Sūrah* "The Cave" [18]:66-83). Let us note that the verses abrogated have in general a more universal meaning than the verses replacing them and that the additional wives—the Koran allowing only four—indicate what might be called the "Krishnaite" aspect of the Prophet.

[10] Traditions advanced by Ghazzali: "The fool does more harm by his ignorance than the wicked man by his wickedness. Furthermore, men reach a higher degree of nearness (*qurb*) to God only in proportion to their intelligence (*ʿaql* = "intellect")." "Because

*

*   *

Innumerable detours and endless discourses result from the fact that Sufi metaphysics is linked with the anti-metaphysical and moralizing creationism of the monotheistic theologies and from the fact, this being so, that it is unable to handle in a sufficiently consequential way the principle of relativity; radicalism in regard to the essential goes hand in hand with inconsequentiality in regard to detail. No doubt the precautions of theology, which are metaphysically unnecessary, give rise to fruitful perplexities, to the sort of wounds that generate mystical intuitions, but this has nothing to do with pure and total truth, to which nonetheless all the Sufis lay claim.

What is it in fact that interests the esoterist, the gnostic, the metaphysician? It is truth in itself and an intelligence proportioned to it: an intelligence that is theomorphic, hence holy, by the very fact that it is proportioned to the highest truths—holy through its transpersonal root, the "uncreated" and immanent Intellect. And what is it that interests the mystical fideist? It is the sublimizing affirmation of a driving idea in and through faith, a faith that has a nearly absolute value because of its dogmatic content on the one hand and its volitive, imaginative, and sentimental intensity on the other. There is only one step from this to believing oneself "inspired" because one abstains from thinking; the fideist is by definition an inspirationist.[11] Admittedly this tension in faith does not exclude intellection properly

for everything there is a support and the support of the believer is his intelligence, his way of worshipping (serving) God (*'ubudiyah* = "servitude") is proportioned to his intelligence." Ghazzali distinguishes four meanings in the word *'aql*: abstract intelligence, which distinguishes man from the animals; the instinct for what is possible and impossible; empirical knowledge; discernment of causes and foresight as to consequences. "Whoever dies knowing that there is no god but God enters Paradise"; commenting on this *hadīth* in his *Futūhāt al-Makkiyah*—in a section on the modes of *Tawhīd*—Ibn Arabi remarks that the Prophet said, "Whoever knows" (*ya'lam*), not "whoever believes" (*yu'min*) or "whoever says" (*yaqūl*); and he adds that Iblis was not unaware that there is no god but God, but that he nullified this knowledge by his sin of "association" (*shirk*). The primacy of "knowledge" is yet a further indication among many others of the fundamentally "gnostic" character of Islam.

[11] A positive inspiration—the only kind we are considering here—can come from God

so called, but in this case intellection is not the "prime mover" of speculations; it appears as a gift or concomitance of faith, which is not false since the Holy Spirit is manifested through the Intellect as well as through inspirations falling from Heaven. The drawback is that one attributes the suggestions of pious sentimentality to the Holy Spirit or inspiration, suggestions that are not necessarily aberrant but may be so.[12]

Jews and Arabs have in common an overactive imagination even when it is poor, which quite paradoxically is not a contradiction. Many Islamic or more particularly Sufic speculations—without forgetting the Shiite sector—fully rival those rabbinical speculations that are most subject to caution; it is thus appropriate to take both *cum grano salis* and not with the illusion that everything laying claim to tradition and containing a modicum of sacred science is necessarily infallible.[13] No doubt playing with complex and exuberant associations of ideas—suggestive by their content as well as their excessiveness—can procure for the Arab or the Arabized soul a satisfaction that is at least stimulating; but there is little likelihood it will have the same effect on other mentalities.[14]

---

or from an angel, which in practice amounts more or less to the same, but it can also come from the subconscious without therefore being false; in this case, however, one is mistaken in attributing it without reservation to a heavenly source, although in the last analysis every true intuition can be traced back metaphysically to the one Truth.

[12] From the first centuries of Islam preacher-storytellers (*qāss*, *qussās*) sought to arouse the imagination of their audience with more or less extravagant stories in order to stimulate piety, fear, hope—a double-edged sword if ever there was one, for the result was an inextricable mixture of the true and fictitious and, in the final analysis, a sort of infantilization of pious literature.

[13] A typical problem: can one see God with one's bodily eyes in certain cases? Were Moses on Sinai and Muhammad during the Night Journey able to see God? Nonetheless, "sight cannot reach Him (*Allāh*)", according to the Koran; and why does one speak of an "eye of the heart" (*'ayn al-qalb*)? For the purpose of the physical eye is precisely to perceive material things as such, and thus it is not suited to a vision of the immaterial in itself or *a fortiori* to a vision of the Archetypes, let alone the Essence. To say that the eye has seen God is to say either that God has made Himself form, light, space or that the eye has ceased to be eye.

[14] Thus the Arab notion of "eloquence" (*balāghah*), which is not unconnected with a

"There is no right superior to that of Truth," proclaims a princely maxim from India; monotheists who stem from the desert—for whom everything begins with faith—would say instead that there is no right superior to that of God or piety. It is perhaps not too hazardous to say that the Aryan spirit, in keeping with the realism—sacred or profane—that is proper to it, tends *a priori* to unveil the truth whereas the Semitic spirit, whose realism is more moral than intellectual, tends toward the veiling of the divine Majesty and those of its secrets that are too dazzling or intoxicating, as is shown precisely by the innumerable enigmas of the monotheistic Scriptures, in contrast with the *Upanishads*, and as is indicated by the allusive and elliptical nature of the corresponding exegesis.

In any case it is only too obvious that the great question that arises for man is not to know whether he is Semitic or Aryan, Oriental or Western, but to know whether he loves God, whether he is spiritual, contemplative, pneumatic; this recalling of the "one thing needful" compensates on the human plane for what may be unfathomable or troubling in the comparison of spiritual modes.

*

*   *

The Arab soul is poor, but heroic and generous; its poverty as well as its ardor qualify it to serve as a vehicle for a faith that is centered on the essential—whether it is a question of doctrine or worship—and that is all the more passionate because it is simple. But this poverty as a psychological fact calls forth compensatory features, which are as it were "quantitative" by reason of their very poverty, whence a tendency toward exaggeration and prolixity, and indeed boastfulness—whence also on another level a tendency toward contrasting simplification, isolating over-accentuation, and too-hasty ostracism; all these features are discernible even in the spiritual literature of the Arabs and those who are Arabized. Paradoxically, the tendency toward simplification or simplistic alternatives finds a sort of compensation in allusive and

deployment of images and speculations that is at once ardent, ingenious, and verbose, can give rise to quite diverse evaluations.

elliptical secretiveness, whence also complication and concealment, detours and veilings.

No doubt the Arab soul has its richness—the contrary would be inconceivable—but it is a poor richness or a poverty enriched by the glistening of nomadic virtues and enhanced by a desert-like acuity of intelligence. Faced with the evidence, however, one is forced to admit that the exuberance attached to this temperament creates a certain problem from the point of view of sapiential esoterism and with regard to its integrity and expression; the thirst for the marvelous is one thing, and metaphysical serenity another.

If there is a poor richness, there is also and no less paradoxically a rich poverty, and it is this that predisposed the Arabs to Islam and with it to a mysticism of holy poverty: the saint in Islam is the "poor one", the *faqīr*, and the spiritual virtue above all others, which moreover coincides with sincerity (*sidq*), is "poverty", *faqr*. Without this spirit of poverty Islam would not have been capable of preserving the Biblical world over an entire sector of the globe or excluding from its universe that literary and artistic, and profoundly worldly, "culture" of which the West is so proud and from which it runs the risk of dying, if indeed it has not already done so. Those who accuse Islam of "sterility" do not understand that one of Islam's greatest claims to glory is that it was able to impress a certain character of the desert on a whole civilization, a character of holy poverty as well as holy childhood.[15]

*

* *

Revelation imposes itself upon Aryans and Semites alike; on the other hand one is right to speak of an Aryan "intellectionism" and a Semitic "inspirationism", even though both intellection and inspiration necessarily belong to all human groups; the entire difference lies in the emphasis. Intellection is sacred because it is derived from the Intellect, which pertains to the Holy Spirit; the same is true for inspiration, with

---

[15] A character preserved—or made visible—especially in the Maghreb; we are not speaking of the caliphs of Damascus and Baghdad or the Turkish sultans.

the difference that it is derived from a particular grace and not, like intellection, from a permanent and "naturally supernatural" capacity.

We do not believe we are over-stylizing things in taking the view that the Aryan tends to be a philosopher[16] whereas the Semite is above all a moralist; in order to be convinced of this one may compare the *Upanishads*, the *Yoga-Vasishtha*, and the *Bhagavad Gītā* with the Bible, or Hindu doctrines with Talmudic speculations.[17] The innermost motive of Muslim mysticism is fundamentally more moral than intellectual—in spite of the intellective character of the *Shahādah*—in the sense that Arab or Muslim, or Semitic, sensibility always remains more or less volitive, hence subjectivist, as we noted above; knowledge itself, if it is not considered a gratuitous gift from Heaven, appears almost as a merit of the will, at least *de facto* and in the general context if not in regard to the deepest intention. To affirm Unity is good while being true as well; and the first reason for accepting that God is One seems to be that He has ordered us to believe it. The highest good is therefore to affirm Unity in the most radical and most sublime manner possible; this subtly and subconsciously moral instinct seems here to be the stimulus for metaphysical speculation. Thus many concepts resulting from this tendency are not to be taken literally: they are "ideals", that is, schematic formulations intended to inspire an impetus toward Unity; it is the operative intensity of faith that counts here more than intellectual coherence. It is quite easy to object that "esoterism" is beyond even elementary logic, that the "profane" understand nothing of these mysteries, and so on—a gratuitous "esoterism", which does not prevent us from sometimes preferring the *'ulamā'* "of the outward" (*zāhir*) to the scholars "of the inward" (*bātin*) or the Hellenizing philosophers to Ghazzali, although we do not fail to recognize the subjective merits of pious extravagances.

---

[16] One might object that the Celtic and Germanic peoples do not answer to this description at least *a priori;* this would be to forget that the Aryan spirit includes two dimensions, one mythological and the other intellectual, and that the groups we have just referred to put all the emphasis on the mythological and heroic side, not to mention the more than probable existence of an esoteric and oral wisdom among the Germans as well as the Celts.

[17] We remarked in one of our first books—and others have since repeated it—that the encounter of Hinduism and Islam on the soil of India has something profoundly

It is important to note in this context that the all-embracing accentuation of the divine Unity in Islam determines and colors the whole perspective, as does the all-embracing accentuation of Christ in Christianity. But whereas in Christianity this conceptual and passional accentuation gives rise first to Trinitarian absolutism and then to the moral and ascetical cult of the cross, in Islam the accentuation of Unity gives rise to the negation of secondary causes and even of the homogeneity of things, hence to an occasionalism that in a certain way dismantles the world *ad majorem Dei gloriam;* in both cases we are altogether removed from the serene contemplation of the nature of things. Thus there is nothing surprising in the fact that thought, which in Christianity always tends toward the "fact" since Christ is a historical phenomenon, readily displays in Islam an occasionalist, hence discontinuous, coloration, and this partly explains certain paradoxical features of Muslim mysticism, beginning with an inspirationism that cares little for coherence.

And this leads to the following parenthesis: whereas the Bible is a book that is directly historical and indirectly doctrinal, the Koran is a book that is directly doctrinal and indirectly historical; this means that in the Koran, which seeks only to proclaim the Unity, Omnipotence, Omniscience, and Mercy of God and correlatively the existential, moral, and spiritual servitude of man, historical facts are only points of reference and have scarcely any interest in themselves. This explains why the Prophets are quoted without any chronological order and why historical occurrences are sometimes related so elliptically as to be unintelligible without commentaries; it is only the relationship Lord-servant that is important here, the rest being but illustration or symbolism. A comparison between the Old Testament and the Koran has no meaning apart from these considerations; as for the New Testa-

---

symbolic and providential about it, given that Hinduism is the most ancient integral tradition and Islam on the contrary is the youngest religion; it is the junction of the primordial with the terminal. But there is more than a symbol here: this encounter means in fact that each of these traditions, even though they are as different as possible, has something to learn from the other, not of course from the point of view of dogmas and practices, but from that of tendencies and attitudes; Islam offers its geometric simplicity, its clarity, and also its compassion, whereas Hinduism brings its influence to bear by its profound serenity and its multiform and inexhaustible universality.

ment, it combines the two styles—it is eminently historical while being explicitly doctrinal—but it is distinctive as compared with the Koran in that it displays different levels of inspiration, which is likewise the case with the Old Testament. The Muslim reproach that the Scriptures have been "falsified" no doubt refers to these differences in an indirect and symbolic manner and with an ostracism that is not at all exceptional in the realm of exoteric oppositions.

As is indicated by the Testimony of Faith, the *Shahādah*, Islam is the religion of Divinity as such—not of divine Manifestation as is Christianity—and therefore of the conformity of the human "form" to the divine "Essence", as is indicated in turn by the second *Shahādah*, that of the Prophet. In relation to the self-evidence of the divine Principle, all other evident and certain things and all the miracles in the world are but little, whence the profound and almost explosive conviction of the Muslim and whence his passionate faith, a faith that is at the same time necessarily serene through its very object, this complementarity indicating in addition the possibility of a certain choice, depending on the level of the doctrine or the soul.

The conviction Islam possesses of being at once the religion-quintessence and the religion-synthesis, that is, the religion that offers everything constituting the essence of every possible religion, is certainly not unfounded: for in the first place Islam affirms—to the point of being nearly reducible to this affirmation—that there is but one sole Absolute, which is both Unique and Total; second, that the universal Law—*Dharma*, as the Hindus would say—is the conformity of contingent beings to the Absolute, and this is what is expressed by the term *Islām*: "Abandonment", "Submission", or "Resignation"; third, that the essence of salvation is the recognition or awareness of the Absolute and nothing else; fourth, that the link between the Absolute and the contingent or between God and the world is that God periodically sends Messengers to remind men of the two fundamental truths, that of the Absolute and that of Conformity to the Absolute: *Allāh* and *Islām*—all this being necessarily prefigured in the personal nature of the Prophet in keeping with the congeniality and complementarity between the sacred content and the providential container. This concise summary we consider to be of decisive importance.

*
*   *

From the doctrinal point of view Sufis seek—whether consciously or not—to combine two tendencies, Platonism and Asharism.[18] For Platonism—as for all true metaphysics—the true, the beautiful, and the good are such because they manifest qualities proper to the Principle, or to the Essence if one prefers, and because God, though supremely free, cannot be free in opposition to His nature, which He obviously cannot change except on pain of absurdity; Asharism proclaims on the contrary that the true, the beautiful, and the good are such because God wills it so without our being able to know why and that the opposite could be the case if by chance God so willed. In this system, which is voluntaristic inasmuch as it is viscerally moralistic and therefore individualistic, God and man are defined as will: God is "absolutely free" will, capable of determining things no matter how and without any other motive than His will, as if will had its sufficient reason in itself and as if freedom could logically and ontologically include the absurd; correlatively, man is defined as will predestined for obedience and apparently free in its choices "if God wills". On this battlefield Sufism obviously approaches pure *gnosis* to the extent it is Platonic—which does not mean that sound doctrine necessarily comes to it from Plato or Plotinus—and it departs from it to the extent it capitulates to Asharism. According to "ontological monism" (*wahdat al-wujūd*), everything that exists is "good" because it is "willed by God"; the notion of evil is in our minds because "God willed it"; evil is what we do not love or what *a priori* God does not love. We are not told why God does not love certain things even though all things are good "in themselves"; we must take note of the fact that He does not love them, and this constitutes all our "knowledge". Here the most vertiginous metaphysics is combined with the most summary Asharism.

Be that as it may, the "Platonic" thesis is expressed in the Koran not only by the formula "in the Name of God, the Clement, the Merciful", but also by all other formulas setting forth the aspects or qualities of God and thus affirming the immutable and at the same time intelligible character of the divine nature; if Ashari does not

---

[18] Indeed the same phenomenon has arisen within Christianity, the Asharite tendency being here replaced by Protestant fideism; the combination and opposition with regard to Platonism go hand in hand.

draw from this the fundamental consequences one would expect, it is because of his immanent moralism, which doubtless coincides with a psychological and social opportunism.

*
*   *

"God doeth what He will," says the Koran, and it is the only thing Ashari seems to remember, at least in a consequential fashion; he forgets that other Koranic formulations implicitly proclaim that "God doeth what He is", which occurs for example when God carries out justice because He is the Just (*al-Hakīm*) or when He produces beauty because, according to a *hadīth*, He is beautiful (*jamīl*) and loves beauty, or again when He forgives because He is always by His very nature "He who forgiveth" (*al-Ghafūr*). God cannot possess the freedom of not being what He is and therefore of not manifesting it, for all the emphasis is in reality on divine Being and not divine Will. God is not "Will" *a priori*; He is Perfection, hence all possible perfections; He is free in the play of possibilities, but not with regard to their essences, which pertain to divine Possibility as such; the imperatives of Possibility take precedence over this play just as Being takes precedence over things.

According to Asharite reasoning God is free to "do what He will" because there is no one above Him; the good is not the good because of an intrinsic quality directly reflecting a given aspect of the divine Perfection, but for the sole reason that God willed it thus; here the error consists on the one hand in confusing Omnipotence or All-Possibility with the arbitrary and on the other hand in forgetting that the foundation of the good is not a decree from God but the intrinsic goodness of the divine Nature. If two and two make four, this is true because God is Truth, not because He is Omnipotence or gratuitousness.

Be that as it may, Islam either had to teach like Mazdeism that there are two "divinities", one for good and one for evil—an idea that emphasizes contingency and not Absoluteness, except for the final Victory—or it had to proclaim that "God doeth what He will", which instead of being interpreted "in an ascending direction", in the sense of All-Possibility and its various consequences, "horizontal" as well as "vertical", has all too often been interpreted "in a descending direction", as an arbitrariness that obviously excludes divine Perfection. Whoever accentuates the side of contingency, manifestation, world must veil the Absolute, which is what was done in Mazdean dualism and in a less abrupt fashion in Christian Trinitarianism; whoever on the contrary accentuates the Absolute—still at the level of a religious voluntarism—cannot help "veiling" in a certain manner the side of contingency by reducing its workings in too unilateral a way to the Transcendent Cause, as is shown precisely in Islam by a certain "atomizing" and occasionalist unintelligibility of the world. This dilemma arises for a dogmatic formulation but not for pure metaphysics, which benefits from a suppleness or mobility dogmatism cannot achieve; thus the role of esoterism is to surmount dogmatist disequilibriums and not prolong or refine them.

Ibn Arabi, in spite of his unevenness and contradictions—the contradictions owing above all to his at least partial solidarity with ordinary theology and the discontinuous, isolating, and over-accentuating quality of its thought—had the great merit of expressing the mystery of radiating and inclusive Unity in a fully Asharite environment, hence of placing the emphasis on the implicitly divine character of cosmic Manifestation, which brings us back to pure and integral metaphysics; it is in this and not in his more or less expeditious argumentation or in his "mythological" imagination or mystical excesses that the whole significance of his work resides. Along with this merit goes that of having positioned Platonic love of the Beautiful at the summit of the universal hierarchy, of having discerned it in God Himself, and of having replaced—but without abolishing—the God-Will of Ashari with God-Beauty, with God-Love.[19]

For us this equation means that the Absolute by definition comprises Infinitude, in which precisely are rooted and from which are therefore derived all beauty and love, so much so that it is the beauty and love perceived in the world that enable us to have a presentiment

---

[19] Mention must also be made of the fundamental doctrine of "Universal Man" (*al-Insān al-kāmil*), which is the *Logos* that prefigures the created universe; it is reflected—or realized existentially—in the microcosm as well as the macrocosm, and it is especially manifested in the Prophets and Sages; the Prophets are summed up in the person of the founder of Islam. This theory derives its justification and inspiration from the theomorphism of man.

of what the radiant nature of God truly is and even to actualize it within ourselves.[20]

*
*   *

The distinction between the necessary and the possible, which concerns all domains of the universe, also applies especially to the domain of thought and activity and in particular to that of mystical inspiration. Thus alongside inspirations pertaining to the necessary or certain it is inevitable that there should be others relating only to the possible and uncertain, while still others are illusory without being harmful; religious enthusiasm, coupled with a thirst for information about heavenly things and a quasi-conventional overestimation of religious mythology as such, cannot but give rise to a margin of dreams, not to say illusions. Christian theology rightly teaches that such mirages are not opposed to sanctity as long as they are simply human and not diabolical;[21] it is appropriate to remember this when confronted with pious fantasies on the margin of the love of God and heroic virtue.[22]

Hence there is a Sufism that is necessary and another that is possible, just as there is a necessary Being and possible existences; the first of these Sufisms is founded on the esoteric evidences resulting from

---

[20] It can be said that Love, together with Beauty, Goodness, and Beatitude, is a mystery or "dimension" of the Essence, but not that the Essence is nothing other than Love; being Absolute, the Essence is ineffable, and it manifests its nature precisely by Spirit and Power. It is *Sat, Chit, Ānanda;* in Arabic, *Wujūd,* "Reality" (or *Qudrah,* "Power"), *Shuhūd,* "Perception" (or *Hikmah,* "Wisdom"), *Hayāt,* "Life" (or *Rahmah,* "Generous, Merciful Goodness").

[21] There is a rather large number of mystics whom the Church has canonized, but without ratifying all their experiences and opinions. More or less innocent inspirationist illusions are possible among particularly imaginative devotees, who are not thereby false mystics and who may even be saints and possibly legitimate philosophers, depending on the case.

[22] Rumi attributes the following discourse to God: "What matter words to me? I have need of an ardent heart; let hearts become inflamed with love, and occupy thyself neither with thoughts nor their expression." This is said in order to excuse human weakness, but not to discredit wisdom; it is at the same time a reference to the mystical unanimity of the religions.

34

the immutable elements of Islam, whereas the second is connected to personal inspirations, philosophical-mystical speculations, religious mythology, hagiography, zeal, and morality.

It can be seen from numerous Sufi treatises that Muslims like to present metaphysical truths—to the extent possible—as a function of subjective experience, whereas Hindus for example present these truths in pure objectivity as if the subject did not exist, which seems paradoxical when one considers the transcendent subjectivism of the *Vedānta;* it is true that Muslims do the same in their Neoplatonic treatises—which are always fundamentally Koranic or Muhammadan—but the most general expression of Sufism unquestionably has the subjectivist character we have indicated, which means that the stages leading toward transcendent Reality are presented less as objective and immutable "envelopes of the Self" than as "moral" stations—in the widest and deepest sense one can give to this adjective. The "states" (*ahwāl*) and "stations" (*maqāmāt*) of Sufism are in principle innumerable, and their description is governed by the author's path, which does not alter the fact that on the one hand these experiences clearly possess a perfectly objective character as points of reference, it being otherwise pointless to speak of them, or that on the other hand—and this must again be stressed—Islam possesses a metaphysical and cosmological doctrine expressed in objective terms, founded on the Koran and the *Sunnah,* and possibly influenced in its conceptualization by the categories of Hellenistic esoterism.

But in Islam spirituality properly so called always retains its solidarity with the "objective subjectivism" of faith—hence with the sincerity of faith and with the inward virtues determined by unitary Truth—of which the Koran and the *Sunnah* are the paradigms; the originality of Sufism is that it presents itself as a metaphysics of the human virtues that are inherent in faith—or, let us say, in consciousness of the Absolute—and that in the final analysis are rendered supernatural by this very inherence.

The distinction between the "possible" and the "necessary" in Sufism leads us to formulate or recall the following precision: esoterism is without a homeland, and it establishes itself wherever it can. Historical Sufism is *grosso modo* a sector of the exoterism in which esoterism has found refuge; esoterism is not like the branch of a tree but like mistletoe, descended from Heaven and placed on the branch; and this association justifies one in saying in a general way that Sufism is esoterism. Thus we do not say that this equation is wrong, but that it is approximate and sufficient for ordinary language; and this is all the more true in that the esoteric tendency in any case contains degrees.

*
*   *

The presence of the element "intoxication" (*sukr*) at the heart of Islam—but then we find ourselves in compensatory esoterism and *bhakti*—is all the more paradoxical in that Islam is indirectly aware of the disequilibrating element contained *de facto* within Christianity, for better or worse: in fact the Renaissance, betrayal though it was, would never have taken hold had it not benefited from a reaction against an idealism of the hereafter—itself contemptuous of an accursed here-below—which weighed upon souls and bodies in an unrealistic and disproportionate fashion. To an accursed "natural", anathematized by an isolated and apparently hostile "supernatural", Islam means to oppose a sanctified and thereby supernaturalized "natural", which it could not realize except at the price of some excesses, in keeping with the ineluctable principle of the "human margin". Islam senses in Christianity a sort of "wine", and the prohibition of intoxicating beverages is in a sense parallel to the rejection of the penitential idealism that characterizes Christianity; intrinsically speaking, this prohibition runs parallel to the affirmation of equilibrium or stability, hence to the integration of the virtualities of disequilibrium.[23]

Still on the subject of "wine" or "intoxication", it is appropriate to note that one of the most authentic expressions of Muslim esoterism is the dance of the dervishes, which has as its basis not the elaborations of theology, but either the Names *Allāh* or *Huwa* ("He") or the

---

[23] During the "Night Journey" (*Laylat al-Mi'rāj*) the Archangel Gabriel allowed the Prophet to choose between three beverages: water, wine, and milk; the Prophet chose milk, which here symbolizes equilibrium or the happy medium. Even the Koranic style can be explained by this rejection of both water and wine, that is, of a logician-like transparency that is felt to be too "easy" and irreverent and a mystical musicality that is too enthralling and thus too dangerous—an observation that is valid at least for the general style of the Koran, which is both dry and sibylline, though at the same time endowed with a virile rhythm.

Shahādah—symbol of all faith and metaphysics—combined with the mystery of the Heart and therefore the mystery of Union. The theme of this dance, like that of the *Dhikr* in general and in the final analysis even of all sacred art, is the return of the accidents to the Substance: in other words art in general and dance in particular express the Substance that has become accident; and it is from this origin that the beauty, profundity, and power of accident-symbols come. Art expresses this relationship in a movement that is at once descending and ascending, for on the one hand it reveals the Archetype in the form and on the other hand it brings the form or the soul back to the Archetype.[24]

The return of the accidental to the Substance, of the formal to the Essence,[25] amounts to the reintegration of plurality into Unity; now Unity, which in the geometrical order is equivalent to the point, includes in reality and as if by compensation a mystery of dilation, precisely as the Absolute by definition includes Infinitude; perfect concentration coincides with an "expansion of the breast" (*inshirāh*), whence the name *dhikr al-sadr* ("invocation by the breast") that is sometimes given to the dance of the dervishes.

This dance pertains, like sexual life, to a magic that is at once vital, existential, and sacramental; it symbolically transfers the finite into the Infinite or the "I" into the Self in a manner that is virtual and yet at the same time effective on its psychological plane. Other dances have the function of evoking a cosmic genius—that of love, for example, or that of war; the sacred dance for its part does not tend toward such and such an essence, but toward the Essence as such. It tends this way in principle and under the veil of less absolute but always interiorizing intentions: virtually bringing form back to Essence, it prefigures the

---

[24] What constitutes the falseness of extra-traditional art is that it wishes to express the accidentality of accidents, thereby losing its entire reason for being—except for the completely negative reason of accidentalizing souls and minds, hence of making them outward and worldly.

[25] The difference between the two expressions is that there is continuity in the case of Substance—even though conditional—whereas there is discontinuity in the case of Essence, hence a "leap into the void"; this is the whole difference between concentric circles and the cross.

mystery of union, the mystical miracle that causes the drop to become again the sea.[26]

Christians readily reproach this type of practice for its "easiness" and "artificial" character, but this is because Westerners rarely have a sense of the metaphysical transparency of phenomena and because they insist as a matter of preference on penitential means; this is the point of view of the moral alternative, not that of contemplative participation in the Archetype by means of the symbol or in the Essence by means of the form. Nevertheless there have always been popular dances in Europe in spite of the ill humor of the religious authorities, and it is probable they were not always profane—those of the month of May for instance—which means that sacred intentions in varying degrees, inherited from Nordic or Mediterranean antiquity, may have found refuge in them.[27]

*
*   *

Since it is in the nature of esoterism to recognize the essence—by definition one—in every form, whether religious or sapiential, and thus to be tolerant as far as possible in practice, one may be surprised to find among Sufis not only denominational narrowness but also intolerance; this is a mere lack of information in many cases, and yet a lack of spiritual imagination in others and an inconsistency with regard to the principle of essentiality and universality. Even when this is not the case, it is necessary to greet declarations of universality with caution, for it can happen that they also embrace idolaters, so that one does not know whether the "tolerance" has in view particular formal reli-

---

[26] Rumi: "In the rhythms of music a secret is hidden: if I were to divulge it, it would overwhelm the world." Like Chaitanya, Rumi had "chosen the way of dance and music" among the "roads that lead to God".

[27] In Judaism the dance of Miriam and that of David left a concrete memory, whence the persistence down to our own day of a dance that is either liturgical or properly mystical: a dance of triumph after the crossing of the "Red Sea" of the passions and a dance of joy before the divine Presence, the *Shekhinah*, actualized first by the "Ark of the Covenant", then by the Holy of Holies in the Temple, and later in the diaspora by the *Sepher Torah*.

gions or simply a sort of underlying and unconscious natural religion that refers to the Divinity because everything does; in the second case the attestation of universality is meant to testify to the loftiness of spirit of the Sufi and not to the validity of other religions. Moreover such declarations are sometimes followed by passages establishing the supremacy of Islam, passages that cannot be explained simply in terms of circumspection, for if one must fear the ʿulamāʾ to so great an extent it would be better not to speak of universality at all—unless what we have here is a kind of dividing of the mind as with the "double truth" of the Christian Middle Ages, in which case it is difficult to know where to place the accent or to what degree the line of demarcation is transparent.

The question that arises here *a priori* is the following, and it is both banal and enigmatic: why are religions and theologies not tolerant of other religions and theologies?[28] This intolerance is often regarded as a needless and regrettable luxury, and it is so regarded by ignorant esoterists as well as profane idealists; in reality, however, it is the only possible means of protection against errors, for if it is assumed that a religion could proclaim that salvation can also come from somewhere else, how could this religion still reject false masters who present themselves in the name of a personal revelation? If a religion is intolerant, it will no doubt exclude many foreign values, but since it offers everything man needs to reach his final end, the harm is in practice quite relative; if it is tolerant, however, it opens the door to the lethal poison of pseudo-spiritualisms without the values of the foreign religions offering the slightest help. What this means is that intolerance is merely an extreme simplification of the self-protection necessary for every spiritual form, hence a kind of preventive war against all possible counterfeits and corruptions; now it is infinitely more important for a religion to keep intact its truths and spiritual means, which are certain and in practice sufficient, than to open itself to foreign values at the risk of losing its own.

As for esoterism, it is necessarily open in principle to all intrinsically orthodox forms, but it compensates for this openness and the

---

[28] Not necessarily with regard to a given philosophy since philosophies are hardly ever presented with religious requirements; if they are, they are either denominational theories or particularly harmful human inventions.

dangers it may include with criteria that are all the more rigorous, which are proper to itself and which in fact are beyond the reach of exoterism; exoterism has no need of them precisely since its nature permits it to simplify the question *a priori*. Intrinsic truth obviously has priority over the problem of its possible forms; metaphysics, combined with human experience, obliges us nonetheless to accept the diversity of the forms of the one Truth.[29]

Among the statements made by Ibn Arabi about the universality of truth and thus about the "religion of the heart", the most explicit—and the one most directly in conformity with the esoteric perspective—is doubtless the following, which comes from the *Fusūs al-Hikam:* "The believer . . . praises only the Divinity contained within his belief (such as it is contained therein), and it is to this he is attached; he cannot perform any act that does not revert to him (its author), and likewise he cannot praise anything without thereby (in effect) praising himself. For to praise the work is without doubt only to praise its author; beauty, like the lack of beauty, reverts to the author (of the work). The Divinity in whom one believes is (so to

---

[29] In principle—although the hypothesis is excluded for more than one reason—Christ could have said that Hinduism is a form of truth, but he could not have enumerated all the Hindu heresies that existed in his time or all the heresies still to come, and so on for all the religions. It sufficed for him to say that he himself is the truth, which is absolutely certain and which in practice is sufficient for a given human cosmos or given predestined men. In his *Tarjumān al-Ashwāq*, Ibn Arabi sings: "My heart has become receptive to every form . . . a temple for idols, a kaaba for a Muslim pilgrim, the tablets of the *Torah* and the book of the Koran. I adhere to the religion of love." All religious forms, Ibn Arabi comments, are united in the love of God, and yet: "No religion is more excellent than the one founded on the love—and need—of God. . . . This religion of love is the prerogative of Muslims; for the station of the most perfect love has been imparted exclusively to the Prophet Muhammad and not the other Prophets; for God accepted him as his well-beloved friend." The extenuating circumstance for this abrupt and unintelligible denominationalism is the fact that for each religion the Prophet who founded it is the sole personification of the total, not the partial, *Logos;* nonetheless one might expect an esoterist not to enclose himself in this concept-symbol but, since he has opted for the essence, to take into account the relativity of forms, even those that are dear to him, and to do so in an objective and concrete, and not merely metaphorical, manner—or else to remain silent, for pity's sake. One is obliged, however, to take note of the *de facto* existence of two esoterisms, one partially formalistic and the other perfectly consistent, all the more so as facts cannot always be at the level of principles.

speak) fashioned by him who conceives (*nādhir*), and it is therefore (in this respect) his work; the praise addressed to what he believes is praise addressed (indirectly and with regard to conceptualization) to himself. And this is why he (the believer insofar as he limits God) condemns every belief except his own: if he were just, he would not do this; but he does it because, fixed on a particular object of worship (*al-maʿbūd al-khāss*), he is beyond all doubt in ignorance; and this is why his belief in God implies the negation of everything that is other than it. If he knew what Junayd said—that the color of the water is the color of the vessel—he would allow every believer (whose belief is other than his own) to believe what he (the other believer) believes; he would know God in every form and in every object of belief. But he (the man limited by his belief) follows his opinions without having (total) knowledge, and this is why God said (through a *hadīth qudsī*): I conform to the opinion my servant forms of Me (*anā ʿinda zanni ʿabdī bī*). That is, I appear to him only in the form of his belief; if he will, let him expand (*atlaqa*) (his conception of Me), and if he will, let him constrict it (*qayyada*). The Divinity in which one believes assumes the limits (of the belief), and this is the Divinity which (according to a *hadīth qudsī*) the heart of the slave contains, the absolute Divinity not being contained in anything since it is the essence of things as well as its own essence." It is important to understand here that the image of the "believer who praises himself" must be applied above all, according to the logic of things, to a given religious point of view and therefore to a given believing collectivity and further that the fact of thus praising "oneself" does not rule out the possibility—obviously since one cannot do otherwise—that at the same time and above all one praises God: not some specific conception of God but, by means of it, the Divinity in itself.

It follows from these considerations that God is the same for all the religions only in the divine "stratosphere", not in the human "atmosphere"; in this "atmosphere" each religion has its own God for all practical purposes, and there are as many Gods as there are religions. In this sense it could be said that esoterism alone is absolutely monotheistic, it alone recognizing only one religion under diverse forms. For if it is true that the form "is" in a certain manner the essence, the essence on the contrary is in no way the form; the drop is water, but water is not the drop.

*

* *

The fact that man tends to conceive in his own image what he worships is also proven by various levels of piety within the same religious collectivity, but here more than ever we must be careful not to attribute to God the limitations of men. Admittedly, God accepts the distinctive piety of the pedantic or excessively servile soul, but not as if He were an accomplice or a despot; otherwise He would not respond to intelligence or nobility, which pierce the fog of a limited mentality.[30] God can assuredly love littleness insofar as it is weak, simple, trusting, and touching; He cannot love in it any possible aspects of pettiness or opacity. Moreover—and confusions are frequent on this plane—God hates arrogance but not a well-inspired pride, hypocrisy but not a dignity that is natural and inherent in the sense of the sacred, profane and impertinent curiosity but not the need for explanation that is a part of understanding. God demands humility but not necessarily modesty, sincerity but not cynicism even if it is well intentioned,[31] obedience but not servility to the extent it takes away from man what God has granted him. And above all: God is supremely free without His freedom giving rise to arbitrariness; He is Necessary Being without His necessity implying the least constraint. "God doeth what He will": this Koranic expression means above all that God is what He is.

---

[30] Every mentality as such includes limits, but it is of particular, not general and existential, limitations that we are speaking here.

[31] As in the case of the *malāmatiyah*, who through sincerism "show the bad and hide the good".

Paradoxes of an Esoterism

A Sufi author was able to write without hesitation that the supreme state, compared to which every other state is but a veil (*hijāb*) and remotion (*buʿd*), consists in there no longer being any place in consciousness for any created thing; in saying this he is not speaking of ecstasy, but intends to describe the habitual state of man—as if this did not ruin the very notion of the human being or the creature as such and as if any saint, beginning with the Prophet himself, had ever shown an example of such sublimity, which in fact is as impossible as it is unnecessary. This sublimity nonetheless offers an "ideal" image, which in its fashion is most suggestive of union with God; this we concede in taking account of a temperament that is sensitive to this type of hyperbolism. It seems to us, however, that it would have been more realistic to say: when a man absents himself from the world for God, God makes Himself present in the world for man; but even if he were the greatest saint, a man does not cease to perceive things; he does not see God in their place, but sees them "in God", and they communicate to him "something of God".

Another example of excessive dialectic is the following, and we have already referred to it: a certain Sufi affirms that everything is good since everything that exists is willed by God, and he feels obliged to conclude that evil is only a matter of perspective. The author of this thesis and his partisans are right to say that everything is good through pure existence and the positive qualities superimposed upon it,[1] but not to subjectivize evil—not to fail in seeing that evil results from the distance necessitated by cosmogonic radiation and manifests the privation of the good precisely, thus marking the absence of the Sovereign Good. We have seen above that a certain kind of monism thinks it can subjectivize evil not only in the case of creatures but even in the case of God: evil, it is said, is what God does not like; this is logic in reverse and is explained by a pious concern not to make divine attitudes depend on external causes and always to leave the initiative or *primum mobile* to the Divinity, as if it were not sufficient to state

---

[1] This moreover is the thesis of Saint Augustine.

that there are phenomena contrary to the divine Prototype—not in their ontological necessity but in their simple phenomenality—and that God is opposed to them on the plane where this opposition has a meaning.

On a completely different level, but in the same category of excessive speculations, is the following example: when the patriarch Joseph made himself known to his brothers and the brothers prostrated themselves before him, he remembered his prophetic dream—the sun and the moon and eleven stars bowing down before him[2]—and he made this remark, according to the Koran: "This is the interpretation of my dream of old that my Lord hath made real"; now quoting this impeccable passage in his *Fusūs* (the chapter *Kalimah Yūsufiyah*), Ibn Arabi thinks it necessary to introduce the *hadīth*: "People are asleep (during their lives), and when they die they wake up"; in other words he takes the opportunity to declare that Joseph did not know this truth, and he does so in order to conclude that Muhammad was wiser: "See then"—he says to the reader—"how excellent are the knowledge and rank of Muhammad!" Question: how can one believe for an instant that Joseph, having the quality of Prophet, did not know that earthly life is a dream and death an awakening? And even if he did not have this quality, how can one prove by referring to the quoted words—which concern a particular fact and not a principle—that he did not know the truth expressed by the *hadīth* in question? Moreover, a Vedantist might make the point—without any Sufi rushing to exalt his "knowledge" or "rank"—that the beyond is likewise but a dream and awakening is only in the Absolute or again that the *jīvan-mukta* has realized this supreme awakening without having had to pass through bodily death, which is therefore not the condition *sine qua non* of ultimate awakening. Finally, if the realization of Joseph's dream is not the homage of his brothers, what then is it and how does Ibn Arabi envisage a realization of this dream in the beyond? This is not even to mention the fact that, according to the Koran, it is God Himself who taught Joseph the interpretation of dreams.[3]

---

[2] The Islamic tradition does not seem to have retained the other dream, that of the sheaves of Joseph's brothers bowing down before Joseph's sheaf.

[3] Moreover, if Joseph's knowledge was imperfect and if it was because of this imperfection that he remembered his dreams when he saw his brothers prostrate

One may think that in writing these lines of the *Fusūs* Ibn Arabi wished to acquit himself of a duty of piety toward the Prophet—to speak well of him, to miss no opportunity of doing so, even to the detriment of other Messengers. When reading passages of this kind, one must in fact take into account the following principle of Muslim piety: it is morally beautiful to seize every opportunity to speak well of the Prophet in whatever way possible, though on condition that one does not say he is the son of God; hence when speaking of other Messengers, it is not a question of defining them, but solely a question of making use of their names to buttress the scale of values proper to Islam. All the same one has a right to expect a more nuanced and objective perspective in an esoteric context.

In a similar vein—not as far as we know in Ibn Arabi but in his favorite disciple, Sadr al-Din Qunyawi—we find reference to the following story, traces of which are also to be found in Attar, in his *Mantiq al-Tayr* as well as his *Elāhi Nāmeh*: Christ, at the moment of his ascension, was stopped at the threshold of the fourth Heaven by angels; they examined him and, having found a pin in his clothing, prevented him from ascending further, or according to another version they prevented him from so doing until he rid himself of the pin. We assume that in its fundamental intention this extravagant story is directed at Christian theology insofar as it divinizes Jesus and reduces God to a Trinity—insofar as it "Christifies" God, if one prefers—but in fact the story implicates the very person of Christ, and there is little likelihood the average reader will guess the polemical intention we have mentioned by way of hypothesis, which would constitute an attenuating circumstance, dogmatic oppositions being what they are.[4] In this same category, one in which storytelling is deprived of a sense of proportion as well as a sense of the ridiculous and where poverty of imagination is readily combined with exaggeration, we find in Attar,

---

themselves before him, his knowledge was also imperfect when he explained their dreams to his two companions in prison and then to the king. According to this opinion, every interpretation of premonitory dreams would have to be reduced to the idea that death is their only realization, and this empties the very notion of "interpretation" (*ta'wīl*) of all its content.

[4] A quite relative attenuating circumstance as far as the Prophet is concerned, for very often, if not always, the Muhammadology of the Sufis amounts in practice to a divinization.

Qunyawi, and other authors an anecdote about the Archangel Gabriel, who, seeking to accompany the Prophet on the "Night Journey" right up to God, was stopped by the scissors of the "no" (*lā*) of the *Shahādah*, which cut a hundred thousand feathers from his wings,[5] only the Prophet having the right and capacity to proceed to the end.

Among exegetes there is an incurable breed who always know better and always insist upon dotting the i's—in short, who always know everything. When the Koran tells us that God, seeing Abraham thrown into the flames, gives them the order "Be cold", the exegetes in question know better what actually occurred: the Archangel Gabriel brought a celestial tunic, which protected Abraham against the fire. And when, three generations later, Joseph sent his tunic to his father, who had become blind and who recovered his sight upon contact with the garment, our commentators know better: it was not Joseph's tunic but Abraham's, inherited by Joseph—as if the tunic of Joseph, prophet and patriarch, would not have sufficed to bring about the miracle and as if the symbolism of the story did not require that Jacob, having become blind because of his having wept for Joseph, should be healed by Joseph precisely, and as if Joseph could have inherited something as precious as Abraham's tunic when, with the exception of Benjamin, he was the youngest of eight brothers, and what brothers! It is just as improbable that they, upon throwing Joseph naked into the well, should have let him keep the miraculous tunic[6] and that the slave merchants and later the Egyptians should have left it with him. Be that as it may, the Koran relates without any ambiguity these words of Joseph: "Take this my tunic; apply it to my father's face; he will recover his sight"—"my tunic" and not "Abraham's tunic".[7] Without being a pedant or perfectionist one may

---

[5] *Lā ilāha illā 'Llāh*: "No divinity except God (*Allāh*) (alone)." In Arabic script the word *lā* resembles a pair of scissors.

[6] Enclosed in a small bag attached to his neck, it seems, which must have made a fairly bulky object; we are asked to believe that the young man always carried it beneath his clothing.

[7] Omar Suhrawardi, although a great theologian, turns to this story when he speaks of the patched robe (*muraqqaʿah*) of the Sufis and even mentions the chain of those who passed it on. Once again we do not contest that such stories may contain a symbolism, even a profound one, but they are nonetheless absurd in their materiality; it is true

conclude that an interpretation, though it may have the function of completing a statement that is elliptical at the literal level, does not on the contrary have the right to seek to correct and contradict a perfectly clear and sufficient text.

Still in the realm of pious one-sidedness and disproportion, though on a less blameworthy scale, tradition or legend attributes acts of goodness to the Prophet—not by inventing them but by presenting them as principles and remaining silent about complementary features[8]—that would in any circumstance have been impracticable, not so much for the Prophet as for the people who would have benefited from them and who could not all have been saints capable of bearing such solicitude without abusing it. What the chroniclers seem to forget is that a kindness must be proportioned to those who receive it, or conversely that the virtue of those who receive it must be proportioned to the kindness; that a sense of proportion, according to the Koran itself, is just as much a virtue as generosity; and that it is a mistake, to say the least, to attribute qualities to a man—or rather the application of qualities—that are foreign to God, which shows precisely that they are the products of a moral idealism and not concrete modes of acting.

Admittedly, the efforts and virtues of Muslims in general and Sufis in particular would be inexplicable without the eminent virtues of the Prophet; Islam itself would be inexplicable without them. We must nonetheless recognize that the traditional stories give only a general idea of these virtues with any certainty and moreover that they suggest to the Christian reader—even if he brings no ill will to the subject—an impression of unreality, for which he cannot be blamed, and this is

that the absurdity can itself indicate a purely symbolic intention, which would be a sufficient explanation if the end always justified the means. In any case everything in this story is explained when one acknowledges that it is a question of an Abrahamic charism inherited only by Joseph, namely, a bodily radiance at once protective and healing; but this has no connection with the patched clothing of the Sufis, which indicates poverty not glory, the earthly not the heavenly.

[8] According to al-Ghazzali and others, the Prophet never became angry; one certainly does not expect this of him, and yet Moses and Jesus did exhibit holy anger; how can one believe that Muhammad—an Arab and a warrior—never did so? Aisha reports that the soul of the Prophet was like the Koran; now the Koran expresses anger by informing us—and assuring us—of the Wrath of God.

because of the inconsistencies in these accounts as much as their quite unnecessary use of hyperbole, objectively speaking.[9]

The desire to attribute the height of all possible perfections to the Prophet—almost automatically and often to him alone—impedes in many cases the definition or description of real qualities: thus when we are told that the Prophet left behind him the two worlds with all their pleasures and that he was thus the greatest of ascetics—he to whom "women and perfumes" were made "lovable"—history gives us no element to corroborate this portrait, or to corroborate it with strength and precision, whereas it does show us with certainty that there was no trace of pettiness in the Prophet's character.[10] If we were told on the contrary, in reference to the principle of a nature sanctified in advance,[11] that the Prophet was *a priori* detached from things because he encountered through them their prefigurations *in divinis*—in which case the question of asceticism does not arise—we would have no difficulty in accepting such a proposition, since we know that what is in question here is a possibility proper to the nature of the Messengers from Heaven.[12]

We have more than once had occasion to quote this formulation by a Church Father: "God became man that man might become God"— and to paraphrase it thus in Vedantic terms: "*Ātmā* became *Māyā* that *Māyā* might become *Ātmā*"; or in Buddhist terms: "*Nirvāna* became *Samsāra* that *Samsāra* might become *Nirvāna*." With regard to the

---

[9] Furthermore, there is not only hyperbolism as such, but also exaggerations of a reductive kind: for example, one extols the "station" of a saint and then adds in essence that he never lied or stole, which is indeed the least of things; or one relates that a saint received such and such a sublime investiture in a given heavenly assembly and then adds that henceforth he had the duty of ensuring the strict observance of the religious prescriptions, which any cadi can do.

[10] Even if the contrary opinion is not always a matter of prejudice or bad faith, it proves at least a complete lack of psychology or even simply of discernment with regard to circumstances as well as with regard to men.

[11] This is expressed by the "opening of the breast" of the infant Muhammad: two angels removed a clot of blood from his breast and replaced it with snow.

[12] The Koran indicates this possibility in these words: "And verily, thou art of a supereminent nature" (*'alā khuluqin azīm*) (*Sūrah* "The Pen" [68]:4), which is certainly a basis for appreciation, but not to the detriment of other "Messengers", who on the contrary are included in this eulogy.

personality of the Prophet as an "avataric" phenomenon, we could say: the *Logos* became "average man" that average man might become the *Logos*; we offer this paraphrase as a key and in connection with what we said above without its being necessary, we hope, to explain it in a detailed manner or justify the terms.

But let us return to the question of moral qualities: Ashari and others, in the name of the Islam of which they seek to be spokesmen, demand a maximum of virtues on the basis of a metaphysical, or simply logical, minimum of intelligibility of God; in other words they present an image of God that makes the effort to be virtuous as difficult as possible. In short they replace logic by threats even more than by enticement, which in the final analysis does wrong to both God and man.

*

* *

According to the Asharite thesis, to which we have already referred, evil comes from God in the same way as good; God created men and made rules for them, but He was not obliged to do either; moreover He can impose obligations on men that they are incapable of carrying out; He can punish a creature who has not sinned and without owing him any compensation, for He "doeth what He will": He owes nothing to man and therefore owes him no goodness; He has no obligation.[13] Still according to the same thesis, the knowledge of God, which is incumbent on man, results from divine Law and not from intelligence; the same applies to the obedience man owes to God: intelligence

---

[13] When the Koran says that "God doeth what He will", this means that the Principle, being infinite, possesses All-Possibility, from which spring forth the indefinitely diverse combinations of particular possibilities. These possibilities are in a constant battle so to speak with the impossible: if the color gray exists, it is to overcome—"as far as possible", precisely—the impossibility that black should be white or that white should be black; if there is a square whose sides are slightly curved, it is to overcome the impossibility—always "to the extent possible"—that a square should be round or a circle square. "With God all things are possible," said Christ; this means that the divine Possible can always intervene "vertically" on planes whose possibilities are only "horizontal"—or "natural", if one prefers.

49

exists only for drawing practical consequences from divine commands. It seems to be forgotten that man, whose privilege of vertical stature and speech is not for nothing, was created "in the image of God", that God created him in order to have an interlocutor and not a slave limited to carrying out divine commands and contravening them when God should so decide. This amounts to saying that Ashari confuses metaphysics with morality, or even with immorality in certain cases: he does not see that God, having created man so as to have a "valid interlocutor", "wishes to owe" something to man, or else He would not have created him;[14] and this is entirely independent of the fact that man, insofar as he is a simple contingency, is nothing with regard to the Absolute, as is the whole world. In short, Asharism denies that God is free to realize the possibility of a reciprocity between Himself and a creature; thus it denies, always in the name of an ill-conceived divine freedom, the immanent logic of natural laws. What we might call the "ontological immoralism" of Ashari arises from a religious anthropomorphism grappling with the disconcerting complexity of *Māyā*: it comes from attributing the divergent effects of divine Radiation to one single divine subjectivity—divergent effects, but perfectly compatible when one recalls that *Māyā* is rooted in the principial order, whence a certain diversity in this order itself.[15] But in a world in which everyone wants to be king it was perhaps better from the theological point of view to say—even in a monstrous fashion—that God is the Master than not to say it at all.

---

[14] "Then We shall save our Messengers and those who believe; thus it is incumbent upon Us (*haqqan ʿalaynā* = "is a duty for Us") to save the believers" (*Sūrah* "Jonah" [10]:104). And likewise: "And We took vengeance upon those who sinned; and it is incumbent upon Us to help the believers" (*Sūrah* "The Romans" [30]:47). In other words what is "incumbent" upon God as a duty is what is in His nature: He must help believers not for the exclusive and accidental reason that He "wills it", but for the principial reason—actualized in specific circumstances—that by virtue of His nature He sustains the true and the good, to which He will necessarily give final victory, being Himself Truth and Goodness. It is in the same sense that God "hath prescribed for Himself Mercy" (*Sūrah* "Cattle" [6]:12, 54); He is not merciful in His essence because He decides to be so, but He exercises Mercy because it is in His nature. He is not what He wills, but He wills what He is.

[15] This is suggested in Hebrew by the plural *Elohim*, at least in a higher and "vertical" sense, the usual and "horizontal" sense doubtless referring to the divine "Names".

No doubt there are grounds for scandal in theological blunderings, but fundamentally no more so than in the formal divergences of the religions: not of course in the simple fact of their plurality, for one readily accepts the diversity of crystals or flowers, but in their flagrant contradictions and reciprocal anathemas. "And the light shineth in darkness; and the darkness comprehended it not": in addition to their immediate sense these words also apply to every Revelation insofar as it is not grasped in all its dimensions by the collectivity—we do not say the few—a collectivity whose spokesmen are the theologians precisely. Religion is to a large extent in the hands of "psychics", not "pneumatics"; in descending, the Word adapts itself to the needs of "sinners" more than to those of the "righteous";[16] the collective soul collaborates in the outward covering of the Revelation owing to the fact that this soul is the Revelation's plane of resonance.

*

*   *

But let us return to the pious excesses of language that seem to be authorized—or not prevented—by the point of view of faith: Ghazzali, who elsewhere criticizes the excesses of fear, relates in his *'Ihyā*—whether rightly or wrongly—that Abu Bakr would have preferred to be a bird rather than a man because of his fear of the Judgment; that Omar for the same reason would have preferred to be a piece of straw; that Hasan al-Basri would have considered himself lucky if he could receive the assurance he would escape from hell after being there for a thousand years; that tens of thousands of people would have died of fright after having heard a sermon by David on hell; and other stories of this kind. What can one conclude from these extravagances? Their demerit lies not only in the exaggeration itself, but also in the isola-

---

[16] In a Christian context this results in exaggerations like the following, which at least is not presented as esoterism: according to Pascal, "There are two classes of men, saints who consider themselves guilty of every fault and sinners who think they are guilty of nothing." One would like to know whether the author of these words considered himself guilty of every fault and, if not, why he attributed this sentiment to the saints; or conversely, since he attributed this sentiment to the saints, why he did not share it.

tion of this exaggeration, an isolation believed to render them more striking and more fully efficacious—one does not wish to adulterate the mystery of terror—though logically it makes them either all the more hopeless or all the more improbable. As a matter of fact these shock-images manifest at one and the same time three values: the sense of the absolute, moral idealism, and indignation at the spectacle of worldly heedlessness. Even so they are incompatible with *gnosis* and are incoherent when referring to the state of soul of a saint; if this state of soul is ephemeral, one ought to say so at once. Let us recall that Ghazzali was a Sufi and not one of the least; otherwise we would have no reason for drawing attention to these things.

One may be surprised that in Islam the perspective of fear, which in its most extreme formulations—when these are accepted at face value—removes practically all meaning from existence, is not opposed to marriage nor in particular to polygamy, as if there were no logical and moral connection between fear and penance,[17] a connection Muslims nonetheless understand very well when it comes to fasting. For Islam nothing is contrary to fear except what diverts us from God *de jure* or *de facto*; now Sufis, while admitting that marriage may include this danger, envisage in the first place the sacred character of sexuality—its quality of Platonic *anamnesis* in particular, which "causes a desire for paradise"—so that sexual pleasure appears to them as at least neutral with regard to fear of the Judgment and as something related to trust and hope. Independently of this aspect of things, they look on conjugal life in a practical and social respect, hence with a view to procreation; finally, they see in it a means of escaping from that distracting preoccupation which is the "goad of the flesh": sexual pleasure being for them something spiritually neutral—and harmful only when it is sought for itself, in which case it becomes "animal" and

---

[17] All the same it must not be forgotten that the numerous marriages of Hasan, the son of Ali, had as their aim the creation of a caste of *sharīfs* as large and diverse as possible. Nevertheless, and this is a completely different point: that a man who has four "legal" wives and several concubine slaves can be considered "chaste" because he does not touch the hand of another woman is for the Westerner one of the enigmas of the Muslim mentality; it is explained by a sort of habitual confusion between legalism and virtue.

separates one from God[18]—they see no reason to expose themselves needlessly to the torment of the sexual instinct and the distracting preoccupation it involves. Some will object that this way of looking at things opens the door to every form of concupiscence, especially the sin of gluttony, for if there is no limit to sexuality there can be none to other satisfactions of the senses; this is false, for eating too much causes illness, degradation, and ugliness, which is not the case with the conjugal life of healthy people, and in this inequality is proof that the two domains are not comparable, except precisely when they are both reduced to animality. Be that as it may, the Muslim "ascetic" (*zāhid*) flees the world, riches, ambitions, comfort, pleasures, food considered to be superfluous, even sleep—everything save woman,[19] which does not prevent him from disparaging her on occasion; we put it this way in order to make the point that, as an Arab dialectician, he will say "woman" and not "some women"—even though he might happen to be circumspect—so that logically he puts himself in the wrong even if he is right a thousand times over.

It goes without saying that a sexual mysticism, which by definition reveals the universality and immanence of Beatitude and thus of Mercy, is incompatible with an accentuation on the fear of hell; now neither Islam in general nor Sufism in particular is founded on this perspective, but they necessarily permit its affirmation either incidentally or occasionally. In any event, if hell is a concrete and quasi-uncontrollable danger even for the holiest of men—something Islam does not teach but certain extravagances seem to suggest, a danger that would drive all other men to despair—everyone would have to become a hermit, and there could be no question either of marrying or even of eating beyond the minimum necessary to prevent us from dying of

---

[18] It should be noted that human animality is situated beneath animality as such, for animals innocently follow their immanent law and thereby enjoy a certain natural and indirect contemplation of the divine Prototype, whereas there is decadence, corruption, and subversion when man willingly reduces himself to his animality.

[19] There are doubtless a few exceptions that "prove the rule". With finesse and profundity and not without humor, Rumi judges that the sage is conquered by woman whereas the fool conquers her, for the fool is brutalized by his passion and does not know the *barakah* of love and delicate sentiments, whereas the sage sees in the lovable woman a ray from God and in the feminine body an image of creative Power.

hunger;[20] this is perhaps a truism, but in fact Sufi authors have not always been consistent in their manner of presenting—explicitly or implicitly—the compatibility between the fear of God and sexual life.[21]

Having spoken of fear, we must now say something about the point of view of trust, which on the one hand compensates in a complementary way for that of fear and on the other hand nullifies the excessively absolute expressions of the latter; in any case the legitimate viewpoint of fear likewise nullifies the possible excesses of the perspective of trust. Trust is no more levity or temerity than is fear dramatics or discouragement.

God created sinners so He could forgive them, Ghazzali tells us: even if the quantity of one's sins should stretch to heaven, God will forgive the believer who both hopes and asks for forgiveness, the idea of hell being "the whip that chases believers toward Paradise". According to Ali, to despair of Mercy is a greater sin on the part of the sinner than all his other sins put together. But there is not only the argument of repentance, trust, and Mercy; there is also that of the graces inherent in the sacramental formulas: above all the *Shahādah*, which effaces sins and leads to Paradise, then the formulas of praise, which cause sins to be forgiven even though they may be as "numerous as the waves on the ocean".[22] No doubt this perspective re-establishes

---

[20] This makes us think of a seeming divergence between Saint John of the Cross and Saint Teresa of Avila: having received a bunch of grapes, Saint John decided that if one thought about the Justice of God, one would never eat them, whereas Saint Teresa was of the opinion that if one thought of the Mercy of God, one would always eat them.

[21] For in the final analysis the man who fiercely intends to renounce the world and who "trembles and sweats" at the very thought of the Judgment cannot in good logic relax with his wives, as the *Sunnah* permits or recommends; if he does so, he has no right to decry too much the world we live in nor for that matter Paradise and the houris. Nor has he the right to proclaim in too shattering a manner that "God alone suffices him"—God alone in His exclusive transcendence—as if the creature did not by definition need the gifts of God and as if the Koran were not the first to affirm this.

[22] One nonetheless insists on the importance of a mind turned toward the hereafter and detached from the here-below, this disposition being both condition and consequence.

equilibrium in the general doctrine, but even so it does not abolish the excesses of the contrary perspective.[23]

There is no symmetry between Goodness and Rigor as such, for the first is ontologically more real than the second; but in practice there is a symmetry between them with regard to the generality of pious men, and even asymmetry in favor of Rigor in connection with some men or some aspect of human nature. Islam teaches nothing else, but it does so by means of an isolating dialectic, both accentuating and discontinuous, which seems characteristic of it as a result of a certain side of the Arab character.

As for the inconsistency of Sufi morals, it is sometimes more apparent than real, for it can be the effect of an ellipsism concealing specific intentions; in fact Sufism has a thoroughgoing casuistry at its disposal, which is largely able to compensate, depending on the case, for the presence of a simplistic moralism and which secretly brings us back into an esoteric climate.

*

*   *

In excesses of the type "God suffices me" there is an attenuating circumstance favoring the polygamist—we need not return to the compatibility in principle between asceticism and sexual life—and it is the following: one must take account of a difference of dimension between the spiritual intention, which pertains to principles, and life in the world and among creatures, which is of a contingent order. The ascetic (*zāhid*), while he is in the *sacratum* of prayer or contemplation, may affirm a single-minded idealism independent of human concessions, contrivances, and nuances, and he may later, outside this *sacratum*, live without contradiction or hypocrisy according to the laws of earthly life; the effects of contemplation will by themselves

---

[23] Nor the logical incompatibility between the two theses. For if it is true that God created sinners to be able to forgive them and that despair of Mercy is a sin greater than all others combined, it cannot be equally true that saints such as Abu Bakr and Omar were right in wishing to be a bird or a straw through fear of the divine Rigor. One and the same doctrine cannot bludgeon us with eschatological threats that objectively lead to despair while ordering us to rejoice in the "licit" goods of this life.

regulate and adapt his behavior in the world rather as a stone that falls into the water produces concentric circles. Excessively absolute declarations of spiritual intention would be unrealistic and hypocritical if the contemplative were not aware of the *distinguo* we have just explained and if he took his own words literally, which is something precisely that the Muslim *zāhid* does not and cannot do.

This brings us back to the question—which we have discussed on other occasions—of the two spiritual subjectivities, one being that of the empirical individual, who cannot sincerely desire a "union" beyond Paradise, and the other that of the spirit, which tends toward its own source and remains independent of every consideration of individual interest. *Advaita Vedānta*, which has nothing individualistic and therefore nothing agitated about it, considers only the second subjectivity and abandons the first to its destiny, as it were, by placing it in the hands of the divine Mother,[24] whereas Sufism accentuates the first subjectivity though without being unaware of the second, sometimes mixing the two in a way that gives rise to a drama akin to that of Christian mysticism. And this is all the more paradoxical in that there is in Islam itself a marked element of serenity, of which the most general manifestation is resignation to the Will of *Allāh* and which finds liturgical expression in the celestial and divinely leveling mantle that is the call to prayer from the top of minarets; now this omnipresent serenity is related to *gnosis* in that it is derived fundamentally from the first Truth, hence from the One, which excludes all that is not it and includes all that through it is possible.

*

* *

Let us return once more to the question of moralistic or ascetical extravagances: attenuating circumstance, we have said, but not a total excuse. Doubtless the excess is accidental and not substantial; it is nonetheless blameworthy owing to the fact that the *zāhid* is not alone but lives in a human society, which for its part has a certain right to understand him or at least not to be scandalized by him through

---

[24] For example, Parvati, Lakshmi, Tripurasundari, Sharada, Sarasvati.

no fault of its own; society would be at fault in this matter if its incomprehension were the result of its lukewarmness or worldliness, which is not the case for the pious persons of whom we are thinking here. In spite of the prejudice of certain esoterists, the mistrust of the 'ulamā—who have a right to exist, as does the "letter" itself—is largely justified by the unintelligibility and paradoxical nature of certain speculations or ascetico-mystical expressions.

Attar relates the following incident in his "Chronicle of the Saints" (*Tadhkirat al-Awliyā*): the serving maid of the famous Rabiah Adawiyyah was going to request an onion from a neighbor, but Rabiah forbade her, for she intended to ask for everything from God alone, wishing to accept nothing from men, whereupon a bird came and dropped an onion in her saucepan, but the saint did not accept it because, she said, it might have come from the demon. The doubtful nature of this story already appears in the fact that it circulates in an older and simpler version as well; but what interests us here is simply what is implied by the version Attar has not hesitated to offer us. There are in fact two important remarks to make: First, it is not normal for a man to ask God for what can or should be given him by men; one does not have the right to expect supernatural aid for things one normally obtains in a natural way. Second, one does not have the right to believe that a legitimate prayer can be answered by a demon or that the demon can respond to our legitimate trust in God; otherwise God would have no reason to fulfill our prayers or reward our trust, for He does not act to no purpose.[25] It will be said that the hagiographer was thinking only of virtues and symbolism; this is obvious, but it does not satisfy every logical need or every sense of proportion.

When we read in "Sufis of Andalusia" (*Rūh al-Quds*) that the hero, having received a luxurious house from the reigning prince,[26] gives it to the first beggar who arrives because he "has nothing else

---

[25] The demon can answer an extravagant prayer that has no chance of being accepted by God, just as it can respond to an excessive and foolhardy trust; Rabiah could thus have been right to doubt the miracle, but in this case her doubt would amount to the condemnation of her prior attitude, which the hagiographer however did not dream of criticizing.

[26] The hagiographer, who is here relating his own adventure, finds it appropriate to specify that the house cost 100,000 *dirhams*, and this in the 12th century.

to give him", we are in the midst of absurdity, and this in several respects, namely, with regard to the hero, the house, the prince, the beggar, the Law; it is clear that the aim of the story is to underscore emphatically—and perish all the rest—the disdain of things here-below and the sublimity of detachment and generosity. That conclusive facts considered in themselves and logic practiced without a moralizing hidden motive can be guarantors of truth and serve the doctrinal or moral intention to be expressed does not seem to impress itself on the attention of our pious authors, who balk at considering a thing in itself, hence "outside God"; it is therefore necessary to read them with patience, which one doubtless owes them in light of their excellent intentions and their love of God and sacred things.[27]

Very often Sufi authors, and religious authors in general, give us the impression of being as uninterested in the exactness of their facts as in the imperatives of logic, as if it were a question here of worldly things, only the landmarks of morals, mystical life, and theology seeming to hold their attention; in other words they seek to make them as striking as possible and believe they cannot achieve this effect except at the expense of objective detail or even common sense. In their minds the materiality of the facts seems to harm the expressivity of the symbol, whereas for the Westerner on the contrary this materiality supports the probability of the image and thus its instructive capacity; it is true that in this order of things everything is a question of appropriateness and degree. No doubt in certain cases the end justifies the means; this does not prevent the means from compromising the end in other cases, and this in our opinion is what occurs in the

---

[27] In pointing out the weaknesses of certain categories of religious writings—and the religious character of Sufi writings is incontestable—some may reproach us for speaking of things of which the majority of Western readers are uninformed and may object that this is not in any case the best way to prepare them for an understanding of Islam and Sufism. Our reply on the one hand is that there exists in our day a rather considerable number of good translations of Islamic works and on the other hand that we are addressing ourselves to readers with a certain knowledge of these works, who are supposed to be interested in them; in the course of their reading they have inevitably encountered—or will encounter—the pitfalls we have spoken of in this chapter. As for those readers who are not at all troubled by these pitfalls—for "East is East, and West is West"—it is obviously not for them we are clearing the ground.

literary genre we are thinking of here. In this connection it is necessary to point out above all the misuse of apologues and the habitual
confusion, born of a tendency to exaggeration, between the real and
imaginary.[28]

We could adduce in this context the fact that the Aryan, to the
extent he is an observer and a philosopher, has a tendency to describe
things as they are, whereas the Semite, who is a moralist, readily
presents them as they ought to be according to his pious sentiment;
he transcends them by sublimizing them before having had time to
extract the arguments comprised in their nature. This tendency obviously does not prevent him from being a philosopher when he wants
to be, but we are speaking here of the most immediate and most general predispositions; the abuse of apologues and quantitative images
incontestably bears witness to this, especially in the case of the Arabs,
although such excesses can be found in every religious climate, the
same psychological causes readily giving rise to the same effects.[29]

We have just contrasted the Oriental cult of the "symbol" with
the Western cult of the "fact"; now if the first can give rise to abuses,
it is only too obvious—and history proves it abundantly—that the
same is true, and *a fortiori*, of the second tendency, and this is not
only as a result of Aristotle and in the scientific domain, but even on
the religious plane. From the beginning Catholics have had attacks of
"pious skepticism" that they confuse with realism, and this in private
spirituality as well as theology;[30] this intermittent temptation has

---

[28] Ibn al-Jawzi, in the 12th century, criticizes these extravagances in his *Kitāb al-
Qussās*.

[29] Buddhists in particular do not deny themselves pious exaggeration, at least in some
aspects or sectors of the *Mahāyāna*.

[30] There is something of this in Thérèse of Lisieux—despite her angelic nature—
when she diminishes the Blessed Virgin in order to bring her "nearer": whereas the
hagiographic tradition takes account of what is implied by the unprecedented privilege
of the "Immaculate Conception" and divine Maternity, Thérèse does not know how
to reconcile the majesty and exceptional graces with simplicity and goodness; when
tradition says that at the age of three Mary went to the Temple with a heart "burning
with love for God", Thérèse considers it more probable—because more banal—that
the Virgin went there "simply to obey her parents"; it appears likewise, according
to the same sentiment, that the life of the Virgin at Nazareth as presented by the
Gospel has to be "completely ordinary" (*Novissima Verba*, collected by Mother Agnes

permitted an increasing infiltration of the profane spirit right up to the triumph of modernism, hence of the "world" and "man"—all this with the help of the creative and innovating obsession of the Europeans, in regard to which the Biblical stability and holy monotony of Islam play the role of divine warnings. Islam has been accused of "sterilizing" an entire sector of humanity, of having "arrested" history; it is one of the most useful things it could do.

*

*   *

Some might take the view that the theological or philosophical framework of an idea that is at once true and fundamental—an idea such as ontological monism (*wahdat al-wujūd*)—is of little importance, even if this framework leaves much to be desired; it is true that in Islam—inasmuch as it is a world of dogma and faith—the important thing is "what" one explains and not "how" one explains it. For the "what" is divine, hence absolute, whereas the "how" is human, hence contingent and provisional; here is the whole opposition between faith and reasoning or between Revelation and thinking. Seen from this angle, weak or even aberrant explanations of indisputable truths represent nothing other than apologetic intentions in the interest of faith; it is not these that count, but the idea they are supposed to make accessible; according to this "intellectual morality", whatever serves the truth is true.

of Jesus); now apart from the fact that the Gospel says nothing about the daily life of Mary, the life of a co-redeeming *Mater Dei* could not in any case be "ordinary" in the stupidly conventional sense of the word. For Thérèse the Blessed Virgin is "mother" more than "queen", as if Mary were not great and mysterious before making herself little and approachable; and it is for the queen, not her subjects, to decide when and how she intends to be mother, the worth and charm of the maternal intimacy residing here precisely in its combination with majesty. Moreover, if one thinks that in order to be able to "imitate" her and love her in a more fatuous manner one must attribute to the Blessed Virgin a sort of bourgeois smallness devoid of extraordinary gifts that would oblige us to an excessive admiration—this is what Thérèse intends—one should also claim the same reassuring mediocrity for Christ, in whom however one cannot deny the most supereminent human gifts; now what is absurd for the Son is equally so for the Mother, for similar reasons.

In conformity with the tendencies of Islamic piety in particular and the Semitic monotheistic perspective in general, the Muslim—if not Hellenized by vocation—does not seek to be a "philosopher", that is, a man who "doubts" and thinks "outside God", outside faith and grace; he therefore expects everything from inspiration since everything has come to him from Revelation; he has no wish to be a Prometheus. Thus it can happen that a quasi-stereotypical zeal takes precedence over logic, the latter being the *ancilla theologiae*, whence sometimes an exorbitant demand to extract from absurdity the elixir of truth, a truth that conveys a right intention nourished by the treasures of Revelation.[31]

It is most fortunate that the choice between a credulous and undisciplined language of "faith" and a skeptical and pedantic language of "reason", or between a language that is absurd but efficacious and another that is logical but inoperative, is not the only alternative.[32] It is nonetheless between these two poles or excesses that the human mind seems to vacillate, something for which neither a healthy faith, which is lucid, nor a healthy intellection, which is pious, is directly responsible.[33]

In a completely different category from the overflowing imagery of an unbridled fideism are phenomena—described in mystical books—pertaining to what we could call an objectivizing symbolist inspiration, which is drawn from the archetypes of the collective religious mind and because of which spiritual intuitions assume objective and sensible forms; in other words inward contacts with heavenly realities become outward experiences as a result of a mechanism that is proper to every religious cosmos and comparable to individual imagination, although operating in the physical world by projecting

---

[31] We have dealt with all these questions—with certain accentuations we shall not repeat here—in our book *Logic and Transcendence* in the chapter "Oriental Dialectic and Its Roots in Faith".

[32] The West, nourished on philosophy, needed the language of faith, which Christianity provided; but Christianity in turn needed the language of reason, which was provided by Scholasticism.

[33] "Lucid" by virtue of a sense of orthodoxy; "pious" by virtue of a sense of the sacred.

into it phenomena-symbols.[34] For this there is both an objective and a subjective condition: the first is a very powerful subtle aura that envelopes and nourishes a religious world, at least as long as it is sufficiently homogeneous; the second is an appropriate receptivity on the part of men—a certain "naiveté", which is nonetheless entirely capable of a "discerning of spirits"—this too being incompatible with the enfeebling and "congealing" of a world become impious. The order of phenomena we have in mind here does not pertain to the miraculous, properly speaking, since the celestial intervention therein is only indirect; but it is not a question of personal fantasies since the phenomena are outward even though their forms are precisely determined by the style of the collective religious mind. It is thus that one can explain the shower of somewhat gratuitous, though not legendary, marvels that occurred during periods of great mystical fervor and within unfissured religious worlds: the partition between the material and the subtle softens, and the psychic is objectified; we might also say that the psycho-spiritual is exteriorized to the extent the believing mentality is interiorized.

*

*   *

Compared with fideists or inspirationists, who are little concerned with coherence, the case of the Greek sophists and scientists and their successors presents exactly the opposite excess: logic on the one hand and phenomena on the other are sufficient in themselves and are therefore used as if they were cut off from their roots, whence the philosophical, scientific, and cultural monstrosities that made, and make, the modern world. And since in every work the essential content or reason for being takes precedence over expression and accident, it is obviously necessary to prefer a faulty expression of the truth to a dialectic that is brilliant but aberrant as a result of its content; one would like to apologize for having to mention this.

---

[34] Of a similar order are the purely symbolical images interspersed with historically adequate facts in the visions of Anne Catherine Emmerich.

What this means—and we are not afraid of repeating ourselves—is the following: just as there may be perfectly formulated arguments on the part of profane thinkers, so conversely the writings of a given gnostic may contain intellections that are badly expressed and even compromised by feeble arguments, but whose function nonetheless is to act as their support; now one owes it to the underlying truth to discern it to the very extent it is lofty and decisive even if in its contingent formulation there are elements of error that disfigure it, though without rendering it unusable—rather as one owes one's parents a favorable consideration even when they err through excess of zeal.

The perfect man, wrote a Sufi—and we spoke of this at the beginning of the present chapter—is one who is extinguished toward the world to the point of no longer seeing anything but God or one who only sees God to the point of no longer seeing the world. The Sufi did not realize this, for on the one hand it is not realizable and on the other hand, for this very reason, it does not have to be realized; this ideal nevertheless bears witness to a heroic tension in relation to the Divine, and this is what counts here; and it may even be that the Sufi did not seek to say anything else, which brings us back to the problem of Oriental ellipsism.[35] In any case someone might still object that the vision of the Principle alone is perfectly within the scope of the "pneumatic"; no doubt, but it does not exclude the simultaneous vision of objects—as is proven by the life of any Sufi or *jivan-mukta*, not to mention the Prophets and *Avatāras*—just as the realization of the "Self" does not exclude an individuality liberated from concupiscence.[36]

In an entirely general manner it must be fully understood that we are not criticizing the incomprehensibility of many Sufi texts, which is inevitable in the absence of commentaries providing keys to this particular language; we would not dream of reproaching a Hallaj or Niffari for the obscurity of their expressions any more than we

[35] Which consists, as we have said more than once, in isolating an idea from its often necessary context and then overemphasizing it to the point of giving it a quasi-absolute character and of ruining, logically speaking, the idea in question, whose overall intention is nonetheless plausible.

[36] This is shown irrefutably by the theological expression—applied to Christ—of "true God and true man".

would dream of reproaching the Song of Songs for such obscurity. In the absence of keys it suffices us *a priori* to perceive the beauty, the grandeur, the profundity, the power of the language, its perfume of truth and majesty, and this is quite apart from the fact that the incomprehensibility cannot be total and that there are keys moreover that end up delivering their secrets, depending on their nature and our receptivity. The fact that keys of this kind should sometimes be combined with the weaknesses of which we have spoken is a completely different matter, which does not concern the keys in themselves or those who use them correctly and with the best of rights.[37]

*

* *

We believe we have alluded more than once to the mistrust shown by the fideists toward rational investigation in matters of faith; a classic example is Hanbalite fideism, which is resistant to all symbolic interpretation of Koranic images, even to the point of absurdity. According to this school it is necessary to take note of Koranic images that express a quality or attitude of God "without asking how", hence without transposition, even in cases where the meaning results from the image itself, as for example when it is said that God is "Light" or that He is "seated" on a "Throne" or when the text speaks of the "Hand" of God. The fideists will say that it is the Koranic word itself which coincides *ipso facto* with its interpretation (*ta'wīl*) and which thus implicitly constitutes it in a certain fashion, so that every explanation of the image becomes superfluous; we would reply that in this case the very notion of *ta'wīl* loses all its meaning and that in reality the symbol-word suggests its intention by its very nature, the sufficient reason of the metaphor being precisely its capacity to transmit a meaning that is superimposed on the raw image and to transmit it without any possible doubt.[38] This is not to say that the fideist point

---

[37] These imperfections, let us say once again, are the inevitable price of what we might call the "moralization of metaphysics".

[38] Consequently, to say with the Mutazilites that the "Throne" is the authority or power of God is not even *ta'wīl*, but simply semantics and good sense. One knows the

of view has no legitimacy in itself; it applies perfectly in cases where the image is mysterious and has to be assimilated in an almost Eucharistic manner, but not when it has no meaning outside of what it signifies by its obviously metaphorical character.[39]

The fact that Ibn Arabi should occasionally support the excessive fideism of the Hanbalites is all the more paradoxical in that he himself practices the most audacious interpretation;[40] this interpretation seems to consist in reducing every Koranic verse to a statement concerned more or less directly with either the divine Essence or supreme Love, which is not only contrary to the immediate sense of the text, but to the very detriment of its coherence and obvious intention; one is entirely justified in being astonished at a procedure as unnecessary as it is paradoxical, since truth has other resources, to say the least. One of the keys to this enigma seems to be the idea that Revelation presents us above all with words and that it is incumbent on sages to explain them even if this means meticulously seeking the most far-fetched etymology and at the risk of contradicting the literal meaning or contradicting it at least on the esoteric, or supposedly esoteric, level; now it seems to us obvious on the contrary that Revelation presents us above all with ideas, not isolated words or images cut off from their necessary context, and that this is the very reason for the existence of divine discourse. These ideas admittedly give rise to a variety of interpretations, but they nonetheless do not give us the authority to isolate each detail by sublimizing it out of its context to

---

incident in which Ibn Taimiyah came down one step of the pulpit (*minbar*) in order to show that "this is how God comes down"; we would say that if these fideists have no wish to use their intelligence, at least they should not forbid others to do so. And since the Arabs make wide use of metaphors, why should God not do so when He speaks to them, especially since He does so in their own language (*lisānun ʿarabiyun mubīn*)?

[39] Ibn Hanbal undoubtedly had a valid presentiment when he excluded speculative thought along with aberrant thought, for it is better to limit oneself to believing that God created the world "from nothing" than to end up in heresy as a result of asking how.

[40] According to a theological opinion, explanatory truth is valid only if it comes from inspiration and not reflection; either this opinion is false—since truth is always truth—or else it is true, but in this case the notion of inspiration includes that of intellection or is combined with it.

the detriment of logic and coherence, and above all to the detriment of the very intentions of the discourse.

Tafsīr, "explanation", is the "outward" (*zāhir*), semantic, historical, and theological exegesis of the Koran; *ta'wīl*, "interpretation",[41] is its "inward" (*bātin*), symbolic, moral, mystical, mythological, metaphysical commentary. According to the Koran, "None knoweth its interpretation but God"; this means that man can know it only by divine inspiration, not by reasoning alone—though inspiration and reason are not mutually exclusive since the one can produce or actualize the other—and this opens the door to an inspirationism that is often problematical inasmuch as it is contemptuous of intelligence. *Ta'wīl* comprises degrees: for example, when the Koran rejects the worship of idols, idols may mean—in addition to the literal sense—things to which we are unduly attached or these attachments themselves; but more profoundly they can also mean forms as such, including the constituent elements of religion and religion itself, in which case we are at the heart of esoterism, not of the "prolonging" but of the "transcending" kind, hence secret by its paradoxical and explosive nature. This is no doubt the source of the opinion—unacceptable in our view—that a word or phrase may "esoterically" have a meaning contrary to the one it has in itself or that this meaning may come to the fore when the word or phrase is applied to the divine nature, an opinion based on the idea that every Koranic expression must have a meaning that applies to God and the love of God, a meaning that is positive as a result of the application in question.[42]

---

[41] Literally: "to return to the origin", that is, to proceed from form to essence.

[42] An example of an inadvertently inadequate interpretation is the assertion that the Koranic prohibition of idol worship means "esoterically" that the *faqīr* should obey only God, which is absurd from the human or social point of view as well as from the spiritual point of view; in fact this idea has nothing to do with idolatry, for the idolater cannot "obey" an idol, which the Koran reproaches precisely for being deaf and dumb; and the man who obeys necessarily does so with regard to a being endowed with consciousness, not an "idol". Ghazzali, who was far from being hostile to Sufism, criticized the extravagances (*tāmmāt*) of certain Sufis; according to him it is forbidden and harmful to divert sacred words or formulations from their obvious meaning, for—as he says—this ruins one's trust in the actual wording of the divine text. This is the condemnation, without appeal, of the exegesis of Ibn Arabi as well as of a certain Shiite exegesis.

*

*　　*

Another matter in this context of semi-esoterism is the frequent disproportion between means and end: in other words there are ascetical
and disciplinary measures that make no sense except for passional men
given to ambition and vanity, not to say pride, and therefore disquali-
fied for *gnosis*; now it is precisely for the sake of *gnosis* that a certain
"esoterism" imposes these measures on the most diverse men; that
is, it imposes them on men who are qualified and thus who have no
need of them as well as on men who have need of them and who by
this very fact are not qualified.[43] In saying this we are not losing sight
of the fact that there is not only profane man but also man insofar as
he carries in his soul the temptation to profanity, which requires or
allows for disciplinary measures; but these measures precisely must be
proportioned to the substance of the individual, even admitting that
there is here no rigorous line of demarcation.

A Westerner who desires to follow an esoteric way would find it
logical to inform himself first of all concerning the doctrine, then to
inquire about the method, and finally to consider its general conditions; but the Muslim of esoteric inclination—and the attitude of the
Cabalist is similar—undoubtedly has the opposite tendency: if one
speaks to him about metaphysics, he will find it natural to reply that
one must begin at the beginning, namely, with pious exercises and all
sorts of religious observances; metaphysics will be for later. He does not
seem to realize that in the eyes of the Westerner, as also the Hindu,[44]
this is to deprive the pious practices of their sufficient reason—not in
themselves of course but in relation to knowledge—and to make the
way almost unintelligible; and above all the Semitic zealot does not
see that the understanding of doctrine cannot result from a moral and
individualistic zeal, but that on the contrary it is there to inaugurate

---

[43] The Imam Abu al-Hasan al-Shadhili is one of the Sufis who very clearly saw this
contradiction and avoided it in their method; he saw nothing objectionable in his
disciples practicing lucrative professions and wearing elegant clothes and did not
dream of sending patricians to beg in front of mosques.

[44] Hence of the Aryan in general, except for groups totally Semiticized by Islam.
Christianity Semiticized Europe only in a partial way and in certain respects.

a new dimension and to elucidate its nature and purpose. The moralistic attitude is blameworthy, of course, only because of its ignorance of the opposite viewpoint or because of its exaggeration, for in fact the doctrine does deserve on our part an element of reverential fear; even our own spirit does not belong to us, and we have full access to it only to the extent we know this. If it is true that doctrine explains the meaning of devotion, it is equally true that devotion has a certain right to precede doctrine and that doctrine deserves this.

With regard to the lower moral disciplines presented as stages leading toward higher intellectual and spiritual results, the great question that arises is knowing whether metaphysical ideas act on the will of a given man or whether on the contrary they remain inoperative abstractions, that is, whether they unleash interiorizing and ascending acts of the will and affective dispositions of the same order. If this is the case, there is no need to seek to create a distaste in the person in question for a world that already hardly attracts him or for an ego that already has no more illusions or ambitions, at least not at the level that would justify coarse disciplines; it is pointless to impose attitudes on the "pneumatic" that are meaningless for him and that instead of humbling him in a salutary fashion can only bore and distract him. To think otherwise—though there are here many degrees to consider—is to place oneself outside esoterism and sapience, whatever the theories to which one thinks one can or must refer; it is to forget in particular that the "pneumatic" is the man in whom the sense of the sacred takes precedence over other tendencies, whereas in the case of the "psychic" it is the attraction of the world and the accentuation of the ego that take priority, without mentioning the "hylic" or "somatic", who sees in sensory pleasure an end in itself. It is not a particularly high degree of intelligence that constitutes initiatic qualification; it is a sense of the sacred—or the degree of this sense—with all the moral and intellectual consequences it implies. The sense of the sacred draws one away from the world and at the same time transfigures it.

Whoever contemplates the divine Majesty assimilates something of it, and he does so in parallel with a consciousness of his own nothingness; this results moreover from the fact, according to a famous *hadīth*, that God becomes "the eye with which he (the contemplative) sees and the hand with which he acts", hence in the final analysis the heart through which he is. This amounts to saying that the sense of the sacred, in spite of its relationship with fear, does not imply servility any more than the sense of truth implies narrowness; esoterism is neither petty nor fanatical. "The soul is all that it knows," as Aristotle said, and the highest function of man is the knowledge of God, which gives its imprint to everything legitimately human.

Conception, meditation, concentration, conformation; in other words, concept of Unity with its intrinsic and extrinsic mysteries;[45] assimilating meditation and unitive concentration upon Unity and its mysteries; moral conformation to Unity, to its mysteries and demands: together with the appropriate traditional supports, these are the constituent elements of the Way. Moral conformation, we said: certainly every spirituality requires the intrinsic virtues as well as discipline in outward behavior and possibly a specific purgative asceticism; this follows from the intelligence as well as from the principle that "God is beautiful and He loveth beauty" (*hadīth*); but it has no connection with ambition and perfectionism, in short with attitudes that are lacking precisely in beauty as well as in intelligence.

*
*   *

Philosophy is one thing, say the Sufis, and inspiration is another; the first comes from men and the second from God. In theory this is completely clear, but in practice what is the significance of the fact that a certain Sufi claims for a given book an inspiration coming from either God or the Prophet? In the first place there can be no question of attributing to mystical books the degree of inspiration of the Koran or *Veda*; but it is possible they are situated at the secondary degree of inspiration, the one Hindus designate by the term *smriti*, which is that of the *Purāna*s, and there are still several other levels to be considered, whose significance is increasingly relative. Relativity of inspiration is connected to the mystery referred to in the saying, which is perhaps a *hadīth*: "The divergence of the learned (of God) is a blessing"—a mystery that also includes at the highest level the divinely foreseen

---

[45] Absoluteness, Infinitude, Perfection, Transcendence, Immanence; then the prefigurations of the cosmos in the Principle on the one hand and the projections of the Principle in the cosmos on the other.

divergences of the religions, though here relativity has another meaning and import. The divine Inspirer—or the "angel of inspiration" (*malak al-ilhām*)—gives rise to many refractions in becoming subjectified: "water takes on the color of the vessel," as Junayd said; even the great revelations must take account of the resources of a collective mentality, and they cannot avoid a certain amount of damage in "shining in the darkness". However paradoxical it may seem, an intrinsically absolute conviction can have an extrinsically relative significance, but in this case there is obviously a different relationship; "no man cometh unto the Father, but by me," said Christ in function of an inward absolute truth, which nonetheless does not prevent other religions from being valid in their turn independently of Christ, though on the basis of the same truth insofar as it is essential and thereby universal, not insofar as it assumes in the case of Christ a particular extrinsic significance personified precisely by Jesus.

Hallaj claimed an inspiration "equal to that of the Koran" for a few lines written by his hand, and this is why Junayd did not hesitate to curse him; a certain number of Sufis blamed or condemned Hallaj for his *Anā 'l-Haqq* ("I am the Truth" = God), and yet tradition finally accepted both Hallaj and Junayd and the Sufis in question. The fact that Ibn Arabi wrote under heavenly inspiration does not bind Islamic orthodoxy; it does not even bind Sufi orthodoxy, as is proven by the negative attitude of the Mawlawiyah regarding the *Shaykh al-Akbar,* and this is all the more plausible in that Sufism does not recognize any absolute authority in matters of metaphysics, whereas Vedantism recognizes itself in Gaudapada, Govindapada, and Shankaracharya. The undisputed authorities of Sufism—those of the first centuries—refer only to the ascetical and mystical method, not to a sapiential doctrine properly so called.

*

*   *

If we note with great reluctance the lack of critical sense and other misdeeds of sentimentalism in many religious books whose level ought to exclude such weaknesses, it must be understood that we do not include in the notion of "sentimentalism" either the sense of beauty or love in itself, any more than we include in it contempt for things that are contemptible; sentimentalism does not consist in having sentiments, but in falsifying the truth as a result of them. To be a sentimentalist does not consist in knowing that two and two make four and at the same time loving something that deserves to be loved, but in persuading oneself that two and two make three or five simply because one desires to shower praise upon something one loves, rightly or wrongly, because one feels able in this way to corroborate or serve some idea one is fond of, or because one thinks that a given truth demands by way of consequence a given excess, whether positive or negative. In short it consists in introducing a quantitative and dynamic element—and an instigator of thoughtlessness—into the domain of the qualitative and the static and in being unaware that truth is beautiful in itself and not because of our zeal, and conversely that our zeal is beautiful only when it flows from truth.

A plausible explanation of the inconsistency one encounters in many Sufi writings is the fact that in certain cases the authors write when they are in a spiritual "state" (*ḥāl*) and because they are in it; we have referred to this above. These states have empirically something quasi-absolute about them; a given state appears unconnected, therefore, with another and equally possible state. Now the authors see sources of inspiration in these states, and of course not without reason; they do not dream of re-reading their productions nor *a fortiori* of submitting them to the scrutiny of a critical intelligence that in their eyes is "profane" because it is not ecstatic and is therefore alien to the breath of the Spirit; they leave to the reader the task of fishing for pearls in the deepest and darkest waters. The Koran nonetheless says, "Approach not prayer when ye are intoxicated," and this precept has many meanings, depending on levels and analogies.[46]

Islam as a whole has escaped that formidable pitfall which is the abuse of intelligence—which neither ancient Greece nor the modern

---

[46] It has been asserted that Ibn Arabi wrote in a state of ecstatic inspiration and that in this state he disdained the laws of logic; now it is necessary to distinguish between inspiration properly so called, which is objective and has nothing to do with ecstasy, and a subjective inspiration, which on the contrary is derived from it, but which it would be wrong in fact to assimilate to inspiration in the ordinary sense of the term. One may in any case ask oneself whether it is legitimate and useful to write in a state of "drunkenness", unless it is a question of texts whose reason for being is to give expression to such a state.

West escaped—and this has enabled it to perpetuate the world of the Bible; but it has not escaped the opposite pitfall, which we have sufficiently described in the course of this book and which is like a ransom of the intelligence for a victory over luciferism. According to an artificial dilemma, but one that is psychologically real for the Semitico-Western mentality, there is an antinomy between science and faith: the man who believes does not think, and the man who thinks does not believe; Islam is not unaware of this dilemma, but in its case faith curbed the insatiable curiosity of science.

In an ardently religious climate where faith is everything and where thought, considered conjectural by definition, amounts to little, one must expect the logic of lovers: everything good—however absurd—that one says about God, the Prophet, and sacred things is true, as if truth were guaranteed by the sublimity of the object; to reflect is then nearly a sin, for thinking appears like the manifestation of doubt and like unhealthy, even luciferian, curiosity. This is the point of view of *bhakti*, which is unaware—whether through inexperience or as a matter of principle—of the humble serenity of pure intellection, humble because impersonal and serene because conforming to That which is. All this doubtless seems like an over-simplification, but one must sometimes choose between the risk of simplifying things and the risk of not being able to say anything at all. Schematic *distinguo*s exist; they have their reason for being and no more exclude implicit compensations or nuances than the distant view of a landscape, necessary for revealing its principal features, excludes the details one observes when traveling through it.

It is important not to lose sight of the fact that the fideistic and dialectical "naiveté"[47] in question here remains completely independent of the eminent lucidity of the Arabs in matters of law, philosophy, science, art, and politics—independent in short of everything

---

[47] Fideistic: to believe what one considers one has to believe on account of dogmatic axioms without asking whether this is essential or "holds water"; dialectical: to deal with a particular point by isolating and intensifying it without asking whether this is suitable in itself and compatible with what one previously said or with other points that are just as valid.

that constituted the prestige of their civilization during the whole of the Middle Ages.[48] The fact is that in the Arab soul, which can jump from the most obstinate incredulity into the most simplistic credulity, an acute rationality opposes an overflowing enthusiasm that is either chivalric and erotic or religious and mystical, and this dilemma gives rise to opposite crystallizations as well as to diverse combinations.

When we speak of the "Arab soul", we are not unaware that it was relatively diverse from pre-Islamic times in the sense that religious indifferentism was characteristic of the Arabs of the Center and the North whereas those of the South were distinguished by a rather contemplative temperament; but all of them were homogeneous regarding their qualities of nobility. The "Arab miracle", the lightning-like expansion of Islam and the glories of medieval Islamic civilization, presupposes and includes a spirit of magnanimity whose roots are plunged in the pre-Islamic Bedouin mentality, a magnanimity that contributed—whatever the falsifiers of history may say—to the nearly unprecedented phenomenon of tolerance on the part of Muslim conquerors in the early centuries, hence at a time when the Arab influence was predominant in Islam. Bedouin magnanimity consisted essentially in "virility" (*murūwah*)—in the sense of the Latin word *virtus*—and "chivalry" (*futuwwah*), which included above all courage, generosity, and hospitality, the most precious, most fragile, and most specifically Arab trait—in the context of the Middle East—being the virtue of generosity.

In a completely general sense and independently of any racial or ethnic question, it must be said that there are gifts that exclude one another, not indeed in principle or in privileged cases, but among the majority of those who benefit from one kind or another; this seems to be the case with mystical intuition and reasoning. To take note of this fact, we must insist, does not mean one considers it a necessity; but this *de facto* incompatibility—which obviously includes many gradations—is something one is very much obliged to keep in mind, whatever explanation one seeks to give it.

---

[48] Conversely, the critical logicism of the Europeans—but everything is relative—by no means precludes passional ideologies, whether philosophical or political, and these are obviously more harmful than the flagrant and ingenuous contradictions of a hasty fideism.

In the same connection there is also another point to consider, and it is crucial: the key to many enigmas in the realm of spiritual thought is the fact that God requires of men that they be pious and virtuous, and not that they be intelligent; this provides the justification for a pious unintelligence, but is unconnected with *gnosis* and esoterism. Obviously God forbids men to make a bad use of their intelligence—persistent error being moreover in the will rather than in the mind—but He cannot blame them for not possessing an intelligence that was not given them. One is forced to admit—though in certain cases one hesitates to do so for fear of being disrespectful or ungracious—that unintelligence can set up house with piety, that it can even enter accidentally and sporadically into the realm of what should be wisdom; in any event one all too often forgets the blindingly obvious fact that it is better to follow truth stupidly than to follow error intelligently, all the more so as truth in any case neutralizes unintelligence, at least to a certain extent, whereas error can only pervert and corrupt the mind. In a word, the world of passions is necessarily also that of stupidity—intelligence showing solidarity with this world by itself becoming stupidity—so that religion, condemned to the same servitude, cannot avoid a few venial sins, which though they are not of course "against the Spirit" are at least against intelligence.

Contrary to a certain sentimental prejudice, the Holy Spirit does not have the role of making up for a lack of intelligence or abolishing stupidity; it can make it inoffensive or limit the harm it may cause and also reduce it to silence, which it does above all by humility. The miracle of humility is precisely that it alone is able to transmute unintelligence into intelligence to the extent this is possible; the humble man is intelligent by his very humility.

God requires from each man what each man can and must give; but from the intelligent man He also requires intelligence in the service of truth, for which it is made and through which it lives.[49] In some people, moreover, intelligence resides less in their words than in their being, less in their theology than in their sanctity; nonetheless the spiritual norm consists in an equilibrium between thought and virtue, between mind and beauty.

Intelligence is beautiful only when it does not destroy faith, and faith is beautiful only when it is not opposed to intelligence.

---

[49] One will recall here the parable of the talents, which refers to all possible gifts and to the duties derived from them.

Human Premises of a Religious Dilemma

If one strives too much to make transcendent truths accessible, one risks betraying them; if one strives too much not to betray them, one risks not making them accessible. This dilemma, which already exists on the level of the general religion, occurs all the more on the level of esoterism.

In speaking of accessibility, what is obviously implied is the kind of understanding it entails; now human mentalities are diverse and give rise to several degrees of receptivity. It is of this diversity or inequality that the caste system in Hinduism takes account, at least in relation to spirituality; admittedly, social functions are not independent of this relationship, but it is not this aspect of caste that concerns us here. The advantage of the Hindu system is that it greatly favors the purity of esoteric spirituality; in the absence of such a system esoterism becomes too closely linked with the average collective mentality, which cannot be proportionate to the demands of a disinterested perspective or, in other words, cannot be entirely free from denominational narcissism.

Islam, like Christianity, is not exclusively addressed to the higher human castes, and this goes without saying since it is a question of religions; furthermore it does not consider "contemplatives" separately from "actives" or "hylics" separately from "psychics", which amounts to saying that in practice it puts *kshatriya*s with a contemplative tendency in the place of *brāhmana*s and *vaishya*s with a hylic tendency in the place of *shūdra*s.[1] This being so, Muslims accentuate the *vaishya* more than the *kshatriya* element in their language and psychology because the *vaishya* is the average, practical, reasonable, and balanced man; his way quite naturally is *karma-mārga*, the way of works and merit, hence also of fear, and this is why the language and the general

---

[1] Let us recall that the *brāhmana* represents the contemplative and sacerdotal mentality; the *kshatriya* the active, combative, dynamic, noble, and heroic mentality; and the *vaishya* the mercantile or artisanal mentality, or that of the peasant in certain cases, the *vaishya* mentality being "horizontal" in a certain sense. As for the *shūdra*, he is a materialist by nature; his virtue is obedience.

climate of Sufism—which is nonetheless "Brahmanical" or "pneumatic" by its nature—are paradoxically molded by the mentality of the *vaishya* and the way of *karma*, even though they combine within this framework with the *kshatriya* spirit,[2] hence with an element of combativeness and *bhakti*. From this amalgam there results a language that is at once sagely moralizing and harshly perfectionistic, which is anything but congenial to disinterested contemplativity, to say the least; but it is also necessary to say that it is precisely the combination of the prudent realism of the merchant with the generous and intrepid idealism of the warrior that is taken to represent synthetic and therefore final perfection in the Islamic perspective;[3] whatever may be the reasons of Providence, however, this has no connection with esoterism and the demands of *gnosis*.

The element "intellection" or "contemplation" is affirmed in Islam by the dogma of unity and the metaphysics pertaining to it and psychologically by the accentuation of the elements "certitude" and "serenity". The element "combativeness" for its part is affirmed by the holy war and its spiritual applications and fundamentally by the Bedouin qualities of nobility and generosity; this chivalrous "verticality" most often provides the framework for contemplative heroism, as is shown by the interiorization of the holy war. As for the "horizontal" element, of which the merchant is perhaps the most readily graspable representative, it is what determines the general or average style of theology and piety, as we have noted above; this mentality is dry, prudent, and practical, being closer to respectability than to greatness; it has in any case the advantage of stability, as does indeed the sacerdotal mentality, but with the heaviness proper to "horizontality".[4] Finally,

---

[2] The idea that man can attain knowledge (*jnāna*) through action (*karma*)—an idea Vedantists reject—is fairly common in average Sufism, knowledge being in practice confused in this case with salvation pure and simple.

[3] The mentality of an Ashari or even a Ghazzali was basically that of a chivalrous merchant; this was the mentality of the Arabs, and other peoples of the Near East were at least predisposed to it. "The essential of the Muslim city is the market," as Massignon said; one might also say—and Ibn Khaldun saw this—that in Islam the merchant element is represented especially by sedentary peoples and the warrior element *a priori* by the nomads.

[4] Among Christians the *kshatriya* element dominates in theology whereas that of the

the "hylic" or "somatic" element is manifested in Islam in the form of an opaque and flat servility, which incidentally—since it exists—penetrates even into theology,[5] as for example when we are assured that good is good and evil is evil because God so decided and for no other reason, or that God rewards the good and punishes the bad without our being able to know why since He would be "free" to do the opposite, or that we must believe obvious things, not because our mind finds them obvious, for obviousness would limit the "freedom" and "sovereignty" of God, but for the sole reason that God has thus informed us without our having a right to the least need for explanation—in short, when everything is made to depend upon a divine arbitrariness that is unintelligible in principle, to which our will and even our intelligence have merely to yield, as if in such conditions it were still worthwhile being man.

The accent Islam places on the horizontal mentality—the prudent and realistic mentality of businessmen and caravaneers, if one will, accompanied of course by warrior qualities—is explained by a concern to speak to the average man and save the largest number possible; in the final analysis it is therefore a manifestation of Mercy. Through the average man, necessarily "horizontal" in certain respects, the Islamic *upāya* seeks to reach every man as such.

For this is inescapable: the masses, whom religion has a mission to win over, seek to recognize themselves in it, which forces religion to prefigure them in a certain way on pain of being unfaithful to its mandate. God Himself condescends in His mercy to assume the character-

---

vaishya can be felt in the sector of lay morality, which is condemned in advance to a certain mediocrity. The *kshatriya* mentality moreover had its share in provoking two divergent explosions within Christianity, the Renaissance and the Reformation; it was at once a factor of idealism and of unrealism, of impulse and of instability. The Islamic *upāya* sought to avoid this pitfall, which it could do only at the cost of new risks.

[5] In a Christian context the equivalent of this *shūdra* piety is a humilitarianism that is blind, irrational, and absurd, though obviously ennobled by its intention. The point here is not to condemn, but to take note and define; if the *shūdra* mentality has a role to play in religion, it is because the very ideas of "servitude" (Islam) and "sin" (Christianity) give it paradoxically a completely natural right to be present, especially since every man carries all potentialities within himself; leveling and pessimistic moralisms insist upon this precisely.

istics of those He would save so that they might recognize themselves in Him; otherwise no dialogue would be possible.

*

* *

It will perhaps be worthwhile to describe further the characteristics of the *vaishya*[6] since they insinuate themselves into the moralistic and sentimental *karma-mārga* of average Islam and are therefore found inappropriately amalgamated with the esoterism of the Sufis, unless one gives up trying to define Sufism as a whole as an esoterism and places the latter in an altogether inward and implicit sector. Thus the characteristics of the *vaishya* are *grosso modo* the following: love of work well done—both the result and the performance—and of wages honestly earned; an emotional accent on the fear of God and on meritorious works conscientiously and piously accomplished, whence also in matters of piety a "top of the class" zeal coupled with a possible tendency to platitude and pedantry; an intelligence solid enough in its own way, but modest, practical, and above all circumspect.[7] On the speculative plane, which scarcely belongs to him, the *vaishya* lacks realism, as if he wished to compensate for his horizontality by an escape into the clouds; thus he readily puts the sublime in place of the true or real, if indeed he ventures into the world of religious speculation, which no one can prevent him from doing.[8]

---

[6] Among European *vaishya*s the elements "peasant" and "craftsman" predominate over the element "merchant", whereas in the Near Easterner the relationship is the opposite. Let us add that in the case of the great artist—unless he is "noble" or "priest" by heredity—his quality as craftsman is no longer a merely outward one, and it rejoins by its inward quality the chivalrous and sacerdotal mentalities; this brings us to the obvious point that a member of a lower collectivity can belong individually to a higher collectivity, and conversely, whatever the outward function of the individual.

[7] *Quidquid agis, prudenter agas, et respice finem*: "Whatever thou doest, do it prudently, and think of the end." This medieval saying, no doubt inspired by Ecclesiastes, reflects well the "horizontal", precautionary, and perfectionistic mentality in question.

[8] A factor that attenuates and may even abolish these generalizations is the fact that each of the castes contains the others in an appropriate manner. Let us also note that each caste—each qualitative type—contains the four temperaments, the order of the castes being vertical and that of the temperaments horizontal; this implies that each mental level includes features at once characteristic and divergent.

It is in the logic of things that a religion or spiritual method, to the extent it stresses the importance of outward observances,[9] assumes in its human substance a psychology in conformity with the one we have just described; for if the *vaishya* tends to be narrowly moralistic because he lacks a sense of proportions, every pedantic moralist is *ipso facto* situated on the same level, whatever his latent possibilities.

As a complement to pious agitation there is pious contraction, the gaze timorously and chastely fixed on the ground, notwithstanding the acceptance—in another dimension—of "legal"[10] pleasures. We would not contest the possible value of such attitudes, for differing mentalities have their requirements just as they have their limits, but we are compelled to criticize them when they become excessive or are presented as the only possible perfections, or as perfection itself. Let all this be said without forgetting that every man carries within himself possibilities inferior to his possibility taken as a whole and that there

---

[9] We must be clear about the meaning of the term "outward observances". When one follows the *Sunnah* for the most contingent actions of daily life or recites the formulas appropriate to the most trivial situations, one practices "outward" or "secondary" observances; but when one performs a rite whose content is essential, this rite is not "outward" simply because it is performed physically. We have read somewhere—in the writings of Omar Suhrawardi—the story of a Sufi who, sensing he was dying, wished for one last time to perform the ritual ablution so as to appear before God in a state of "legal purity"; not having the strength to carry out this final act, he took the hand of one of those present to perform with it the missing act. We do not say he was wrong from his point of view, but we do say this point of view is not everything, and we would also say—no doubt a little schematically—that a Hindu in his situation would have pronounced a *mantra* or *nāma*, which purifies from all defilement and constitutes a central sacrament, hence a qualitatively "inward" practice. Ramakrishna tells the story of a holy *brāhmana* who asked a *shūdra* near a well to draw some water for him; the man did not dare to do so because of his impurity of caste. "Say *Shiva*," replied the Brahman, "and you will be pure." And let us recall that the *Bhagavad Gītā* specifies that "there is no lustral water like unto Knowledge".

[10] Without ruling out more subtle cases and without seeking to be displeasingly schematic, the following remark is called for: it is logical that a man should be chastely apprehensive to the extent his sense of pleasure is opaque and quantitative; certain *ahādīth* on Paradise, along with the accompanying speculations, make allowance for this opaqueness. This perhaps constitutes an attenuating circumstance for Sufis who do not wish to listen to talk about the "Garden" and what it contains, in spite of all that is hasty and ill sounding in their point of view.

can always be circumstances in which he must take account of these in a concrete fashion; no man can behave heedlessly like a god.

A striking aspect of the "horizontality" of the *vaishya* is his conventionalism, which may take the place of a more or less direct vision of things. Conventionalism is a protection against the lack of a sense of proportion for those who are not sufficiently endowed with discernment, whence the advantages of even a blind practice of the complete *Sunnah.* The weight of "conventions" can also be useful if necessary for men of high caste who, although contemplatives, may lack discrimination:[11] convention provides a sure framework for their mystical impulses, which may be too colored by individualism, thus preventing extravagant consequences on the social plane; it then serves as an anchor and a normative criterion in the comings and goings of inspirations that are difficult to verify.

*
*   *

No doubt it is not only the inward that counts, for there is also the outward; there are not merely great things, but also small things; Muslims insist on this, and rightly so as long as they do not dramatize in favor of a disproportionate and invasive *karma-mārga.*[12] Rightly so, we say, but let no one tell us that the quantity and affective intensity of observances actually constitutes esoterism or leads to supreme Knowledge or that pious agitation is an integral part of the sapiential way or even constitutes *gnosis* in practice.

---

[11] We are speaking throughout about personal castes, not necessarily social castes.

[12] We use the term *karma-mārga* in a special and restricted sense, for in Hinduism the "way of works" can be much more than that; it is even above all—on the level of the *kshatriyas*—the accomplishment of the duty pertaining to one's function without attachment to the fruit of the works (*nishkāma karma*), which proves moreover that the simple fact of practicing multiple outward observances does not constitute in itself a phenomenon of outwardness or a horizontal mentality. As for the cult of small outward observances, it is certainly also pronounced in Judaism, but here it takes on a less personalistic and less sentimental character than in Islam. No Jew would ask himself how Moses sat in order to eat grapes.

Its excesses aside, exteriorizing moralism is no doubt founded on the idea that since the loss of Paradise everyone carries inferior elements within himself; in fact all believers participate in the same observances—although assuredly these include certain margins—but this does not mean that because of this loss everyone is a *vaishya* or *shūdra*; it is incumbent upon traditional wisdom, whether exoteric or esoteric, not to overlook real lines of demarcation. Since the enigma of the Arab-Muslim soul comes from a certain mixture and at the same time a certain conflict between the mentality of the "knight" and that of the "merchant"—the heroism that charges ahead and if necessary simplifies and the prudence that appraises and readily overemphasizes details—it is not surprising that certain lines of demarcation should be particularly fluctuating and that the esoteric domain should thereby be affected.

A possible objection is the following: the esoteric perspectives of love and knowledge must be protected against any usurpation of their privileges of inwardness and essentiality; esoterism itself is therefore obliged to erect a barrier made of pious outwardness and thus exclude every temptation of ambition and hypocrisy. This is all very well, but the whole question has to do with knowing where one wishes to locate the boundary between this concern for integrity and the adulteration of esoterism. The man who is qualified, it will be said, will find his way: "God knows his own"; let us just hope this is sufficient consolation in the face of so much ambiguity.

Another objection might be based on the psychological influence of the *ahādīth*, hence the *Sunnah*; for from them is derived the meticulous and fussy *karma-yoga* that so often veils esoterism properly so called, sometimes in so impenetrable a way. It is readily forgotten that in providing rules for living, and in doing so in detail, the Prophet did not say that this was the supreme wisdom; moreover, responsibility for these compilations does not fall upon the Prophet himself—who in many cases merely acted in his own manner—but upon his Companions, who sought to preserve the least gesture and least remark of the Prophet and who did so with all the dryness and meticulousness of which the Arabs are capable, to the point of not always being able to avoid a certain "pettiness", if this word may be permitted in such a matter. The Koran says that in order to be loved by God we must follow the Prophet; the Companions deduced from this that the integral example of the Prophet is a kind of sacrament, a kind of sanctifying and salvific mold into which one must flow without being concerned with the why of things.[13] If on the one hand the *ahādīth* and the accounts connected with them often give the impression of pettiness because of their content, whether because it is too modest or too human—we have in mind, for example, some of the stories regarding the Prophet's wives—the very existence of the *ahādīth* nonetheless bears witness on the other hand to an extraordinary cause; for the fact that one has taken the trouble of religiously collecting the least gestures of a man proves the immensity of his prestige and the greatness of his nature. The argument that the way of multiple observances and their mystical accentuation is the exclusive way of the Prophet is altogether disproportionate, for every founder of a religion inevitably provides an example of all kinds of attitudes and ways of acting without this constituting his message properly so called, and the fact that these manifestations can contradict one another proves precisely that they constitute a choice and that no single one of them totally or exclusively involves the authority of the Messenger.

It is true that the meticulous imitation of the slightest deeds and gestures of the Prophet, the scrupulous and extinctive entering into the mold of his person, is a kind of Eucharistic participation in the man-*Logos*; nonetheless this participation is limited to the plane of the individuality and assumes importance only insofar as the way is that of the individual, something having no direct connection with metaphysical realization. Realization certainly does not exclude this imitation, but on the one hand simplifies it and on the other interiorizes it, the spiritual accentuation in this case being beyond the human pure and simple.

In any case if an outward activity, however multiple, is in itself reconcilable with a methodic contemplation of the Essence—of the "kingdom of God which is within you"—the same is not true of an individualistic and exteriorizing accentuation of numerous observances, for this is a quantitative search for personal merits; the

---

[13] The Christian point of view is completely different; indeed Saint John, far from compiling "information" (*hadīth, ahādīth*), limits himself to the essential: "There are also many other things which Jesus did, the which, if they should be written every one, I suppose that even the world itself could not contain the books that should be written."

accentuation of the individual and the outward necessarily excludes that of the universal and the inward.[14] What is blameworthy is not pious pettiness and its fragmentariness, but its potential claim to totality and greatness.

But let us return to a more general consideration. The *Sunnah* seeks to keep in mind the security, equilibrium, and sincerity of the man who knows he is little, whereas the Christian perspective has inward values in mind first and foremost, as well as the risks of the ideal and of heroism. It goes without saying that each of the two ways of seeing includes the perspective of the other *a posteriori* and to a certain degree: Christians have their monastic rules and their courtesy just as Muslims for their part have their antisocial and, when necessary, anti-ritualistic idealism, the second adjective pertaining at least to supererogatory practices. "And the remembrance of God is greater," says the Koran—greater than the canonical prayer and therefore greater in principle than all observances.[15]

*
* *

We would like to provide a few supplementary details regarding the hierarchy of fundamental human mentalities, employing Hindu terminology as always because of its greater convenience, despite the Islamic context; and we do so without scruple since the nature of things has no denominational coloring.

What the two higher castes have in common—and we are speaking of typological castes, not of social castes and even less of classes—is acuity of intelligence, the capacity for spontaneously placing oneself above oneself, hence the predominance of the qualitative over the quantitative and, in spirituality, the accentuation of inwardness and verticality, whether it is a question of wisdom or heroism. On the contrary, what unfavorably characterizes the third caste—that is, leaving aside its qualities—is a mentality that is more or

---

[14] Of course, anecdotes pertaining to this *distinguo* are not lacking in Sufism.

[15] Likewise, the remembrance of God is the reason for the existence of every rite and every practice, as the Shaykh al-Alawi remarked in one of his treatises.

less mercantile or, let us say, a certain intellectual and moral pettiness resulting from outwardness and horizontality;[16] but compared to the fourth caste, the third has in common with the first two an inward incentive toward the good, whereas the fourth cannot maintain itself in the good except under a pressure coming from outside and above, for this human type does not dominate itself and does not like to dominate itself. Finally, what the second and the third castes—and still more the fourth—have in common is a certain "worldliness", though in very different respects.

Compared with the outcastes, who because of their heterogeneous psychic make-up and their lack of a center are "unbalanced", the four normal and normative types are "balanced": among them the first three types are "disciplined", and among these the two higher types are "noble". We do not mean "nobility" in the sociological sense of the term, but in the sense that the spirit is "free", hence "sovereign", for it is naturally conformed to the universal Law, whether in "heroic" or "sacerdotal" mode; man is noble to the extent he carries the Law within himself; in other cases he is ennobled to the extent that his obedience is perfect and to the extent that, having been quantitative, it becomes qualitative.

If on the one hand the *brāhmana* and the *kshatriya* are close to one another because of their superior intelligence and the authority that springs from it, there is on the other hand a meeting point between the *brāhmana* and the *vaishya* inasmuch as both are peaceful and inasmuch as the second possesses a certain contemplativity that also relates him to the first. It is easy to see the peaceful character of the peasant, the craftsman, the merchant; none of them has any interest in coming to blows, and each of the three functions possesses an aspect that binds or unites human groups rather than placing them in opposition; as for contemplativity, it results for the peasant from his life in nature and for the craftsman from his concern with symbolism and the sacred; for the merchant it results from his constant contact with useful and beautiful objects whose worth he knows, and in this

---

[16] It could also be said that this mentality considers the whole from the starting point of details—whence its specific moralism—whereas the higher mentality considers the details from the starting point of the whole. In the first case analysis takes precedence over synthesis; in the second synthesis takes precedence over analysis.

respect he is disinterested, which he shows by his perspicacity and honesty.[17] All in all the peaceful and contemplative *vaishya* is morally and spiritually superior to a *kshatriya* who is merely ambitious and quarrelsome,[18] even though the *kshatriya* is in himself superior because of his liveliness of intelligence, strength of decision, and heroic vocation. The pitfall of the *kshatriya* spirit is an intelligence with too little contemplativity, that of the *vaishya* a contemplativity with too little intelligence; but it is the objective content that is important, not the subjective bearing.

In the same line of compensatory phenomena, it is necessary to call attention to a possible superiority of the *kshatriya*, not over the *brāhmana* in himself and as sage, of course, but over the professional priest who has become narrow and pedantic, even pharisaical, through "specialization".[19] On the other hand the *brāhmana* in the absolute sense eminently possesses all the capacities of the *kshatriya*,[20] which is not the case with the functional and social *brāhmana*; in other words the intrinsic *brāhmana* is *ativarna*, "without color" (of caste), and he is thus identifiable with the *hamsa*, the primordial man.[21]

We spoke above of the peaceful nature shared by the first and third castes, and we would like to add the following: if Islam is a

---

[17] The important role of the *vaishya* spirit in Islam—and let us not forget that Islam is a world religion and not a brotherhood of gnostics—is prefigured in the fact that the Prophet married a rich businesswoman and was himself employed in business before his prophetic career.

[18] "Blessed are the peacemakers: for they shall be called the children of God"; these words of Jesus, apart from their general meaning, apply to both the *brāhmana* and the *vaishya* in connection with their affinity.

[19] In the West the emperor and other princes were often more realistic than the clergy, including the pope; Dante knew this well.

[20] The Pharaoh in Egypt, as well as the emperors of China and Japan, sought to realize this primordial synthesis, but rather belatedly.

[21] The saint who is withdrawn from the world, the *sannyāsin*, is said to be "beyond-caste", *ativarna*; this characteristic amounts to primordial wisdom, *sophia perennis*, hence esoterism. If every saint is personally a *brāhmana* from the simple fact of his sanctity, even though socially he may be a pariah like Tiruvalluvar, every sage sharing in the *sophia perennis* is *ativarna*, beyond caste. We would add that the *brāhmana* priest can be bound by his form and function, whereas the *ativarnāshrāmin* as such and in principle is neither limited nor bound by anything outside him.

doctrine of the *brāhmana* conveyed by a *vaishya* piety—the *kshatriya* element not being predominant overall—it is precisely by reason of its being rooted in the mystery of Peace (*Salām*), which includes *a priori* the sage, but paradoxically also the small and weak. Islam is itself an invitation to "appeasement" in the sense that the root of the word *islām* is the same as that of the word *salām*: to "resign oneself" or "surrender" (*aslama*) is to be reintegrated into "Peace", which is an aspect of God. *Al-Salām* is one of the ninety-nine divine Names.[22] "And God summoneth to the abode of Peace (*dār al-Salām*), and leadeth whom He will to a straight path."[23]

*

*   *

According to the Koran man is essentially two things: "servant" (*'abd*) and "vicar" (*khalīfah*), and not "servant" exclusively as a "quantitative" and ill-inspired piety would have it. The Prophet is at once "servant" and "messenger" (*rasūl*), not one without the other, which should be enough for us to recognize in the man who believes the dignity that he possesses by definition and that results from his deiformity; we say "in the man who believes", for the dignity of "vicar" is dependent upon the individual's consent to the specific vocation of man.

We referred above to the leveling that exoterism entails. Exoterist "reasoning" is basically as follows: it is necessary to be able to save all men, including the most earthbound, and since these are the most difficult to save, it is necessary to adapt to their needs more than to those of others; and consequently all men must to some extent be *shūdras*. From this arises all too often the paradox of a spirituality that applies to all a psychology—and imposes upon all a morality—of *vaishyas* and *shūdras*, whereas it is precisely in this domain that the distinction of human levels is most essential; let us recall in this connection the Gnostic distinction between the *pneumatikos*, the *psychikos*, and the *hylikos*.[24]

---

[22] In the same way the blessed in Paradise utter no "vain or harmful" word, but only the words: *Salāman Salāma* (*Sūrah* "The Event" [56]:25-26).

[23] *Sūrah* "Jonah" [10]:26.

[24] To this it might be objected that before God every man is *shūdra*, which is both true and false; it is true in a transposed sense that removes from the word all its

With regard to their status as responsible, free, and weak individuals, men are equal before the saving Law; with regard to their supra-individual participation in the immanent Intellect, which is also salvific, they are unequal. The first relationship concerns exoterism, and the second esoterism: esoterism accepts, and even requires, a submission of the individual to the Law—of the individual, but not of what within him pertains to the Intellect. The Intellect is the Law of the microcosm just as the Law is the Intellect of the macrocosm; there is parallelism in keeping with what is required by the nature of things, but not confusion.[25]

In fact the term "Sufism" includes the most shallow fanaticism as well as the most profound speculation; now neither one nor the other constitutes plenary *Tasawwuf*, which goes without saying in the case of the first attitude, whereas the second amounts to integral esoterism only on condition that it is accompanied by an appropriate

---

psychological implications, and it is false as a result of this very reservation. Referring to a *hadīth* that condemns all rich men to hell, Ibn Arabi declares that the maxim applies only to coarse people who are attached to their riches and not to sages who know for themselves that it is not to be taken literally. This opinion shows that there are sayings that concern only a given moral or intellectual level and that there is no question, especially from the Sufi point of view, of reducing all men to a single rudimentary type; nonetheless this error is frequently committed, and precisely on the basis of canonical formulations.

[25] According to the *Brahmasūtras* (3.4.36-38), "Man can acquire Knowledge even without observing the prescribed rites; and in fact one finds in the *Veda* many examples of people who failed to accomplish particular rites or were prevented from doing so, but who nonetheless, because their attention was perpetually fixed on the supreme *Brahma*, acquired the true Knowledge that concerns it." Likewise, Shankara in his *Ātmā-Bodha*: "There is no other means of obtaining complete and final Deliverance than by Knowledge; this alone removes the bonds of the passions. . . . Action (*karma*), not being opposed to ignorance (*avidyā*), cannot remove it; but Knowledge dissipates ignorance just as light dissipates darkness." Such remarks concern only "pneumatics"; now the fact that the majority of pneumatics have practiced certain actions—ritual, moral, or other—does not mean that they were ignorant of the relative character of action nor all the more that they attained Knowledge by means of action; and if a given *hadīth* appears to make mystical Union dependent on supererogatory acts, this is solely because it takes as its starting point the tendencies of exteriorized man, not to mention the fact that certain rites can be supports for cognitive actualization. Action collaborates with intellection and contemplation but does not replace them, nor is it a condition *sine qua non*.

method and not merely by pious observances, whose emotional accentuation moreover is scarcely compatible with the perspective of *gnosis*. Authentic esoterism—let us say it again—concerns a way that is founded on total or essential, and not merely partial or formal, truth and that makes an operative use of intelligence and not just of the will and feelings. The totality of truth demands the totality of man.

We have seen that the price of the providential leveling realized by Islam is a certain predominance of the *vaishya* spirit,[26] a spirit which is so paradoxical in a Sufi context, but which has contributed to sparing Islam a luciferian experience analogous to the Renaissance; nonetheless this unquestionably simplistic mentality tends to produce among Muslims, upon contact with the modern world, an aberrant intellectualist reaction and finally apostasy. This for us is one more reason for describing without euphemism the disadvantages of the leveling in question, in order to be able to point out its occasionally attenuating or compensatory causes and above all in order to be able to demonstrate its relativity in light of the essential and decisive values of Tradition.

[26] "A fusion of the elite and the common, the Islamic aristo-democracy can be brought about without violence or promiscuity because of the peculiarly Islamic institution of a conventional type of humanity, which for want of a better term I shall call average man or human normality. . . . It is precisely the 'average man' who is the object of the *Sharīʿah* or sacred Law of Islam. . . . Certain Shariite prescriptions may seem absurd in the eyes of Europeans. They nonetheless have their reason for being. A universal religion must take into account every intellectual and moral degree. The simplicity, weaknesses, and peculiarities of other people have, to a certain extent, a right to consideration. But intellectual culture also has its rights and requirements. The average man establishes a sort of neutrality around each person, which guarantees all individualities while obliging them to work for the whole of (Muslim) humanity" (Abdul Hadi, "L'universalité en l'Islam", *Le Voile d'Isis*, January, 1934).

Tracing the Notion of Philosophy

Were Ibn Arabi, Jili, and other theoreticians of Sufism philosophers? Yes and no, depending on the meaning given to this word.

According to Pythagoras, wisdom is *a priori* the knowledge of the stellar world and all that is situated above us, *sophia* being the wisdom of the gods and *philosophia* that of men. For Heraclitus the philosopher is one who applies himself to knowledge of the profound nature of things, whereas for Plato philosophy is knowledge of the Immutable and the Ideas, and for Aristotle it is knowledge of first causes and principles, together with the sciences derived from them. In addition philosophy implies for all the Ancients moral conformity to wisdom: he alone is wise, *sophos*, who lives wisely. In this particular and precise sense, the wisdom of Solomon is philosophy; it is to live according to the nature of things on the basis of piety—the "fear of God"—for the sake of what is essential and liberating.

All this shows that the word "philosopher" itself has nothing restrictive about it, to say the least, and that one cannot legitimately impute to this word any of the vexing associations of ideas it may elicit; usage applies this word to all thinkers, including eminent metaphysicians—some Sufis consider Plato and other Greeks to be prophets—so that one would like to reserve it for sages and simply use the term "rationalists" for profane thinkers. It is nonetheless legitimate to take into account a misuse of language that has become conventional, for unquestionably the terms "philosophy" and "philosopher" have been seriously compromised by ancient and modern sophists; in fact the major disadvantage of these terms is that they imply conventionally that the norm for the mind is reasoning pure and simple,[1] in the absence not only of intellection but of indispensable objective data.

---

[1] Naturally the most "advanced" of the modernists seek to demolish the very principles of reasoning, but this is simply fantasy *pro domo*, for man is condemned to reason as soon as he uses language, unless he wishes to demonstrate nothing at all. In any case one cannot demonstrate the impossibility of demonstrating anything, if words are still to have any meaning.

Admittedly one is neither ignorant nor rationalistic just because one is a logician, but one is both if one is a logician and nothing more.[2]

In the opinion of all profane thinkers, philosophy means to think "freely", as far as possible without presuppositions, which is precisely impossible; on the other hand *gnosis*, or philosophy in the proper and original sense of the word, is to think in accordance with the immanent Intellect and not by means of reason alone. What favors confusion is the fact that in both cases the intelligence operates independently of outward prescriptions, although for diametrically opposite reasons: that the rationalist draws his inspiration if necessary from a pre-existing system does not prevent him from thinking in a way he deems to be "free"—falsely, since true freedom coincides with truth; and likewise *mutatis mutandis* that the gnostic—in the orthodox sense of the term—bases himself extrinsically on a given sacred Scripture or on some other gnostic cannot prevent him from thinking in an intrinsically free manner by virtue of the freedom proper to the immanent Truth or the Essence, which by definition escapes formal constraints. Or again: whether the gnostic "thinks" what he has "seen" with the "eye of the heart" or whether on the contrary he obtains his "vision" thanks to the intervention—preliminary and provisional but in no way efficient—of a thought, which then takes on the role of occasional cause, is a matter of indifference with regard to the truth or its quasi-supernatural springing forth in the spirit.

*
*   *

The reduction of the notion of intellectuality to that of simple rationality often has its cause in the prejudice of a school: Saint Thomas

---

[2] A German author (H. Türck) has proposed the term "misosopher"—"enemy of wisdom"—for those thinkers who undermine the very foundations of truth and intelligence. We would add that misosophy—without mentioning some ancient precedents—begins *grosso modo* with "criticism" and ends with subjectivisms, relativisms, existentialisms, dynamisms, psychologisms, and biologisms of every kind. As for the ancient expression "misology", it designates above all the fideist hatred for the use of reason.

is an empiricist, which means that he reduces the cause of all non-theological knowledge to sensible perceptions in order to be able to underestimate the human mind to the advantage of Scripture—because this allows him, in other words, to attribute to Revelation alone the glory of "supernatural" knowledge. And Ghazzali inveighs against the "philosophers" because he wishes to reserve for the Sufis a monopoly of spiritual knowledge, as if faith and piety, combined with intellectual gifts and grace—all the Arab philosophers were believers—did not provide a sufficient basis for pure intellection.

According to Ibn Arabi, the "philosopher"—which for him practically means the skeptic—is incapable of knowing universal causality except by observing causations in the outer world and drawing from his observations the conclusions that impose themselves on his sense of logic. According to another Sufi, Ibn al-Arif, intellectual knowledge is merely an "indication" pointing to God: the philosopher knows God only by way of a "conclusion"; his knowledge has content only "with a view to God" and not "by God", as does that of the mystic. But this *distinguo* is valid only if we assimilate all philosophy to unmitigated rationalism and forget moreover that in the doctrinaire mystics there is an obvious element of rationality. In short, the term "philosopher" in current speech signifies nothing other than the fact of expounding a doctrine while respecting the laws of logic, which are those of language and common sense, without which we would not be human; to practice philosophy is first and foremost to think, whatever the reasons that rightly or wrongly incite us to do so. But it is also more especially and according to the best of the Greeks to express by means of reason certainties "seen" or "lived" by the immanent Intellect, as we have remarked above; now the explanation necessarily takes on the character imposed on it by the laws of thought and language.

Some will object that the simple believer, who understands nothing of philosophy, can derive much more from scriptural symbols than does the philosopher with his definitions, abstractions, classifications, and categories—an unjust reproach, for in the first place theorizing thought does not exclude supra-rational intuition, which is completely obvious, and in the second place it does not pretend to provide by itself anything that it cannot offer by virtue of its nature. What it can offer may be of immense value, or else it would be necessary to suppress all doctrines; Platonic *anamnesis* can have doctrinal concepts as its occasional cause as well as symbols provided by art or virgin nature. If in intellectual speculation there is a human danger of rationalism and thus—at least in principle—of skepticism and materialism, mystical speculation for its part includes, with the same reservation, a danger of excesses or even of rambling and incoherence, whatever may be said by esoterizing zealots who take pleasure in question-begging and sublimizing euphemisms.

*
*   *

We must say a few words here in defense of the Arab philosophers, who have been accused among other things of confusing Plato, Aristotle, and Plotinus. We believe on the contrary that they had the merit of integrating these great Greeks in one and the same synthesis, for what interested them was not systems but truth as such. We shall no doubt run counter to certain esoterist prejudices if we say that metaphysically orthodox philosophy—that of the Middle Ages as well as antiquity—is derived from sapiential esoterism, whether intrinsically by its truth or extrinsically in relation to the simplifications of theology; it is "thinking", if one will, but not ratiocination in the void. If it is objected that the errors one may find in some philosophers who overall are orthodox prove the non-esoteric and consequently profane nature of all philosophy, this argument can be turned against theology and the mystical or gnostic doctrines, for in these sectors erroneous speculations can also be found on the margin of real inspirations.

To give a concrete example, we shall mention the following case, which in any event is interesting in itself and apart from any question of terminology: the Arab philosophers rightly accept the eternity of the world, for, as they say, God cannot create at a given moment without putting Himself in contradiction with His very nature and thus without absurdity;[3] most ingeniously Ghazzali replies—and others have repeated the same argument—that there is no "before" with regard to creation, that time "was" created with, for, and in the world. Now this argument is invalid since it is unilateral: for though

---

[3] Indeed the unicity of God excludes that of the world in both succession and extent; the infinity of God demands the repetition of the world in both respects: creation cannot be a unique event anymore than it can be reduced to the human world alone.

it safeguards the transcendence, absolute freedom, and timelessness of the Creator with regard to creation, it does not explain the temporality of this creation, which is to say that it does not take account of the temporal limitation of a unique world projected into the void of non-time, a limitation that involves God since He is its cause and it exists in relation to His eternity;[4] the very nature of duration demands a beginning. The solution of the problem is that the co-eternity of the world is not that of our "actual" world—which of necessity had an origin and will have an end; rather this co-eternity consists in the necessity of successive worlds: God being what He is—with His absolute Necessity and absolute Freedom—He necessarily cannot not create, but He is free in the modes of creation, which never repeat themselves since God is infinite. The whole difficulty comes from the fact that Semites envisage only one world, namely ours, whereas the non-Semiticized Aryans either accept an indefinite series of creations—this is the Hindu doctrine of cosmic cycles—or else envisage the world as a necessary manifestation of the divine Nature and not as a contingent and particular phenomenon. In this confrontation between two theses, the theological and the philosophical, it is the philosophers and not the theologians—even if they were Sufis like Ghazzali—who are right; and if doctrinal esoterism is the explanation of problems posed but not clarified by faith, we do not see why those philosophers who provide this explanation thanks to intellection—for reasoning pure and simple would not succeed in doing so, and it is moreover metaphysical truth that proves the worth of the intuition corresponding to it—do not have the same merit as recognized esot-

---

[4] All the same, there is in favor of this argument—which moreover is repeated by Ibn Arabi—the attenuating circumstance that it is the only way of reconciling emanationist truth with creationist dogma without giving the latter an interpretation too far removed from the "letter"; we say "emanationist truth" in order to emphasize that what is in question is an authentic metaphysical idea and not some pantheist or deist emanationism. Be that as it may, Ibn Arabi, when speaking of creation—at the beginning of his *Fusūs al-Hikam*—cannot help expressing himself in a temporal mode: "When the divine Reality willed to see . . . its Essence" (*lammā shāʾa ʾl-Haqqu subhānahu an yarā . . . ʿaynahu*); it is true that in Arabic the past tense has in principle the sense of the eternal present when it is a question of God, but this applies above all to the verb "to be" (*kāna*) and does not prevent creation from being considered an "act" and not a "quality".

erists, especially since, to paraphrase Saint Paul, one cannot testify to great truths except by the Holy Spirit.

For theologians, to say that the world is "without beginning" amounts to saying that it is eternal *a se*—this is why they reject the idea—whereas for philosophers it means that it is eternal *ab alio,* for it is God who lends it eternity. Now an eternity that is lent is a completely different thing from eternity in itself, and it is precisely for this reason that the world is both eternal and temporal: eternal as a series of creations or a creative rhythm and temporal by the fact that each link in this flux has a beginning and end. It is universal Manifestation as such that is co-eternal with God because it is a necessary expression of His eternal Nature—the sun being unable to abstain from shining—but eternity cannot be reduced to a given contingent phase of this divine Manifestation. Manifestation is "co-eternal", which is to say that it is not eternal in the same way as the sole Essence; and this is why it is periodically interrupted and totally reabsorbed into the Principle, to such an extent that it is both existent and nonexistent and does not enjoy a plenary and so to speak "continuous" reality like the Eternal itself. To say that the world is "co-eternal" nevertheless means that it is necessary as an aspect of the Principle, that it is therefore "something of God", which is already indicated by the term "Manifestation"; and it is precisely this truth theologians refuse to accept—for obvious reasons, since in their eyes it abolishes the difference between creature and Creator.[5]

The world's "co-eternity" with God evokes the universal *Materia* of Empedocles and Ibn Masarrah, which is none other than the *Logos* as Substance (*'amā* = "cloud" or *habā* = "dust"):[6] it is not creation as such that is co-eternal with the Creator; it is the creative virtuality,

---

[5] The total Universe can be compared to either a circle or a cross, the center in both cases representing the Principle; but whereas in the first image the relationship between the periphery and the center is discontinuous, this being the dogmatist perspective of theology, analogically speaking, in the second image the same relationship is continuous, this being the perspective of *gnosis*. The first perspective is valid when phenomena as such are considered—something *gnosis* would not contest—whereas the second perspective adequately takes account of the essential reality of things and the Universe.

[6] This idea, like the terms used to express it, belongs to Islam, apart from the Greek analogies noted later; there is nothing surprising in this since truth is one.

which comprises—according to these doctrines—four fundamental, formative principles. These are, symbolically speaking, "Fire", "Air", "Water", "Earth",[7] which recall the three principial determinations (*gunas*) included in *Prakriti*: *Sattva, Rajas, Tamas*, the difference in number indicating a secondary difference in perspective.[8]

*

*   *

Regarding the confrontation between Sufis and philosophers, the following remark must be made: if Ghazzali had limited himself to asserting that there is no possible esoteric realization without an initiation and corresponding method and that philosophers in general demand neither,[9] we would have no reason to reproach him; but his criticism is leveled at philosophy as such—that is, it is situated above all on the doctrinal and epistemological plane. In fact the Hellenizing philosophy here in question is neutral from the initiatic point of view, given that its intention is to provide an exposition of truth and nothing else; particular opinions—such as those of rationalism properly so called—do not enter into the definition of philosophy.[10] Be that as it may, the Ghazzalian ostracism makes us think of those theologians of

[7] This Empedoclean quaternity is found in another form in the cosmology of the Indians of North America and perhaps also of Mexico and other more southern regions: here it is Space that symbolizes Substance, the universal "Ether", while the cardinal points represent the four principial and existentiating determinations.

[8] *Sattva*—analogically speaking—is "Fire", which rises and illumines; *Tamas* then is "Earth", which is heavy and obscure. *Rajas*—by reason of its intermediary position—includes an aspect of lightness and another of heaviness, namely, "Air" and "Water", but both considered in violent mode: it is on the one hand the unleashing of the winds and on the other that of the waves.

[9] This possible silence proves nothing in any case against the rightness of a given philosophy; moreover Plato said in one of his letters that his writings did not include all his teachings. It may be noted that according to Synesius the goal of monks and philosophers is the same, namely, the contemplation of God.

[10] In our first book, *The Transcendent Unity of Religions*, we adopted the point of view of Ghazzali regarding "philosophy": that is, bearing in mind the great impoverishment of modern philosophies, we simplified the problem as others have done before us

old who sought to oppose the "vain wisdom of the world" with "tears of repentance", but who finally did not refrain from constructing systems of their own and who in doing so could not manage without the help of the Greeks, to whom nevertheless they denied the assistance of the "Holy Spirit" and therefore any supernatural quality.

Sufis do not wish to be philosophers—that is understood; and they are right if they mean by this that their starting point is not doubt and that their certainties are not rational conclusions. But we do not at all see why when they reason wrongly they would do so in a manner different from philosophers, nor why a philosopher when he conceives a truth whose transcendent and axiomatic nature he recognizes would do so in a manner different from the Sufis.

It was not as a gnostic but as a "thinker" that Ibn Arabi treated the question of evil, explaining it by subjectivity and relativity with an entirely Pyrrhonic logic. What is serious is that in abolishing evil, practically speaking—since it is reduced to a subjective point of view—one abolishes good with the same stroke, whether this was the intention or not; and in particular one abolishes beauty by depriving love of its content, whereas it is precisely upon their reality and necessary connection that Ibn Arabi's doctrine insists. It is beauty that determines love, not conversely: the beautiful is not what we love and because we love it, but what by its objective value obliges us to love it; we love the beautiful because it is beautiful even if we lack judgment, which does not invalidate the principle of the normal relationship between object and subject. Likewise, the fact that one may love because of an inward beauty and in spite of an outward ugliness or that love may be mixed with compassion or other indirect motives cannot invalidate the nature either of beauty or love.

On the contrary, it is as a gnostic that Ibn Arabi responded to the question of freedom; every creature does what it wills because every creature is basically what it wills to be: in other words, because a possibility is what it is and not something else. Freedom in the last analysis coincides with possibility, and this moreover is attested to by

by making "philosophy" synonymous with "rationalism". According to Ghazzali, to practice philosophy is to operate by syllogisms—though he cannot do without them himself—and thus to use logic; the question is whether one does so *a priori* or *a posteriori*.

the Koranic story of the initial pact between human souls and God; destiny is therefore what the creature wills by his nature and thus by his possibility. One may wonder which we should admire more here: the gnostic who penetrated the mystery or the philosopher who knew how to make it explicit.

But if a man does what he is or if he is what he does, why strive to become better and why pray to this end? Because there is a distinction between substance and accident: demerits as well as merits come from either one or the other without man being able to know from which they come, unless he is a "pneumatic", who is aware of his substantial reality, an ascending reality on account of its conformity to the Spirit (*Pneuma*). "Whoso knoweth his soul knoweth his Lord"; but even then the effort belongs to man and the knowledge to God; in other words it suffices that we strive while being aware that God knows us. It suffices us to know we are free in and through our movement toward God, our movement toward our "Self".

*
*   *

In a certain respect the difference between philosophy, theology, and *gnosis* is total; in another respect it is relative. It is total when one understands by "philosophy" only rationalism, by "theology" only the explanation of religious teachings, and by *gnosis* only intuitive and intellective, thus supra-rational, knowledge; but the difference is only relative when one understands by "philosophy" the fact of thinking, by "theology" the fact of speaking dogmatically about God and religious things, and by *gnosis* the fact of presenting pure metaphysics, for then the categories interpenetrate. It is impossible to deny that the most illustrious Sufis, while being "gnostics" by definition, were at the same time to some extent theologians and to some extent philosophers or that the great theologians were to some extent philosophers and to some extent gnostics, the last word having to be understood in its proper and not sectarian meaning.

If we wish to retain the limitative, or even pejorative, sense of the word "philosopher", we could say that *gnosis* or pure metaphysics starts with certainty, whereas philosophy on the contrary starts from doubt and serves to overcome it only with the means that are at its disposal and that are intended to be purely rational. But since neither

97

the term "philosophy" as such nor the use that has always been made of it obliges us to accept only the restrictive sense of the word, we shall not censure too severely those who employ it in a wider sense than may seem opportune.[11]

Theory by definition is not an end in itself; it is only—and seeks only to be—a key for becoming conscious through the "heart". If a taint of superficiality, insufficiency, and pretension is attached to the notion of "philosophy", it is precisely because all too often—and indeed always in the case of the moderns—it is presented as being sufficient unto itself. "This is only philosophy": we readily accept the use of this turn of phrase, but only on condition that one does not say, "Plato is only a philosopher"—Plato who knew that "beauty is the splendor of the true", a beauty including or demanding all we are or can be.

When Plato maintains that the *philosophos* should think independently of common opinions, he is referring to intellection and not logic alone; whereas Descartes, who did everything to restrict and compromise the notion of philosophy, maintains this while starting from systematic doubt, to such an extent that for him philosophy is synonymous not only with rationalism but also with skepticism. This is a major suicide of the intelligence, inaugurated moreover by Pyrrho and others as a reaction against what was believed to be metaphysical "dogmatism". The "Greek miracle" is in fact the substitution of reason for Intellect, of the fact for the Principle, of the phenomenon for the Idea, of the accident for the Substance, of the form for the Essence, of man for God; and this applies to art as well as thought. The true Greek miracle, if miracle there be—and in this case it would be related to

---

[11] Even Ananda Coomaraswamy does not hesitate to speak of "Hindu philosophy", which at least has the advantage of making clear the "literary genre", more especially as the reader is supposed to know what the Hindu spirit is in particular and what the traditional spirit is in general. In an analogous manner, when one speaks of the "Hindu religion", one knows perfectly well that it is not a case—and cannot be a case— of a Semitic and Western religion, hence a religion that resists every differentiation of perspective; one also speaks traditionally of the Roman, Greek, and Egyptian "religions", and the Koran does not hesitate to say to the pagan Arabs: "Unto you your religion, and unto me mine", even though the religion of the pagans had none of the characteristic features of Judeo-Christian monotheism.

the "Hindu miracle"—is doctrinal metaphysics and methodic logic, providentially utilized by the monotheistic Semites.

*

*   *

The notion of philosophy, with its suggestion of human fallibility, evokes *ipso facto* the problem of infallibility and thereby the question of knowing whether man is condemned by his nature to be mistaken. The human mind, even when disciplined by a sacred tradition, remains exposed to many flaws; that these should be possible does not mean they are inevitable in principle; on the contrary they are the result of causes that are not at all mysterious. Doctrinal infallibility pertains to the realm of orthodoxy and authority, the first element being objective and the second subjective, each having a bearing that is either formal or non-formal, extrinsic or intrinsic, traditional or universal, depending on the case. This being so, it is not even difficult to be infallible when one knows one's limits; it is enough not to speak of things of which one is ignorant, which presupposes that one knows that one is ignorant of them. This amounts to saying that infallibility is not only a matter of information and intellection, but also includes, and essentially so, a moral or psychological condition, without which even men who are in principle infallible become accidentally fallible. Let us add that it is not blameworthy to offer a plausible hypothesis on condition that it is not presented in the form of certitude *ex cathedra*.

In any case there is no infallibility that *a priori* encompasses all possible contingent domains; omniscience is not a human possibility. No one can be infallible with regard to unknown or insufficiently known phenomena; one may have an intuition for pure principles without having one for a given phenomenal order, that is, without being able to apply the principles spontaneously in a given domain. The importance of this possible incapacity diminishes to the extent that the phenomenal domain in question is secondary and where, on the contrary, the principles infallibly enunciated are essential. One must forgive small errors on the part of one who offers great truths— and it is these truths that determine how small or how great are the errors—whereas it would obviously be perverse to forgive great errors when they are accompanied by many small truths.[12]

Infallibility, in a sense by definition, pertains in one degree or another to the Holy Spirit in a way that may be extraordinary or ordinary, properly supernatural or quasi-natural; now in the religious domain the Holy Spirit adapts itself to the nature of man in the sense that it limits itself to preventing the victory of intrinsic heresies, a victory that would falsify the "divine form" that is the religion; for the *upāya*, the "salvific mirage", is willed by Heaven, not by men.[13]

---

[12] There is certainly no reason to admire a science that enumerates insects and atoms but is unaware of God, a science that professes ignorance concerning Him and yet claims omniscience as a matter of principle. It should be noted that the scientist, like every other rationalist, does not base himself on reason as such; he calls "reason" his lack of imagination and knowledge, and his ignorances are for him the "data" of reason.

[13] Always respectful of this form, the Holy Spirit will not teach a Muslim theologian the subtleties of Trinitarian theology nor those of *Vedānta*; from another angle it will not change a racial or ethnic mentality—neither that of the Romans with regard to Catholicism nor that of the Arabs with regard to Islam. Humanity must have not only its history but its histrionics.

The Quintessential Esoterism of Islam

The Islamic religion is divided into three constituent parts: *Īmān*, Faith, which contains everything one must believe; *Islām*, the Law, which contains everything one must do; *Ihsān*,[1] operative Virtue, which confers upon believing and doing the qualities that make them perfect—in other words, that intensify or deepen both faith and works. *Ihsān*, in short, is the sincerity of the intelligence and the will: it is our complete adherence to the Truth and our total conformity to the Law, which means that we must on the one hand know the Truth entirely, not only in part, and on the other hand conform to it with our deepest being and not only with a partial and superficial will. Thus *Ihsān* opens onto esoterism—which is the science of the essential and total—and is even identified with it; for to be sincere is to draw from the Truth the maximal consequences from the point of view of both intelligence and will; in other words, it is to think and will with the heart, hence with our entire being, with all we are.

Ihsān is right believing and right doing, and it is at the same time their quintessence: the quintessence of right believing is metaphysical truth, *Haqīqah*, and that of right doing is the practice of invocation, *Dhikr*. *Ihsān* comprises as it were two modes, depending on its application: the speculative and the operative, namely, intellectual discernment and unitive concentration; in Sufi language this is expressed precisely by the terms *Haqīqah*[2] and *Dhikr* or by *Tawhīd*, "Unification", and *Ittihād*, "Union". For Sufis the "hypocrite" (*munāfiq*) is not merely someone who gives himself airs of piety in order to impress people, but it is the profane man in general, someone who fails to draw all the consequences implied in the Dogma and Law, hence the man who is not sincere since he is neither consequential nor whole;

---

[1] Literally *Ihsān* means "embellishment", "beautiful activity", "right doing", "charitable activity"; and let us recall the relationship that exists in Arabic between the notions of beauty and virtue.

[2] It is to be noted that in the word *haqīqah*, as in its quasi-synonym *haqq*, the meanings "truth" and "reality" coincide.

now Sufism (*tasawwuf*) is nothing other than sincerity (*sidq*), and the "sincere" (*siddīqūn*) are none other than Sufis.

Ihsān, since it is necessarily an exoteric notion as well, may be interpreted at different levels and in different ways. Exoterically it is the faith of the fideists and the zeal of the ritualists; in this case it is intensity and not profundity and thus has something quantitative or horizontal in it when compared with wisdom. Esoterically one can distinguish in *Ihsān* two accentuations: that of *gnosis*, which implies doctrinal intellectuality, and that of love, which requires the totality of the volitive and emotive soul, the first mode operating with intellectual means—without however neglecting the supports that may be necessitated by human weakness—and the second with moral and sentimental means. It is in the nature of things that this love can exclude every element of intellection and that it can readily if not always do so—precisely to the extent it constitutes a way—whereas *gnosis* on the contrary always contains an element of love, doubtless not violent love but one akin to Beauty and Peace.

*

*   *

Ihsān includes many ramifications, but it is obviously constituted most directly by quintessential esoterism. At first sight the expression "quintessential esoterism" looks like a pleonasm; is esoterism not quintessential by definition? It is indeed so "by right" but not necessarily "in fact", as is amply proven by the unequal and often disconcerting phenomenon of average Sufism. The principal pitfall of this spirituality—let it be said once again—is the fact that it treats metaphysics according to the categories of an anthropomorphist and voluntaristic theology and of an individualistic piety that is above all servile in character. Another pitfall, which goes hand in hand with the first, is the insistence on a certain hagiographic "mythology" and other preoccupations that enclose the intelligence and sensibility within the phenomenal order; finally there is the abuse of scriptural interpretations and metaphysico-mystical speculations, which are derived from an ill-defined and poorly disciplined inspirationism or from an esoterism that is in fact insufficiently conscious of its true nature.

An example of "moralizing metaphysics" is the confusion between a divine decree addressed to creatures endowed with free will and the ontological possibility that determines the nature of a thing; as a result of this confusion one asserts that Satan, by disobeying God—or Pharaoh, by resisting Moses—obeyed God in that by disobeying they obeyed their archetype, hence the existentiating divine "will", and that they have been—or will be—pardoned for this reason. Now the ideas of "divine will" and "obedience" are being used here improperly, because in order for an ontological possibility to be a "will" or an "order" it must emanate from the legislating *Logos* as such, and in this case it is expressly concerned with free and therefore responsible creatures; and in order for the submission of a thing or a being to constitute an "obedience", it is clearly necessary for there to be a discerning consciousness and freedom, hence the possibility of not obeying. In the absence of this fundamental *distinguo* there is merely doctrinal confusion and misuse of language, as well as heresy from the legitimate point of view of theologians.

The general impression given by Sufi literature must not cause us to forget that there were many Sufis who left no writings and were strangers to the pitfalls we have just described; their influence has remained practically anonymous or blends with that of well-known individuals. Indeed it may be that certain minds instructed in the "vertical" way—which refers to the mysterious filiation of al-Khidr—and outside the requirements of a "horizontal" tradition shaped by an underlying theology and dialectical habits, may have voluntarily abstained from formulating their thought in such an environment, without this having prevented the radiance proper to every spiritual presence.

To describe known or what one may call literary Sufism in all its *de facto* complexity and paradoxes would require a whole book, whereas to give an account of the necessary and therefore concise character of Sufism, a few pages can suffice. "The Doctrine—and the Way—of Unity is unique" (*al-Tawhīdu wāhid*): this classic formula succinctly expresses the essentiality, primordiality, and universality of Islamic esoterism as well as esoterism as such; and we might even say that all wisdom—all *Advaita Vedānta* if one prefers—is contained for Islam within the *Shahādah* alone, the twofold Testimony of faith.

Before going further and in order to situate Islam within the totality of Monotheism, we wish to draw attention to the following: from the point of view of Islam, which is the religion—analogically and principially speaking—of the primordial and universal, Mosaism appears as a kind of "petrifaction" and Christianity by contrast as a kind of "disequilibrium". Indeed Mosaism—every question of exaggeration or stylization notwithstanding—has the vocation of being the preserving ark of both the Abrahamic and Sinaitic heritage, the "ghetto" of the One and Invisible God, who speaks and acts, but who does so only for an Israel that is impenetrable and turned in on itself and that puts all the emphasis on the Covenant and obedience; whereas the sufficient reason for Christianity, at least with regard to its specific mode, is to be the incredible and explosive exception that breaks the continuity of the horizontal and exteriorizing stream of the human by a vertical and interiorizing irruption of the Divine, the entire emphasis being placed on sacramental life and penance. Islam, which professes to be Abrahamic, hence primordial, seeks to reconcile the oppositions within itself, just as the substance absorbs the accidents but without abolishing their qualities; by referring to Abraham and thereby to Noah and Adam, Islam seeks to restore the value of the immense treasure of pure Monotheism, whence its accentuation of Unity and faith; it frees and reanimates this Monotheism, the Israelization and Christification of which had actualized specific potentialities while dimming its substantial light. All the unshakable certitude and propulsive power of Islam are explained by this and cannot be explained otherwise.

*

* *

The first Testimony of faith (*Shahādah*) contains two parts, each of which is composed of two words: *lā ilāha* and *illā 'Llāh*, "no divinity—except the (sole) Divinity". The first part, the "negation" (*nafy*), corresponds to universal Manifestation, which is illusory in relation to the Principle, whereas the second part, the "confirmation" (*ithbāt*), corresponds to the Principle, which is Reality and which in relation to Manifestation is alone real.

Nevertheless Manifestation possesses a relative reality without which it would be pure nothingness; in a complementary way there must be within the principial order an element of relativity without which this order could not be the cause of Manifestation, hence of what is relative by definition; this is visually expressed by the Taoist symbol of the *Yin-Yang*, which is an image of compensatory reciprocity.

This means that at a level below its Essence the Principle contains a prefiguration of Manifestation, which makes Manifestation possible; and Manifestation for its part contains in its center a reflection of the Principle, without which it would be independent of the Principle, which is inconceivable, relativity having no substantiality of its own.

The prefiguration of Manifestation in the Principle—the principial *Logos*—is represented in the *Shahādah* by the word *illā* ("except" or "if not"), whereas the name *Allāh* expresses the Principle in itself; and the reflection of the Principle—the manifested *Logos*—is represented in turn by the word *ilāha* ("divinity"), whereas the word *lā* ("there is no" or "no") refers to Manifestation as such, which is illusory in relation to the Principle and therefore cannot be envisaged outside it or separately from it.

This is the metaphysical and cosmological doctrine of the first Testimony, that of God (*lā ilāha illā 'Llāh*). The doctrine of the second Testimony, that of the Prophet (*Muhammadun Rasūlu 'Llāh*), refers to a Unity not exclusive this time but inclusive; it expresses not distinction but identity, not discernment but union, not transcendence but immanence, not the objective and macrocosmic discontinuity of the degrees of Reality but the subjective and microcosmic continuity of the one Consciousness. The second Testimony is not static and separative like the first, but dynamic and unitive.

Strictly speaking, the second Testimony—according to its quintessential interpretation—considers the Principle only in relation to three hypostatic aspects, namely: the manifested Principle (*Muhammad*), the manifesting Principle (*Rasūl*), and the Principle in itself (*Allāh*). The entire accent is placed on the intermediate element, *Rasūl*, "Messenger"; it is this element, the *Logos*, which links the manifested Principle to the Principle in itself. The *Logos* is the "Spirit" (*Rūh*), of which it has been said that it is neither created nor uncreated or again that it is manifested in relation to the Principle and non-manifested or principial in relation to Manifestation.

The word *Rasūl*, "Messenger", indicates a "descent" of God toward the world; it also implies an "ascent" of man toward God. In the case of the Muhammadan phenomenon, the descent is that of the Koranic Revelation (*laylat al-qadr*), and the ascent is that of the Prophet during the "Night Journey" (*laylat al-mi'rāj*); in the human microcosm, the descent is inspiration, and the ascent is aspiration; the descent is divine grace whereas the ascent is human effort, the content of which is the "remembrance of God" (*dhikru 'Llāh*), whence the name *Dhikru 'Llāh* given to the Prophet.[3]

The three words *dhākir, dhikr, madhkūr*—a classic ternary in Sufism—correspond exactly to the ternary *Muhammad, Rasūl, Allāh*: *Muhammad* is the invoker, *Rasūl* the invocation, *Allāh* the invoked. In the invocation, the invoker and the One invoked meet, just as *Muhammad* and *Allāh* meet in *Rasūl* or in the *Risālah*, the Message.[4]

The microcosmic aspect of *Rasūl* explains the esoteric meaning of the "Blessing upon the Prophet" (*salāt 'alā 'n-Nabī*), which contains on the one hand the "Blessing" properly so called (*Salāt*) and on the other hand "Peace" (*Salām*), the latter referring to the stabilizing, appeasing, and "horizontal" graces and the former to the transforming, vivifying, and "vertical" graces. Now the "Prophet" is the immanent universal Intellect, and the purpose of the formula is to awaken within us the Heart-Intellect in the twofold relationship of receptivity and enlightenment—of the Peace that extinguishes and the Life that regenerates, by God and in God.

*

*   *

The first Testimony of faith, which refers *a priori* to transcendence, includes secondarily and necessarily a meaning according to immanence: in this case the word *illā*, "except" or "if not", means that every positive quality, every perfection, every beauty belongs to God or even "is" God in a certain sense, whence the divine Name "the Outward" (*al-Zāhir*), which is the complementary opposite of "the Inward" (*al- Bātin*).[5]

---

[3] Jacob's Ladder is an image of the *Logos*, with the angels descending and ascending, God appearing at the top of the ladder and Jacob remaining below.

[4] Another ascending ternary is that of *makhāfah, mahabbah, ma'rifah*: fear, love, knowledge—modes at once simultaneous and successive; we shall return to this later.

[5] This interpretation has given rise to the accusation of pantheism, wrongly of course since God cannot be reduced to outwardness, that is, since outwardness does not exclude inwardness any more than immanence excludes transcendence.

In a similar but inverse manner, the second Testimony, which refers *a priori* to immanence, includes secondarily and necessarily a meaning according to transcendence: in this case the word *Rasūl*, "Messenger", means that Manifestation—*Muhammad*—is but the trace of the Principle, *Allāh*, hence that Manifestation is not the Principle.

These underlying meanings must accompany the primary meanings because of the principle of compensatory reciprocity to which we referred when speaking of the first Testimony and with regard to which we mentioned the well-known symbol of *Yin-Yang*. For Manifestation is not the Principle while nonetheless being the Principle by participation because of its "non-inexistence"; and Manifestation—the word says as much—is the Principle manifested, but without being able to be the Principle in itself. The unitive truth of the second Testimony cannot be absent from the first Testimony any more than the separative truth of the first can be absent from the second.

And just as the first Testimony, which has above all a macrocosmic and objective meaning, necessarily includes a microcosmic and subjective meaning,[6] so the second Testimony, which has above all a microcosmic and subjective meaning, necessarily includes a macrocosmic and objective meaning.

The two Testimonies culminate in the word *Allāh*, which being their essence contains them and thereby transcends them. In the name *Allāh* the first syllable is short, contracted, absolute, whereas the second is long, dilated, infinite; it is thus that the Supreme Name contains these two mysteries, Absoluteness and Infinitude, and thereby also the extrinsic effect of their complementarity, Manifestation, as is indicated by this *hadīth qudsī*: "I was a hidden treasure, and I wanted to be known; hence I created the world." Since absolute Reality includes intrinsically Goodness, Beauty, Beatitude (*Rahmah*) and since it is the Sovereign Good, it includes *ipso facto* the tendency

---

[6] An initiatic, or if one prefers "advaitic", meaning: "There is no subject ("me") except the sole Subject (the "Self")." It should be noted that Ramana Maharshi and Ramakrishna seem to have failed to recognize in their teachings the vital importance of the ritual and liturgical framework of the way, whereas neither the great Vedantists nor the Sufis ever lost sight of it.

to communicate itself, hence to radiate; this is the Absolute's aspect of Infinity, and it is this aspect that projects Possibility, Being, whence spring forth the world, things, creatures.

The Name *Muhammad* is that of the *Logos*, which is situated between the Principle and Manifestation or between God and the world. Now the *Logos* is on the one hand prefigured in the Principle, which is expressed by the word *illā* in the first *Shahādah*, and on the other hand projects itself into Manifestation, which is expressed by the word *ilāha* in the same formula. In the Name *Muhammad* the whole accent and all the fulgurating power are situated at the center between two short syllables, one initial and one final, without which this accentuation would not be possible; it is the sonorous image of the victorious Manifestation of the One.

*

*   *

According to the school of *Wujūdiyah*,[7] to say that "there is no divinity (*ilāha*) if not the (sole) Divinity (*Allāh*)" means that there is only God, that as a consequence everything is God, and that it is we creatures who see a multiple world where there is only one Reality; the question that remains is why creatures see the One in multiple mode and why God Himself, insofar as He creates, legislates, and judges, sees the multiple and not the One. The correct answer is that multiplicity is objective as well as subjective—the cause of diversifying contingency being in each of the two poles of perception—and that multiplicity or diversity is in reality a subdivision, not of the divine Principle of course, but of its manifesting projection, which is existential and universal Substance. Diversity or plurality is therefore not opposed to Unity; it is within it and not alongside it. Multiplicity as such is the outward aspect of the world; but it is necessary to look at phenomena according to their inward reality, hence as a diversified and diversifying projection of the One. The metacosmic cause of the

---

[7] The ontological monism of Ibn Arabi. It should be noted that even in Islam this school does not have a monopoly on unitive metaphysics despite the prestige of its founder.

phenomenon of multiplicity is All-Possibility, which coincides by def-inition with the Infinite, the latter being an intrinsic characteristic of the Absolute. The divine Principle, being the Sovereign Good, tends by this very fact to radiate, hence to communicate itself—to project or make explicit all the "possibilities of the Possible".

To say radiation is to say increasing distance, hence progressive weakening or darkening, which explains the privative—and finally subversive—phenomenon of what we call evil; we speak of it thus for good reason and in conformity with its nature and not because of a particular, even arbitrary, point of view. But evil must have a positive function in the economy of the universe or else it would not be possible, and this function is twofold: first of all there is contrasting manifestation, that is, the highlighting of the good by means of its opposite, for to distinguish a good from an evil is a way of un-derstanding better the nature of the good;[8] then there is transitory collaboration, which means that it is also the role of evil to contribute to the realization of the good.[9] It is in any case absurd to assert that evil is a good because it is "willed by God" and because God can will only the good; evil always remains evil in relation to the privative or sub-versive character that defines it, but it is indirectly a good by virtue of the following factors: by existence, which detaches it so to speak from nothingness and causes it to participate, with everything that exists, in the divine Reality, the only one there is; by superimposed qualities or faculties, which as such always retain their positive character; and finally, as we have said, by its contrasting function with regard to the good and its indirect collaboration in the realization of the good.

---

[8] At first sight one might think that this highlighting is a merely circumstantial and therefore secondary factor, but this is not the case, for it is a question here of the quasi-principial opposition of phenomena—or categories of phenomena—and not of accidental confrontations. Qualitative "contrasting" is indeed a cosmic principle and not a question of encounters or comparisons.

[9] Evil in its aspect of suffering contributes to the unfolding of Mercy, which in order to be plenary must be able to save in the fullest meaning of this word; in other words divine Love in its dimension of unlimited compassion implies evil in its dimension of unfathomable misery; to this the Psalms and the Book of Job bear witness, and to this the final and quasi-absolute solution is the *Apocatastasis*, which reintegrates everything in the Sovereign Good.

To consider evil in relation to cosmogonic Causality is at the same stroke and *a priori* to consider it in relation to universal Possibility: if manifesting Radiation is necessarily prefigured in the divine Being, the privative consequences of this Radiation must be so in a certain manner as well, not as such of course but as "punitive" functions—morally speaking—pertaining essentially to Power and Rigor and thus making manifest the "negation" (*nafy*) of the *Shahādah*, namely, the exclusiveness of the Absolute. These functions are expressed by the divine Names of Wrath, such as "He who contracts, tightens, tears away" (*al-Qabid*), "He who avenges" (*al-Muntaqim*), "He who injures" (*al-Darr*), and several others;[10] these are altogether extrinsic functions, for "Verily, my Mercy (*Rahmah*) precedeth my Wrath (*Ghadab*)", as is declared by the inscription on the throne of *Allāh*: "precedeth", hence "takes precedence over" and in the final analysis "annuls". Moreover the wrathful functions are reflected in creatures in just the same way as the generous ones, whether positively by analogy or negatively by opposition; for holy anger is something other than hatred, just as noble love is something other than blind passion.

We shall add that the function of evil is to permit or introduce the manifestation of divine Anger, which means that this Anger in a certain way creates evil for the sake of its own ontologically necessary manifestation: if there is universal Radiation, there is by virtue of the same necessity both the phenomenon of evil and the manifestation of Rigor, and then the victory of the Good, hence the eminently compensatory manifestation of Mercy. We could also say very elliptically that evil is the "existence of the inexistent" or the "possibility of the impossible", this paradoxical possibility being required as it were by the limitlessness of All-Possibility, which cannot exclude even nothingness, for however null in itself, this nothingness is nonetheless "conceivable" existentially as well as intellectually.

Whoever discerns and contemplates God, first in a conceptual way and then in the Heart, will finally see Him also in creatures—in the

---

[10] Vedantic doctrine discerns in the substantial or feminine pole (*Prakriti*) of Being three tendencies: one ascending and luminous (*Sattva*), one expansive and fiery (*Rajas*), and one descending and obscure (*Tamas*); the last does not in itself constitute evil but prefigures it indirectly and gives rise to it on certain levels or under certain conditions.

manner permitted by their nature and not otherwise. From this comes on the one hand charity toward one's neighbor and on the other hand respect toward even inanimate objects, always to the extent required or permitted by their qualities and defects, for it is not a question of deluding oneself but of understanding the real nature of creatures and things;[11] this means that one must be just and—depending on the case—more charitable than just, and also that one must treat things in conformity with their nature and not with a profaning inadvertence. This is the most elementary manner of seeing God everywhere, and it is also a way of feeling that we are everywhere seen by God; and since there are no strict lines of demarcation in charity, we may say that it is better to be a little too charitable than not charitable enough.[12]

*

*   *

Each verse of the Koran, even if it is not metaphysical or mystical in itself, includes a meaning in addition to its immediate sense that pertains to one or the other of these two domains; this certainly does not authorize setting aside an underlying meaning in favor of an arbitrary and forced interpretation, for neither zeal nor ingenuity can replace the real intentions of the Text, whether these are direct or indirect, essential or secondary. "Lead us on the straight path": this verse refers first of all to dogmatic, ritual, and moral rectitude, but it cannot but refer also and more especially to the way of *gnosis;* on the other hand, when the Koran institutes some rule or other or when it relates some incident, no higher meaning imposes itself in a necessary way, which is not to say that this is excluded *a priori,* provided that the symbolism is plausible. It goes without saying that the exegetical science (*'ilm al-usūl*) of theologians, with its classification of explanatory categories,

---

[11] Love of beauty and the sense of the sacred are also situated in this context.

[12] According to the Koran God rewards merits much more than He punishes faults, and He more readily forgives a fault on account of a small merit than reduces a reward on account of a small fault—always according to the measures of God, not according to ours.

does not take account—and this is its right—of the liberties of an esoterist reading.

A point we must take into account here, even if only to mention it, is the discontinuous, allusive, and elliptical character of the Koran: it is discontinuous like its mode of revelation or "descent" (*tanzīl*) and allusive and therefore elliptical through its parabolism, which insinuates itself in secondary details that are all the more paradoxical in that their intention remains independent of context. Moreover it is a fact that the Arabs, and with them the Arabized, are fond of a separating and accentuating discontinuity, of allusion, ellipsis, tautology, and hyperbolism; all this seems to have its roots in certain characteristics of nomadic life, with its alternations, mysteries, and nostalgias.[13]

---

[13] With regard to allusive ellipsism, here are some examples: Solomon arrives with all his army in the "Valley of the Ants", and one of these says to the others: "O ants! Enter your dwellings lest Solomon and his armies crush you unknowingly." The meaning is first that even the best of monarchs, to the very extent he is powerful, cannot prevent injustices committed in his name and second that the small, when confronted with the great, must look to their own safety by remaining in a modest and discrete anonymity, not because of a voluntary ill will on the part of the great, but because of an inevitable situation; the subsequent prayer of Solomon expresses gratitude toward God, who gives all power, as well as the intention of being just, of "doing good". Then Solomon, having inspected his troops, notices that the hoopoe is absent, whose important function is to discover water holes, and he says: "Verily I shall punish it with a severe chastisement, or I shall slay it, unless it bring me a valid excuse"; the teaching, which slips here into the general narrative, is that it is a grave matter to fail without a serious reason in fulfilling the obligations of an office, the degrees of seriousness being expressed by the degrees of punishment. Finally, the hoopoe having recounted that it had seen the Queen of Sheba, a worshipper of the sun, Solomon says to it: "We wish to see whether thou speakest truth or whether thou liest." Why this distrust? To emphasize that a leader must verify the reports of his subordinates not because they are liars but because they may be so; but the distrust of the king is also explained by the extraordinary nature of the account, and it thereby includes an indirect homage to the splendor of the kingdom of Sheba. These are so many psychological, social, and political teachings inserted into the story of the meeting between Solomon and Queen Bilqis (*Sūrah* "The Ant" [27]:18, 21, 27). That these incidents can also have profound meanings we have no reason to doubt, but we nonetheless do not wish to abolish the distinction between interpretations that are necessary and those that are merely possible. Let us add, regarding the quotations we have presented here, that it is completely in the style of Islam to mention—explicitly or implicitly—practical details that at first sight seem obvious and thus to provide points of reference for the most

Let us now consider the Koranic "signs" in themselves. The following verses—and many others as well—have an esoteric significance that is at least certain and therefore legitimate even if it is not always direct; or more precisely, each verse has several meanings of this kind, if only because of the difference between the perspectives of love and *gnosis* or between doctrine and method.

"God is the Light of the heavens and of the earth" (*Sūrah* "Light" [24]:35), that is, the Intellect at once "celestial" and "terrestrial", which is to say principial or manifested, macrocosmic or microcosmic, the transcendent or immanent Self; "And unto God belong the East and the West, and wheresoever ye turn, there is the Face of God" (*Sūrah* "The Cow" [2]:115); "He is the First and the Last, and the Outward (the Apparent) and the Inward (the Hidden); and He knoweth infinitely all things" (*Sūrah* "Iron" [57]:3); "He it is who sent down profound peace (*Sakīnah* = Tranquility through the divine Presence) into the hearts of the believers (the heart being either the deep soul or the Intellect) in order to add faith unto their faith", a reference to the illumination that superimposes itself on ordinary faith (*Sūrah* "Victory" [48]:4); "Verily we are God's, and verily unto Him we shall return" (*Sūrah* "The Cow" [2]:156); "And God calleth to the house of Peace, and leadeth whom He will (whoever is qualified) upon the straight (ascending) Path" (*Sūrah* "Jonah" [10]:26); "Those who believe and whose hearts find peace through the remembrance (mention = invocation) of God. Is it not through the remembrance of God that hearts find peace?" (*Sūrah* "The Thunder" [13]:28); "Say *Allāh*, then leave them to their vain discourse" (*Sūrah* "Cattle" [6]:92); "O men, ye are the poor (*fuqarā* from *faqīr*) in relation to God, and God is the Rich (*al-Ghanī* = the Independent), the universally Praised", every cosmic quality referring to Him and bearing witness to Him (*Sūrah* "The Angels" [35]:15); "And the hereafter (the principial night) is better for thee than the here below (the phenomenal world)" (*Sūrah* "The Morning Hours" [93]:4); "And worship God until certitude (metaphysics, *gnosis*) cometh unto thee" (*Sūrah* "Al-Hijr" [15]:99).

We have quoted these verses as examples without undertaking to explain the specifically esoteric implications hidden in their respec-

---

diverse situations of individual and collective life; the *Sunnah* is an abundant proof of this.

tive symbolisms. But it is not only the verses of the Koran that are important in Islam; there are also the sayings (*ahādīth*) of the Prophet, which obey the same laws and in which God sometimes speaks in the first person; a saying in this category, to which we referred above on account of its doctrinal importance, is the following: "I was a hidden treasure, and I wanted to be known; hence I created the world." Or a saying in which the Prophet speaks for himself: "Spiritual virtue (*ihsān* = right doing) is that thou shouldst worship God as if thou sawest Him, for if thou seest Him not He nonetheless seeth thee."

A key formula for Sufism is the famous *hadīth* in which God speaks through the mouth of the Messenger: "My slave ceaseth not to draw nigh unto Me by devotions freely accomplished[14] until I love him; and when I love him, I am the Hearing whereby he heareth and the Sight whereby he seeth and the Hand wherewith he smiteth and the Foot whereon he walketh." Thus the absolute Subject, the Self, penetrates the contingent subject, the ego, and thus the ego is reintegrated into the Self; this is the principal theme of esoterism. The "devotions freely accomplished" culminate in the "Remembrance of God" or are directly identified with it, all the more so since the profound reason for every religious act is this remembrance, which in the final analysis is the very reason for the existence of man.

But let us return to the Koran: the quasi-"Eucharistic" element in Islam—that is, the element of "heavenly nourishment"—is chanted recitation of the Book; canonical Prayer is the obligatory minimum of this, but it contains as if by compensation a text that is considered to be the equivalent of the entire Koran, namely the *Fātihah*, the "*Sūrah* that opens". What is important in the rite of reading or reciting the revealed Book is not only a literal understanding of the text, but also—and almost independently of this understanding—an assimilation of the "magic" of the Book, whether by elocution or audition, with the intention of being penetrated by the divine Word (*Kalamu*

---

[14] Exoterizing Sufism, which prolongs and intensifies the *Sharī'ah*, deduces from this passage the multiplication of pious practices, whereas the Sufism that is centered on *gnosis* deduces the frequency of the quintessential rite, *Dhikr*, emphasizing its contemplative quality and not its character of meritorious act. Let us remember, however, that there is no strict line of demarcation between the two conceptions, although this line does exist by right and can always be emphasized.

'Llāh) as such and thus by forgetting the world and the ego.[15] From the twofold point of view of doctrinal content and "real Presence", ejaculatory prayer—*Dhikr*—has in principle the value and virtue of a synthesis of Koranic recitation.

*
*   *

The Muhammadan sayings sometimes contain judgments that appear excessive, which prompts us to give the following explanation. Ibn Arabi has been reproached for placing the Sages above the Prophets— wrongly so, for he regarded all the Prophets as Sages too, though their quality of wisdom took precedence over that of prophecy. Indeed the Sage transmits truths as he perceives them whereas the Prophet as such transmits a divine Will, which he does not spontaneously perceive and which determines him in a moral and quasi-existential manner; the Prophet is thus passive in his receptive function whereas the Sage is active by his discernment, although in another respect the Truth is received passively, just as inversely and by way of compensation the divine Will confers upon the Prophet an active attitude. And here is the point we wish to make: when a Prophet proclaims a point of view whose limitations one can perceive without difficulty, whether from the standpoint of another religious system or from a perception of the nature of things, he does so because he incarnates in this case a particular divine Will: for example, there is a divine Will which, for a given mentality, inspires the production of sacred images just as there is another divine Will which, for another mentality, pro- scribes images; when the Arab Prophet, determined by this second Will, proscribes the plastic arts and anathematizes artists, he does not do so on the basis of prevailing opinion or as the result of a personal intellection, but under the effect of a divine Will that seizes him and makes of him its instrument or spokesman.

All this is said to explain the "narrowness" of certain positions taken by the founders of religion. The Prophet as Sage has access to

---

[15] As it happens, non-Arab Muslims, who to a large extent do not know the language of the Koran, recite or read parts of the Book in order to benefit from its *barakah*, a practice considered perfectly valid.

115

every truth, but there are some truths which do not actualize themselves concretely in his mind or which he places in parentheses unless an occasional cause makes him change his attitude, and this depends on Providence, not chance. The Prophet does not belie by his nature as Sage what he must personify as Prophet, except in some exceptional cases, which believers may understand or not and of which they are not meant to be judges.

*

* *

The twofold Testimony is the first and most important of the five "Pillars of the Religion" (*arkān al-Dīn*). The others have a meaning only in reference to it, and they are canonical Prayer (*Salāt*), the Fast of Ramadan (*Siyām*), Almsgiving (*Zakāt*), Pilgrimage (*Hajj*). The esoterism of these practices is not only in their obvious initiatic symbolism but in the fact that our practices are esoteric to the extent we ourselves are, first by our understanding of the Doctrine and then by our assimilation of the Method,[16] these two elements being contained in the twofold Testimony precisely. Prayer marks the submission of Manifestation to the Principle; the Fast is detachment with regard to desires, hence with regard to the ego; Almsgiving is detachment with regard to things, hence with regard to the world; finally, the Pilgrimage is the return to the Center, the Heart, the Self. A sixth Pillar is sometimes added, Holy War: this is combat against the profane soul by means of the spiritual weapon; it is therefore not the Holy War that is outward and "lesser" (*asghar*), but the Holy War that is inward and "greater" (*akbar*), according to a *hadīth*. Islamic initiation is in fact a pact with God for the sake of this "greater" Holy War; the battle is fought by means of the *Dhikr* and on the basis of *Faqr*, inward "Poverty", whence the name of *faqīr*, given the initiate.

What is distinctive about Prayer among the "Pillars of the Religion" is that it has a precise form and includes bodily positions, which as symbols necessarily have meanings specific to esoterism; but these

---

[16] Which essentially includes the virtues, for there is no path that is limited to an abstract and in a sense inhuman *yoga*; Sufism is precisely one of the most patent proofs of this.

meanings are simply explanatory and do not enter consciously and operatively into the accomplishment of the rite, which requires only a sincere awareness of the formulas and the pious intention of the movements. The reason for the existence of the canonical Prayer lies in the fact that man always remains an individual interlocutor before God and that he need not be anything else; when God wants us to speak to Him, He does not accept from us a metaphysical meditation. As for the meaning of the movements of the Prayer, all we need to say here is that the vertical positions express our dignity as free and theomorphic "vicar" (*khalīfah*) and that the prostrations on the contrary manifest our smallness as "servant" (*'abd*) and as dependant and limited creature;[17] man must be aware of the two sides of his being, made as he is of clay and spirit.

*
*   *

For obvious reasons the Name *Allāh* is the quintessence of Prayer just as it is the quintessence of the Koran; containing in a certain manner the whole Koran, it thereby also contains the canonical Prayer, which is the first *sūrah* of the Koran, "that which opens" (*al-Fātihah*). In principle the supreme Name (*al-Ism al-A'zam*) even contains the whole religion and all the practices it requires, and it could therefore replace them;[18] but in fact these practices contribute to the equilibrium of the soul and society, or rather they condition them.

---

[17] The gestures of the ritual ablution (*wudū'*), without which man is not in a state of prayer, constitute various so to speak psychosomatic purifications. Man sins with the members of his body, but the root of sin is in the soul.

[18] "Remembrance (*dhikr*) is the most important rule of the religion. The law was not imposed upon us nor the rites of worship ordained except for the sake of establishing the remembrance of God (*dhikru 'Llāh*). The Prophet said: 'The circumambulation (*tawāf*) around the Holy House, the passage to and fro between (the hills of) Safa and Marwah, and the throwing of the pebbles (at three pillars symbolizing the devil) were ordained only for the sake of the Remembrance of God.' And God Himself has said (in the Koran): 'Remember God at the Holy Monument.' Thus we know that the rite that consists in stopping there was ordained for remembrance and not specifically for the sake of the monument itself, just as the halt at Muna was ordained for remembrance and not because of the valley. Furthermore He (God) has said on the

In several passages the Koran enjoins the faithful to remember God, hence to invoke Him and frequently repeat His Name. Likewise the Prophet said: "It behooves you to remember your Lord (to invoke Him)." He also said: "There is a means of polishing everything and removing rust; what polishes the heart is the invocation of *Allāh*; and there is no act that removes God's punishment as much as does this invocation." The Companions of the Prophet said: "Is the fight against infidels equal to this?" He replied: "No, not even if one fights until one's sword is broken." And he said further on another occasion: "Should I not teach you an action that is better for you than fighting against infidels?" His Companions said: "Yes, teach it to us." The Prophet said: "This action is the invocation of *Allāh*."

Dhikr, which implies spiritual combat since the soul tends naturally toward the world and the passions, coincides with *Jihād*, Holy War; Islamic initiation—as we said above—is a pact for the sake of this War, a pact with the Prophet and with God. The Prophet on returning from a battle declared: "We have returned from the lesser Holy War (performed with the sword) to the greater Holy War (performed with invocation)."

Dhikr contains the whole Law (*Sharīʿah*), and it is the reason for the existence of the whole Law;[19] this is declared by the Koranic verse: "Verily, prayer (the exoteric practice) preventeth man from committing what is shameful (degrading) and blameworthy; and certainly remembrance (invocation) of God (the esoteric practice) is greater" (*Sūrah* "The Spider" [29]:45).[20] The expression "the remembrance of

subject of the ritual prayer: 'Perform the prayer in remembrance of Me.' In a word, our performance of the rites is considered ardent or lukewarm according to the degree of our remembrance of God while performing them. Thus when the Prophet was asked which spiritual strivers would receive the greatest reward, he replied: 'Those who have remembered God most.' And when asked which fasters would receive the greatest reward, he replied: 'Those who have remembered God most.' And when the prayer and the almsgiving and the pilgrimage and the charitable donations were mentioned, he said each time: 'The richest in remembrance of God is the richest in reward'" (Shaykh Ahmad al-Alawi in his treatise *Al-Qawl al-Maʿrūf*).

[19] This is the point of view of all invocatory disciplines, such as Hindu *japa-yoga* or the Amidist *nembutsu* (*buddhānusmriti*). This *yoga* is found in *jnāna* as well as in *bhakti*: "Repeat the sacred Name of the Divinity," said Shankaracharya in one of his hymns.

[20] "God and His Name are identical," as Ramakrishna said; and he was certainly not the only one or the first to say so.

God is more important" or "the greatest thing" (*Wa la-dhikru 'Llāhi akbar*) evokes and paraphrases this formula from the canonical Prayer: "God is greater" or "the greatest" (*Allāhu akbar*), and this indicates a mysterious connection between God and His Name; it also indicates a certain relativity—from the point of view of *gnosis*—of the outward rites, however indispensable in principle and in the majority of cases. In this connection we could also cite the following *hadīth*: one of the Companions said to the Prophet: "O Messenger of God, the prescriptions of Islam are too numerous for me; tell me something I can hold fast to." The Prophet replied: "Let thy tongue always be supple (in motion) with the mention (the remembrance) of God." This *hadīth*, like the verse we just quoted, expresses by allusion (*ishārah*) the principle of the inherence of the whole *Sharīʿah* in *Dhikr* alone.

"Verily in the Messenger of God ye have a fair example for whosoever hopeth in God and the Last Day, and remembereth God much" (*Sūrah* "The Clans" [33]:21). "Who hopeth in God": this is he who accepts the Testimony, the *Shahādah*, not merely with his mind but also with his heart; this is expressed by the word "hopeth". Now faith in God implies by way of consequence faith in our final ends; and to act in consequence is quintessentially to "remember God"; it is to fix the mind upon the Real instead of squandering it in the illusory, and it is to find peace in this fixation, according to the verse we have quoted above: "Verily in the remembrance of God do hearts find rest!"

"God maketh firm those who believe by the firm Word, in the life of the world and in the hereafter" (*Sūrah* "Abraham" [14]:27). The "firm Word" (*al-qawl al-thābit*) is either the *Shahādah*, the Testimony, or the *Ism*, the Name, the nature of the *Shahādah* being *a priori* intellectual or doctrinal and that of the *Ism* being existential or alchemical, though not in an exclusive manner, for each of the two divine Words participates in the other, the Testimony being in its way a divine Name and the Name being implicitly a doctrinal Testimony. By these two Words man becomes rooted in the Immutable, in this world as in the next. The "firmness" of the divine Word refers quintessentially to the Absolute, which in Islamic language is the One; thus the affirmative part of the *Shahādah*—the words *illā 'Llāh*—is called a "confirmation" (*ithbāt*), which indicates reintegration into immutable Unity.

The whole doctrine of *Dhikr* is brought out by these words: "So remember Me (*Allāh*); I will remember thee (*Fadhkurūnī adh-*

kurkum)" (*Sūrah* "The Cow" [2]:152). This is the doctrine of mystical reciprocity, such as appears in the following formulation of the early Church: "God became man that man might become God"; the Essence became form that form might become Essence. This presupposes a formal potentiality within the Essence and a mysterious immanence of the essential Reality within form; the Essence unites because it is one.

*

* *

Every way includes successive stages, which can at the same time be simultaneous modes; these are the "stations" (*maqāmāt*, singular: *maqām*) of Sufism. The fundamental stations are three: "Fear" (*Makhāfah*), "Love" (*Mahabbah*), and "Knowledge" (*Ma'rifah*); the number of the other stations, which in principle is indeterminate, is obtained by the subdivision of the three fundamental stations, whether the ternary is reflected in each of them or each is polarized into two complementary stations, each of which may in its turn contain various aspects, and so on. Moreover the "stations" are also manifested as passing "states" (*ahwāl*, singular: *hāl*), which are anticipations of the stations or which cause a given station already acquired to participate in another station still unexplored.

That each of the three fundamental modes of perfection or the way is repeated or reflected in the other two appears to us obvious and easy to imagine; we shall therefore not seek to describe these reciprocal reverberations here. On the other hand we must give an account of a subdivision that is not self-explanatory and that results from the bipolarization of each mode because of the universal law of complementarity; this complementarity is expressed fundamentally, for example, by the divine Names "the Immutable" (*al-Qayyūm*) and "the Living" (*al-Hayy*). We may thus distinguish within *Makhāfah* a static pole, Abstention or Renunciation (*Zuhd*), and a dynamic pole, Accomplishment or Effort (*Jahd*), the first pole realizing "Poverty" (*Faqr*), without which there is no valid work, and the second giving rise to "Remembrance" (*Dhikr*), which is work in the highest sense of the word and which eminently contains all works, not from the point of view of worldly necessities or opportunities, but from that of the fundamental divine requirement.

In *Mahabbah* there are likewise grounds for distinguishing between a static or passive pole and a dynamic or active pole: the first is Contentment (*Ridā*) or Gratitude (*Shukr*), and the second is Hope (*Rajā*) or Trust (*Tawakkul*). Moreover the second pole implies Generosity (*Karam*), just as Contentment for its part implies or requires Patience (*Sabr*); these virtues are necessarily relative, hence conditional, except toward God.[21]

As for *Maʿrifah*, it includes an objective pole, which refers to transcendence, and a subjective pole, which refers to immanence: on the one hand there is the "Truth" (*Haqq*) or Discernment of the One (*Tawhīd*), and on the other hand there is the "Heart" (*Qalb*) or Union with the One (*Ittihād*).

The three formulas of the Sufi rosary retrace the three fundamental degrees or planes: the "Asking of forgiveness" (*Istighfār*) corresponds to "Fear", the "Blessing on the Prophet" (*Salāt ʿalā 'n-Nabī*) to "Love", the "Testimony of faith" (*Shahādah*) to "Knowledge". The higher planes always include the lower whereas the lower planes prefigure or anticipate the higher if only by opening onto them; for Reality is one, in the soul as in the Universe. Moreover Action reunites with Love to the extent it is disinterested, and it reunites with Knowledge to the extent it is accompanied by an awareness that God is the true Agent; and the same applies to Abstention, *Vacare Deo*, which likewise can have its source only in God in the sense that mystical emptiness prolongs the principial Void.

It is a fact that classical Sufism has a tendency to seek to obtain cognitive results by volitive means rather than seeking to obtain volitive results by cognitive means, that is, by what is intellectually self-evident;[22] the two attitudes must in reality be combined, especially since in Islam the supreme and decisive merit is acceptance of a truth and not a moral attitude. There is no question that profound virtues predispose to Knowledge and can even bring about its blossoming in

---

[21] We give here only the "archetypes" or "keys" of the virtues—or "stations"—which sum up their multiple derivations. The *Risālah* of Qushayri or the *Mahāsin al-Majālis* of Ibn al-Arif, and other treatises of this kind, contain enumerations and analyses of these subdivisions, which have been studied by various Arabists.

[22] As was understood by the best of the Greeks, the word "philosophy" implied for them virtue through wisdom.

cases of heroism, but it is no less true, to say the least, that when Truth is well assimilated it produces the virtues in the very measure of this assimilation or—what amounts to the same—this qualification.

*

*　　*

The Koran repeatedly cites the names of earlier Prophets and relates their stories; this must have a meaning for the spiritual life, as the Koran itself attests. It can happen indeed that a Sufi is attached— within the very framework of the Muhammadan Way, which is his by definition—to some pre-Islamic Prophet; in other words the Sufi places himself under the symbol, influence, affective direction of a Prophet who personifies a congenial vocation. Islam sees in Christ— Sayyidna Isa—the personification of renunciation, interiorization, con- templative and solitary sanctity, Union; and more than one Sufi has claimed this spiritual filiation.

The series of the great Semitic Prophets includes only one woman, Sayyidatna Maryam; her prophetic—but not law-giving—dignity is made clear by the way the Koran presents her and also by the fact that she is mentioned in the *Sūrah* of "The Prophets" together with other Messengers. Maryam incarnates inviolable purity, to which is joined divine fecundation;[23] she also personifies spiritual retreat and abundance of graces[24] and, in an altogether general manner and *a priori*, celestial Femininity, Purity, Beauty, Mercy. The Message of the Blessed Virgin was Jesus, not Jesus as the founder of a religion but the Child Jesus[25]—not such and such a *Rasūl* but the *Rasūl* as

---

[23] "And Mary, daughter of Imran, who kept her virginity intact; and We (*Allāh*) breathed into her of our Spirit (*Rūh*)" (*Sūrah* "Banning" [66]:12).

[24] According to the Koran, Mary spent her early youth in the "prayer-niche" (*mihrāb*) of the Temple and was nourished there by angels. When Zachariah asked her whence came this food, the Virgin replied: "It is from God; verily God giveth to whom He will without reckoning" (*Sūrah* "The Family of Imran" [3]:37). The image of the "prayer- niche"—or spiritual retreat (*khalwah*)—is found in the following verse: "And make mention of Mary in the Book (O Prophet), when she withdrew from her people (from the world) to a place toward the East (toward the Light); and she placed a veil between herself and them" (*Sūrah* "Mary" [19]:16, 17).

[25] "And We (*Allāh*) made the Son of Mary and his Mother a sign (*āyah*)" (*Sūrah* "The

such, who contains all possible prophetic forms in their universal and primordial indifferentiation. Thus the Virgin is considered by certain Sufis as well as Christian authors to be Wisdom-Mother or Mother of Prophecy and all the Prophets; thus Islam calls her *Siddīqah*, the "Sincere"—sincerity being none other than total conformity to the Truth—which is indicated by the identification of Mary with Wisdom or Sanctity as such.

*
*   *

The Sufi readily calls himself "son of the Moment" (*ibn al-Waqt*), which means that he is situated in God's Present without concern for yesterday or tomorrow, and this Present is none other than a reflection of Unity; the One projected into time becomes the "Now" of God, which coincides with Eternity. The Sufi cannot call himself "son of the One", for this expression would evoke Christian terminology, which Islam must exclude because of its perspective; but he could call himself "son of the Center"—according to a spatial symbolism in this case—and he does so indirectly by his insistence on the mysteries of the Heart.

The whole of Sufism, it seems to us, is summed up in these four words: *Haqq, Qalb, Dhikr, Faqr,* "Truth", "Heart", "Remembrance", "Poverty". *Haqq* coincides with the *Shahādah,* the twofold Testimony: the metaphysical, cosmological, mystical, and eschatological Truth. *Qalb* means that this Truth must not be accepted with the mind alone but with the Heart, hence with all we are. *Dhikr,* as we know, is the permanent actualization of this Faith or *Gnosis* by means of the sacramental word; while *Faqr* is simplicity and purity of soul, which make this actualization possible by imparting the sincerity without which no act is valid.[26]

Believers" [23]:50). It will be noted that the "sign" is not Jesus alone, but he and his Mother.

[26] "Blessed are the pure in heart: for they shall see God" (Matt. 5:8).

The four most important formulas in Islam, which correspond in a sense to the four rivers of Paradise gushing forth from beneath the Throne of *Allāh*—the earthly reflection of this Throne being the Kaaba—are the first and second *Shahādah*, then the Consecration and the Praise: the *Basmalah* and the *Hamdalah*. The first *Shahādah*: "There is no divinity except the (sole) Divinity"; the second *Shahādah*: "Muhammad is the Messenger of God (of the sole Divinity)"; the *Basmalah*: "In the Name of God, the Clement, the Merciful";[27] the *Hamdalah*: "Praise be to God, the Lord of the worlds."

---

[27] God is clement or benevolent in Himself in the sense that Goodness, Beauty, and Love are contained in His very Essence (*Dhāt*), and He therefore manifests them necessarily in and through the world; this is expressed by the Name *Rahmān*, which is almost synonymous with the Name *Allāh*. And God is also good in relation to the world in the sense that He manifests His goodness toward creatures by according them subsistence and all possible gifts, including above all salvation; this is expressed by the Name *Rahīm*.

Hypostatic Dimensions of Unity

Since our intentions converge upon the quintessence, let us now return by way of conclusion to the metaphysical synthesis we outlined when referring to the esoteric symbolism of the *Shahādah*. The fundamental idea of Islam, that of divine Unity, implies inevitably the idea of diversity, that is, the idea of the relationships between the One and what seems to invalidate or contradict it; here we shall deal with this problem in a manner that is necessarily concise and without of course losing sight of the fact that a doctrinal outline can offer no more than landmarks, if only for the simple reason that an expression is inevitably something other than the reality expressed. Identity between the outline and the reality is in any case as unnecessary as it is impossible, precisely because this outline is capable of providing perfectly sufficient points of reference; otherwise there would be no adequate and effective symbolism or consequently any doctrine.

The whole problem of creation or universal manifestation is rooted in the very nature of the divine Principle. The absolutely Real projects the world because its infinite nature requires that it also be known starting from and within relativity; to say that God "created" and not that He "creates" is a way of expressing the contingency or relativity of the world, and in a certain sense it is to sever the world from its transcendent Cause. God "wants to be seen" not only "starting" from the world, but also "in" the world and even "as" world: either directly in qualities or indirectly and by contrast in their absence; and He wants to be seen not only by man but also by the lower creatures, who contemplate Him in a certain fashion by their specific form itself—or at least by whatever is positive in their form or state, as the case may be.

Absolute, Infinite, Perfection: these, we might say, are the primary definitions of the divine nature. Geometrically speaking, the Absolute is like the point, which excludes everything that is not itself; the Infinite is like the cross or star or spiral, which prolongs the point and in a sense makes it inclusive; and Perfection is like the circle or a system of concentric circles, which reflects the point or transposes it into extension. The Absolute is ultimate Reality in itself; the Infinite is its Possibility, hence also its Omnipotence; Perfection is Possibility to the extent it realizes a given potentiality of the absolutely Real or realizes all potentialities. Creation or manifestation is an effect of the divine nature: God cannot prevent Himself from radiating, hence manifesting Himself or creating, because He cannot prevent Himself from being infinite.

Divine Perfection is the sum or quintessence of all possible perfections, and we know them as a whole through experience; these perfections are manifested thanks to the Infinite, which offers them existential space—or substance if one prefers—and which actualizes and projects them; and it is thanks to the Absolute that things exist or are not "nonexistent". The Absolute, imperceptible in itself, makes itself visible by the existence and logic of things; in a similar way the Infinite reveals itself by their inexhaustible diversity; likewise Perfection manifests itself by their qualities, and in so doing it communicates both the rigor of the Absolute and the radiation of the Infinite, for things have their musicality as well as geometry. In other words, when everyday natural experience is combined with metaphysical intuition or faith—and faith always actualizes intuition to a certain degree—the recognition of the positive qualities in things and beings obliges us to acknowledge their archetypes or essences within the divine Order; likewise the inconceivability of limits in space-time obliges us to acknowledge the Infinite in itself; likewise again the fact that the least existence is absolute in relation to its absence—or the fact that physical, mathematical, and logical laws are ineluctable—bears witness in the final analysis to the Absolute and leaves us with no other choice than to accept it.[1]

*
* *

The ternary "Absolute-Infinite-Perfection" is reflected in the progression of numbers: the number one corresponds to the Absolute, the

---

[1] No doubt this way of thinking is meaningless to rationalists, but what matters is that they can in no way prove the opposite, either from the objective point of view of the Real or from the subjective point of view of knowledge.

progression itself to the Infinite, and the particular character—the form—of each number to Perfection.[2] The progression of numbers is not strictly comparable to an indefinite series of points where one is necessarily first, as if there could be a progression with a beginning but not an end; in reality it is necessary to compare the number one to a central point and the progression to an indefinite series of concentric circles; the center has by definition the value of an absolute and is therefore not a beginning, properly speaking; it is as it were outside number, and yet number is inconceivable without it. The same is true of the unlimited diversity of forms: the central form is circular or spherical, and there is no common measure between it and the square or cube; roundness has something absolute about it in relation to all other possible forms. Another example of existential progression is provided by matter, where the four sensible elements and all the chemical substances and aggregates emerge from ether, which—being simple and inherent in every sensible substance—is the center of this unfolding. Here too the central element cannot be merely a quantitative beginning, so to speak; on the contrary, it is quasi-transcendent in relation to its modalities or projections. The modalities being "infinite" in number, unity or the center must have an "absolute" character.

The ternary "Absolute-Infinite-Perfection" finds its most direct expression in Islamic language in the terms *Jalāl*, *Jamāl*, and *Kamāl*: "Majesty", "Beauty", and "Perfection". Traditionally Rigor or Justice is attributed to Majesty, and Gentleness or Mercy to Beauty; now Beauty like Mercy pertains to the Infinite, and Majesty like Justice to the Absolute.

*
*   *

There is a profound significance in the fact—at first sight paradoxical—that Islam, jealous as it is of the unity of God and so scrupulous in its fundamental formulations, places at the head of each *sūrah* the quasi-Trinitarian formula, "In the Name of God, the Clement, the

---

[2] As is shown by geometrical figures insofar as they express numbers, which in this respect are qualities and not quantities.

127

Merciful", and that it employs this formula on every occasion as a con-
secratory blessing. We think we have already provided the key to this
enigma: when we speak of the Absolute we speak by the same token
of the Infinite and the Perfect.[3] *Rahmah*—a term most often translated
as "Clemency"—implies more profoundly, like the Sanskrit term
Ānanda, all the aspects of Harmony:[4] Goodness, Beauty, and Beatitude; and *Rahmah* is integrated into the divine Essence itself inasmuch
as it is fundamentally none other than the radiating Infinitude of the
Principle, an identity the Koran expresses by saying: "Call upon *Allāh*
or call upon *al-Rahmān*; to Him belong the most beautiful Names."[5]

For one cannot appeal to the One without Mercy responding.

*
*   *

God is manifested in the world, as we have said, by the miracle of
existence, the gulf between the least grain of dust and nothingness
being absolute; He manifests His Infinity *a priori* by the cosmic container space-time, which has no imaginable limits, any more than do
the multiplicity and diversity of its contents; and He manifests His

---

[3] In Christianity the element "Absolute" is represented either analogically or directly
by the "Father", the element "Infinite" or "Radiation" being the Holy Spirit, and the
element "Perfection" being the "Son" or Word, who is the "Wisdom of the Father". In
Buddhism it is the Buddha who represents Perfection, whereas in a manner that is at
first sight paradoxical Radiation is represented in the form of the *Bodhisattva*, who in
fact carries the message of *Nirvāna*—the Absolute—to the extremity of *Samsāra*.

[4] *Sat* referring to the Absolute and *Chit* to the Consciousness that *Ātmā* possesses of
its inexhaustible Perfection, hence its Qualities.

[5] A remark: the Trinity that the Koran attributes to Christianity—namely, "God,
Jesus, Mary"—is justified in the sense that the Blessed Virgin is by her nature, and
not by adoption, the human receptacle of the Holy Spirit (whence *gratia plena* and
Dominus tecum); as "Immaculate Conception" she is *a priori* the vehicle of the Spirit
and thereby personifies it. It follows that an invocation of Mary, such as the *Ave*, is
practically, implicitly, and quintessentially an invocation of the Holy Spirit, which in
Islam pertains to the hypostatic mystery of *Rahmāniyah*, divine "Generosity", which
is Life, Radiation, Light; the Virgin, like the Spirit, is the "womb" (*rahim*)—at once
inviolable and generous—of all graces.

Perfection by the qualities of things and beings, which bear witness to their divine archetypes and thereby to the divine Perfection.

This triple manifestation constitutes divine "Outwardness", which is expressed by the Name "the Outward" (*al-Zāhir*). According to Sufis the *Shahādah* comprises two meanings, depending on whether we are considering transcendence or immanence: first, the truth that God alone is real, in contrast to the world, which—being contingent—is illusory; second, the truth that no existence can be situated outside of God, that all that exists "is not other than He" (*lā ghayruhu*), or else the world would not exist. The first meaning corresponds to the mystery of the "Inward" (*al-Bātin*) and the second to that of "the Outward".

It is not true that we cannot know what God is and can only know what He is not; but it is true that we cannot imagine God any more than we can hear light or see thunder. On the one hand space and time, then the existence of things, and then their qualities "prove" God; on the other hand they "are" God, but seen through the veil of "Outwardness" or "Distance" (*buʿd*), hence contingency. This veil produces by definition the privative or subversive phenomenon of evil, which is the ransom of projection outside the Principle, a projection that is nonetheless necessary and finally benefic inasmuch as "I was a hidden treasure, and I wanted to be known", universal Radiation being the very consequence of the "Sovereign Good".

The Absolute or the Essence intrinsically comprises Infinitude; it is as the Infinite that it radiates. Divine Radiation projects the Essence into the "void", but without there being any "going out" whatsoever, for the Principle is immutable and indivisible, and nothing can be taken from it; by means of this projection upon the surface of a "nothingness" in itself nonexistent, the Essence is reflected in the mode of "forms" or "accidents". But the "life" of the Infinite is not only centrifugal; it is also centripetal: it is alternately or simultaneously—depending on the relationships considered—Radiation and Reintegration; Reintegration is the apocatastatic "return" of forms and accidents into the Essence, but without there being anything added to the Essence, for it is absolute Plenitude. Moreover, and even above all, Infinitude—like Perfection—is an intrinsic characteristic of the Absolute: it is as it were its inward life or its love, which by overflowing, so to speak, prolongs itself and creates the world.

*

*　*

Certitude and serenity: the fundamental intention of Islam is contained in these two words. For everything begins with certitude: certitude with regard to the Absolute (*Wujūd al-mutlaq*), "necessary" Being, which projects and determines "possible" existences; certitude with regard to what, being necessary, cannot not be, whereas contingencies can either be or not; and serenity through finding one's roots in what is.

Certitude is salvific to the extent it is objectively lofty and subjectively sincere, that is, to the extent its object is the Absolute, not mere contingency, and to the extent its subject is the heart, not thought alone. This certitude is the very essence of man, encompassing the whole of his being and all his activity; man was made for it, and he is man because of it.

Certitude produces serenity, which penetrates the soul, being the radiation of liberating certitude. Serenity is to certitude what the Infinite is to the Absolute or what Possibility is to Reality or Totality to Unity. Certitude and serenity are prolonged in faith.

Certitude, serenity, and faith: by this necessary and free Being, which alone gives a meaning to all that is, both in the world and in man, and which is Light, Peace, and Life.

APPENDIX

Selections from Letters and
Other Previously Unpublished Writings

1

How is *Tasawwuf* to be defined? One Sufi has said that *Tasawwuf* is "poverty"; another has said it is "fasting"; still another has said it is "the five prayers and awaiting death". These are pious associations of ideas; they are not definitions.

If we were asked what *Tasawwuf* is, we would say it is (1) Discernment between the Real and the illusory, (2) permanent Remembrance of the Real, and (3) Beauty of soul, conformity to the Real.

Discernment between the Real and the illusory: between *al-Haqq*, the True, and *al-hijāb*, the veil; *lā ilāha illā 'Llāh*. This is *Hikmah*, the wisdom mentioned by the Koran: "He (*Allāh*) giveth wisdom unto whom He will, and he unto whom wisdom is given, he hath truly received abundant good" (*Sūrah* "The Cow" [2]:269).

Permanent Remembrance of the Real: *Dhikru 'Llāh*. As the Koran says: "And the Remembrance of *Allāh* is of all things the most great" (*Sūrah* "The Spider" [29]:45).

Beauty of soul, conformity to the Real: for God loves all Beauty—*Jamāl*—since it reflects His Infinitude, His Harmony, His Goodness, and His Beatitude; and He particularly loves Beauty of soul since the inward takes precedence over the outward, and the immortal over the perishable. *Hadīth*: "Verily *Allāh* is beautiful, and He loveth Beauty."

2

"Say: *Allāh*! then leave them to their vain discourse." Thus it is that the *Dhikr* cuts through the Gordian knot of the soul's obscurities and troubles, its states of heaviness and dispersion—in short, the inward problems that appear insoluble, whether their causes are objective or subjective or both at once.

This means that the *Dhikr* cuts through the inextricable and absurd knot of lower *māyā*, which is found in the microcosm as well as the macrocosm, in the soul as well as the world.

Man tends to argue with his own absurdity as well as with that of the world, and the adversary, who has an interest in our having troubles and forgetting God, takes advantage of the situation by involving us in an indefinite movement; this is what is called "going round in circles". Now what we do not understand, God understands, and we attest to this fact by saying *Allāh* and turning away from all discussion about the uncertain, conjectural, indefinite, insoluble. In any event, it is necessary to know that there is always an unintelligible point in *māyā*: on the higher plane it is mystery, and on the lower it is the absurd; in one case as in the other we say *Allāh*.

To say *Allāh* is to show Confidence and Faith. For *Allāh* is the reply to everything; the soul is a question, and the supreme Name the response; or the soul is a wound, and the Supreme Name a balm.

3

What distinguishes us above all from Muslim-born or converted individuals—"psychologically", one could say—is that our mind is *a priori* centered on universal metaphysics (*Advaita Vedānta, Shahādah, Risālat al-Ahadiyah*) and the universal path of the divine Name (*japa-yoga, nembutsu, dhikr,* prayer of the heart); it is because of these two factors that we are in a traditional form, which in fact—though not in principle—is Islam. The universal orthodoxy emanating from these two sources of authority determines our interpretation of the *sharīʿah* and Islam in general, somewhat as the moon influences the oceans without being located on the terrestrial globe; in the absence of the moon, the motions of the sea would be inconceivable and "illegitimate", so to speak. What universal metaphysics says has decisive authority for us, as does the "onomatological" science connected to it, a fact that once earned us the reproach of "de-Islamicizing Islam"; it is not so much a matter of the conscious application of principles formulated outside of Islamism by metaphysical traditions from Asia as of inspirations in conformity with these principles; in a situation such as ours, the spiritual authority—or the soul that is its vehicle—becomes like a point of intersection for all the rays of truth, whatever their origin.

One must always take account of the following: in principle the universal authority of the metaphysical and initiatic traditions of

Asia, whose point of view reflects the nature of things more or less directly, takes precedence—when such an alternative exists—over the generally more "theological" authority of the monotheistic religions; I say "when such an alternative exists", for obviously it sometimes happens, in esoterism as in essential symbolism, that there is no such alternative; no one can deny, however, that in Semitic doctrines the formulations and rules are usually determined by considerations of dogmatic, moral, and social opportuneness. But this cannot apply to pure Islam, that is, to the authority of its essential doctrine and fundamental symbolism; the *Shahādah* cannot but mean that "the world is false and *Brahma* is true" and that "you are That" (*tat tvam asi*), or that "I am *Brahma*" (*aham Brahmāsmi*); it is a pure expression of both the unreality of the world and the supreme identity; in the same way, the other "pillars of Islam" (*arqān al-Dīn*), as well as such fundamental rules as dietary and artistic prohibitions, obviously constitute supports of intellection and realization, which universal metaphysics—or the "Unanimous Tradition"—can illuminate but not abolish, as far as we are concerned. When universal wisdom states that the invocation contains and replaces all other rites, this is of decisive authority against those who would make the *sharīʿah* or *sunnah* into a kind of exclusive *karma-yoga*, and it even allows us to draw conclusions by analogy (*qiyās, ijtihād*) that most Shariites would find illicit; or again, should a given Muslim master require us to introduce every *dhikr* with an ablution and two *rakaʿāt*, the universal—and "antiformalist"—authority of *japa-yoga* would take precedence over the authority of this master, at least in our case. On the other hand, should a Hindu or Buddhist master give the order to practice *japa* before an image, it goes without saying that it is the authority of Islamic symbolism that would take precedence for us quite apart from any question of universality, because forms are forms, and some of them are essential and thereby rejoin the universality of the spirit.

4

I am glad to learn you have finally desisted from fasting, for the body needs all its strength when it is ailing, that is, one needs strength to eliminate an ailment that risks establishing itself if it can profit from a weakening and lack of resistance. In short, one has the right to be prudent, especially at our age; there are *fuqarā* who are not so, although our perspective does not require any quasi-heroic zeal on the plane of the *sharī'ah*; the emphasis being on the *Dhikr*.

5

A word presupposes silence: it cannot be heard in the midst of noise. Silence must be perfect to the extent the word is noble. This is why *dhikr* requires *faqr*: the Name *Allāh* is fully pronounced only if the soul is extinguished for it.

When there is extinction of soul there is virtue. The soul is virtuous when it is as God created it: vices are privations, or they are superimposed defects. The primordial soul—extinguished, silent—is the "lotus" (*padma*) that contains the "jewel" (*mani*); it is this lotus the Blessed Virgin personifies. She is the "peace" (*salām*) that conveys "blessing" (*salāt*). Or she is the holy "silence" (*hesychia*) that contains the divine Word (*Logos*), the Name.

But in reality this "silence" is life: "I am black, but beautiful." Let the fallen soul remain silent—*vacare Deo*—and the divine Qualities will be mirrored in it, Qualities whose traces it bears in its very substance.

Truth and beauty are paths toward holy silence: they bring about the remembrance of our paradisiacal substance. For this silence is made of truth and beauty; it is an emptiness that in reality is plenitude.

6

You ask whether I meant to say in one of my books that "intelligence cannot discern truth without reference either to esoterism, on the one hand, or the Revelation and its commentators, on the other, beginning with the Prophet Muhammad". What I meant to say is the following: in principle pure intelligence—the Intellect—can know all that is knowable; in principle it can know this on its own without the intervention of an outward teaching. But in fact it is much more likely that even the most gifted mind cannot draw all of metaphysics from itself; if Shankara had grown up in total ignorance, never having heard of the *Veda, Ātmā, Māyā*, can it be affirmed with certainty

136

that he could have drawn these notions out of himself? Revelation, whether Vedic or otherwise, not only communicates key ideas to us, but also—and above all—awakens or actualizes the latent knowledge we bear within ourselves. You say: "But the Muslim philosophers, like their predecessors in Greece, talked about many things not mentioned by the Prophet and the early notables of Islam." Of course, for the Prophet—or the Koran—gave no more than the impulsion; the Greek philosophers themselves also needed certain traditional stimuli. Every man has parents, and parents always have ideas; I am thinking now of Antiquity. Once the impulsion is given—Koranic and Hellenist for the Arabs—metaphysical and mystical authors can have completely original ideas, whether from inspiration or simply reflection.

7

Tawhīd, Dhikr, Faqr. "Testimony to Unity", "Remembrance of God", "Poverty"; that is, Truth, Way, and Virtue.

What is the relationship between Virtue and "Poverty"? To be "poor" is to be as God created us, without adding any artifice, any attitude of pride; it is to remain conformable to the *Fitrah*, the primordial Nature.

The Koran says: "O men, ye are the poor in relation to God, and God is the Rich, the universally Praised." This means that everything the creature possesses *a priori*—his qualities and faculties—he has from the Creator, who is the source of every good and to whom belong all merits. This is why it may be said that virtue is "to be what we are", what we are through the creative Will.

Tawhīd, Dhikr, Faqr. On the one hand there is something we must know, which is the True; something we must will, which is the Good; and something we must love, which is the Beautiful. On the other hand there is something we must at once know, will, and love, which is the True, the Good, and the Beautiful: Truth, Way, and Virtue. One knows the Truth, but at the same time one wills and loves it, for it is likewise a Good and a Beauty.

To know is to be aware of the nature of a given reality; to will is to be incited to action by a given reality; to love is to experience happiness through a given reality. In a certain sense to love and to be coincide: what we love calls us to union; what we must love is also what we must be. To love God is to "be" God within the limits of our possibilities, and this means precisely that we must tend toward God "with all our being".

"Love God with all thy strength, and love thy neighbor as thyself", which means that we must *a priori* love ourselves; now to love myself is to love what God wished to realize in creating me, hence to love my primordial Nature, the *Fitrah*, and as a consequence *Faqr*, Virtue aiming toward the Creator; it is in sum to love the "Kingdom of God that is within you". And what I am, the "neighbor" is also; to love myself is to love him. And since we want God to have pity on us—"the spirit is willing, but the flesh is weak"—we must have pity on others; this is another reason for loving our neighbor.

From another point of view, Heaven asks us to "hate our soul"; in this case it is not our primordial Nature that is in question—obviously—but that counterfeit which is the concupiscent soul; this soul we must "hate" in the neighbor just as we do in ourselves, for otherwise there would be neither intelligence nor justice. To hate our soul is to realize, precisely, that it is not ourselves; for what Love asks us to become is what we are in the depths of our Heart.

8

Concerning the question of the "formal" and "informal" or the "letter" (which may kill) and the "spirit" (which vivifies), I would like to note that there is always, or nearly always, an intermediate region between exoterism and esoterism, a *barzakh*, which appears both as an esoterized exoterism and an exoterized esoterism; Christianity is nothing else, whence its paradoxical character, and with regard to Islam we find this *barzakh* in the ritualism of a Ghazzali and in popular Sufism, but also throughout the collective forms of *Tasawwuf*. Between exoterism and esoterism there always exists a ritualistic and moral *karma-yoga*; now this *yoga*, by the very fact of its individualistic nature—for action and merit necessarily belong to the individual—is opposed to the metaphysical perspective as well as to the way of the saving Name. The rationalizing individualism of Muslim piety is as non-metaphysical as the sentimental individualism of Christians. There is a marked tendency toward a transcendence of forms in any esoterism inasmuch as this viewpoint is directly affirmed—on the doctrinal plane, where every formulation becomes an *upāya*, an "unavoidable artifice", as well as on the methodical plane, where concentration and its direct supports absorb most of the exterior rites; to deny this tendency is to go against the nature of things.

The whole emphasis must be placed on metaphysical truth and the divine Name; this is a "religion" that runs through all traditional forms just as the thread runs through the cloth. Starting from a source of doctrinal, hence intellectual, evidence, one must realize faith and find—in and by the Name—inner certitude, which is our very being.

9

It is necessary to pass from the abstract notion to concrete awareness; this is the passage from hypocrisy to sincerity. Most men who admit that God takes precedence over everything and that the hereafter is better than the here-below behave as if they did not admit it; this is the most usual hypocrisy.

The *Shahādah* expresses an alternative not only between the Real and the illusory—this is its metaphysical meaning—but also between the here-below and the hereafter and between the Remembrance and heedlessness. The *Nafy* expresses the illusory, or the here-below—the world of impermanence—or heedlessness; the *Ithbāt* expresses the Real, or the hereafter—the world of permanence—or the Remembrance.

In the *Nafy* the word *lā* symbolizes the separative, illusory, and impermanent side of the world; the word *ilāha* refers then to the participative, symbolic, unitive side, that is, to things that allow celestial archetypes to appear through them; this symbolism encompasses everything that by its nature brings us nearer to God, whether these values are objective or subjective, natural or spiritual. In the *Ithbāt* the word *illā* symbolizes the created element within the celestial hereafter; the Name *Allāh* very clearly expresses the Uncreated.

The Invocation, and all that favors it, is the "earthly Heaven"; Paradise is the "heavenly Earth".

Terrestrial beauty attaches the *ghāfil* to the world and removes the *dhākir* from the world; it draws the *dhākir* closer to Heaven, for he knows that it manifests the divine *Rahmah*; and since he sees how

Rahmah is already beautiful in its earthly manifestation, he chooses *Rahmah*, not the world.

Among believers the *dhākirūn* are those who accept the *Shahādah* with sincerity to some degree or other, contrary to the *ghāfilūn*. To realize spiritual sincerity it is necessary for the soul to pass from abstract thought to concrete awareness: it does not suffice to believe in Paradise; it is necessary to live within it in a certain fashion, and one does so in and by the *Dhikr*, which is like a prolongation and anticipation of Paradise or which—more profoundly and truly—is even identified with the celestial Abode in the sense that it is of the same substance of *Rahmah*.

For where the Name of God is, there is *Rahmah*, and there is Paradise.

10

I must always repeat to the *fuqarā* that if some expression of destiny upsets them they should submit to it in their personal prayers and even thank God for the trial, only then asking Him to free them from it. Likewise, when a person bothers us and we even come to criticize him, which is inevitable in some cases, we must reestablish equilibrium by praying for him, provided the person is not a *kāfir*.

11

The Name *Allāh* contains two syllables, one short and one long, which betoken two hypostatic mysteries, namely, the Absolute and the Infinite, or the combination—one could say—between the Absolute and its dimension of Infinitude. The absolute is what admits no augmentation or diminution, hence what excludes all relativity; and the infinite is what contains no limitation, either extrinsic or intrinsic. With regard to spatial symbolism the Absolute and the Infinite suggest, respectively, the geometric point and extension, the first indicating pure Essence, and the second All-Possibility. The potentiality of the Absolute Principle is infinite; it is because necessary Being includes possible being that the world exists.

In addition to spatial symbolism there is also temporal symbolism: the relationship point-extension corresponds to the relationship instant-duration; such a parallelism at the very basis of existence must have a metaphysical foundation. Incontestably, space is static and time dynamic; now space relates to Substance—ether gives proof of this—and time to Energy; the divine Principle is at once Substance and Energy, and each of these aspects implies both Absoluteness and Infinitude, which is another way of saying that the Absolute is at once static and dynamic—if it can be so expressed—and the same is true of the Infinite. It is therefore not only the *hypostases* of Absoluteness and Infinitude that meet or are combined in the divine Nature, but also the *hypostases* of Substantiality and Energy or of Consciousness and Power—Consciousness because the Principle is the Self, and Power because the Principle radiates and determines all. God is Intelligence and Will and is such absolutely and infinitely, Will being the intrinsic consequence of Intelligence. To know is to will, and to know the Good is to love; "God is Love".

God is "He Who is"; "I am that I am." To be is to radiate; a reality radiates to the extent it is; pure Being is pure Radiation.

The Name *Allāh* not only contains two syllables, one short and one long, but also—within each syllable—two sounds, a vowel and a consonant, namely, the sounds *a* and *l*, the vowel indicating Substance and the consonant Energy. The *hā* at the end is a final synthesis, which is proven by its association with the word *Huwa*, "He", which signifies the Essence. The vowel *a* is static, and it expresses Substance because it is in itself an invariable "extension"; the consonant *l* is dynamic, and it expresses Energy because it is a "compression", hence a "becoming".

To this doctrine of the *Ism* is joined that of the *Shahādah*, the four words of which—*lā ilāha illā 'Llāh*—signify respectively: Manifestation as such, the reflection of the Principle in Manifestation, the prefiguration of Manifestation in the Principle, the Principle as such.

12

The psychological cleansing of a man should be accomplished *a priori* and fundamentally by religion: it is the Truth that heals, and it is our sincerity and fervor that contribute to this healing. If we have realized the elementary equilibrium that religion, by definition, is capable of conferring upon us and if there remains within us nonetheless— within the framework of this elementary equilibrium—some defect or psychic asymmetry that needs correction, we may consider using secondary supports, of the artistic order for example, provided these supports are compatible with Islam in particular and spiritual dignity in general. But once again it should not be a question of commencing with such supports, for the beginning of a spiritual career should be based exclusively on spiritual and traditional elements; one must begin with the fear of God! On the level of esoterism I would say that one does not initiate an abnormal man and that a normal man has no need for psychological treatment; on the level of exoterism I would say that religion by its very nature possesses sufficient resources to stabilize the soul.

13

By "Islamic esoterism" we mean that esoterism comes first and Islam afterward: in other words the esoterism is the sole essence, sufficient unto itself, and Islam is the form or framework, although there are other forms and frameworks.

By "esoteric Islam" we mean on the contrary that Islam comes first and esoterism afterward: in other words Islam is the divine Revelation and thus the basis, and esoterism is its essence perceived *a posteriori*; the essence is given by Islam, which thus presents itself as the *conditio sine qua non* of *gnosis*. According to this way of looking at things, Islam is the starting point of esoterism, whereas according to the preceding perspective metaphysics is the starting point, choosing for itself this or that exoteric framework if it does not find itself within one already, for in the latter case what is involved is more a question of taking advantage of a preexisting framework than an actual choice. But in no case can the path of *gnosis* have as its starting point an anthropomorphist, voluntaristic, individualistic, and sentimental theology, or a legalism of the same kind.

In Islamic terms: is the beginning of the Path (*Tarīqah*) the exoteric Law (*Sharī'ah*) or the esoteric Truth (*Haqīqah*)? The whole question is to know the level of the esoterism; if it is pure, its starting point must be an element already stemming from Knowledge.

142

14

The supreme Name, like the *Shahādah,* is an answer. It answers the world, and it answers the ego; every time the world holds up before us one or another of its masks, let us answer: *Allāh;* and every time the ego puffs itself up, let us answer: *Allāh.*

The world is a vast current of forms; the ego is its living kernel, which vivifies illusion with its blood. The Name, like an icebreaker, traverses the current of forms, this hardened web of world and ego, which at the same time consists only of mist. The world is the nothingness that hides itself behind a thousand masks; each of these masks wants to draw the ego away from God. The ego is a drop of the Self that has become ice, mask, and nothingness, and yet at the same time remains itself; this is its inner contradiction.

God has given us His Name so that we might become once again what we are; the Name melts our ice, removes the mask, and vanquishes the nothingness. When the ego swells up, it forgets its Self and wants to become a mask; it denies its profound otherness and professes its belief in the delusive current of forms. And the nothingness is as it were a mask of God; to vanquish the nothingness means to see God behind all things.

Life, with its two dimensions of past and future, is our participation in the current of forms, our inwovenness in the world; whoever answers the world with *Allāh* and the ego with *Allāh* answers life also with *Allāh.* World, life, ego: in the center is the supreme Name, which nothing can withstand.

15

I am sending you here an article in which I have attempted to offer a synthesis of what is essential and sufficient in Sufism. Indeed it sometimes happens that the *fuqarā* draw their inspiration from all kinds of Sufi readings that are very uneven, believing they are going to find doctrinal and methodical directives that are authoritative; in reality what is authoritative for us is only what is essential and what therefore coincides with the *sophia perennis,* as I demonstrate in my article included here, precisely. The *fuqarā* readily believe that Ibn Arabi above all is for us an absolute authority or the authority as such, but this is not the case, for whatever his merits or prestige, this author is most uneven, sometimes professing opinions that are questionable, to say the least; and this is to say nothing of the fact that the Sufis contradict one another and that there are in Sufism, as in all traditional spirituality, certain variations in perspective—*ikhtilāf al-'ulamā' rahmah*—or uneven abilities in discernment and perspicacity; not everyone is a *jnānin* in the full sense of this word. I therefore wrote this article in order to provide points of reference for what I shall term our *tarīqah's* perspective, which is "special" precisely in virtue of its character as a synthesis; each thing comes in its own time. *Allāhu karīm.*

Before writing this article, I wrote another on weaknesses found in "average Sufism", which is too involved with Asharite theology; I have just written a third article as well, on the notion of "philosophy". All of this is connected, but the article included here is by far the most important for the *fuqarā'*. If I mention the other two articles, it is because I intend to send you some copies when they are ready so that you can have a complete picture; for all this concerns our perspective, hence our doctrine.

16

Concerning Ibn Arabi, I recall that someone once questioned whether Sufism admits traditional universality; Ibn Arabi supposedly would have denied this because he said that Islam is the pivot of the other traditions. Now every traditional form is superior to others in a certain respect, and this is in fact the sufficient reason for such a form; and it is always this respect that a person speaking in the name of his tradition has in mind; what matters in the recognition of other traditional forms is the fact—exoterically astonishing—of this recognition, not its mode or degree. In fact the Koran offers the prototype of this way of seeing: on the one hand it says that all the Prophets are equal, and on the other hand it says that some are superior to others, which means—according to the commentary by Ibn Arabi—that each Prophet is superior to the others owing to a particularity belonging to him alone, that is, in a certain respect.

Ibn Arabi belonged to a Muslim civilization and owed his spiritual realization to the Islamic *barakah* and the masters of Sufism, hence to the Islamic form; he was therefore obliged to take a position consistent with this aspect of things, the aspect according to which this form contains a superiority with respect to other forms; if this relative superiority did not exist, Hindus who became Muslims throughout the centuries would never have had any positive reason for doing so; the fact that Islam constitutes the last form of the *Sanātana Dharma* in this *mahāyuga* implies that it possesses a certain contingent superiority over the preceding forms; in the same way the fact that Hinduism is the most ancient traditional form still living implies that it possesses a certain superiority or "centrality" compared to later forms; there is quite obviously no contradiction here since the relationships to be considered are in each case different.

17

All our happiness must come from the holy mystery of His Name.

The worldly or imperfect man goes through life as if on a long road; if he is a believer, he sees God above him in the far distance and also at the end of this road. The spiritual man, however, stands in God, and life passes before him like a stream.

One must think of God when in plenitude that He may think of us when in emptiness.

Happiness is where holiness is. Holiness is like an opening toward Heaven; it is being recollected within the Unique. Every man is holy when he thinks of God if he is thinking of nothing else.

The brethren must be told that all should be done with concentration: ablution, ritual prayer, rosary, invocation, individual prayer, Koranic reading. In the regular practices in particular—ablution, ritual prayer, rosary—one must know what one is doing and what one is saying. For the invocation, the need for concentration goes without saying.

In the ablution, the hands refer to profane actions; the mouth to the impurities contracted knowingly; the nose to the impurities contracted unwillingly and unconsciously; the face to the shame of sin; the forearms to impure intention; the ears to deafness with regard to the divine Word; the head to pride; the feet to waywardness. Or in positive terms: the purified hands to spiritual actions; the mouth to active purity; the nose to passive and unconscious purity; the face to the state of grace; the forearms to purity of intention; the ears to receptivity to the divine Word or to spiritual or angelic inspirations; the head to humility before God, hence to awareness of our nothingness; the feet to our qualification for the path of contemplation.

This is a teaching I found in a text of the *Shaykh al-Akbar*, which I read years ago.

18

In one of L.'s letters, I was surprised to find the following assertion: "As a Muslim, I had incurred no responsibility toward anyone, and I was thus, and still am, entirely free to do whatever seems in my best interest." The author of this sentence does not seem to know that there is no traditional form that allows its members to leave it; for example, it is impossible for a Hindu to become a Muslim without being expelled from his caste, which signifies civic death; and is it necessary to recall that no religion allows passage into another religion? Islamic Law reserves capital punishment for apostasy (*irtidād*); therefore, I do not see how one can think oneself independent with respect to Islam by virtue of one's quality "as a Muslim". As for esoterism—Islamic or otherwise—there can be exceptional cases where a change of traditional form cannot be excluded, which amounts to saying that esoterism alone can see in such a change something other than "apostasy"; nonetheless it is clear that in esoterism one depends upon one's Master and that nothing can be done without him. L. became a Muslim to be a *faqīr*, he did not become a *faqīr* to be a Muslim; it is therefore all the more illogical to lay a claim as a *faqīr* to one's "freedom" as a "Muslim". It should be added that for a change of traditional form to be legitimate the first condition is that the motive must be one of "technical" opportuneness, the change not being a conversion pure and simple, as is the case for L. and M.; in other words this change must really be considered a passage from one form to another and not a passage from error to truth.

19

According to the Shaykh al-Alawi, the profound meaning of religious practices and the reason they exist is the remembrance of *Allāh*, which means that all the *sharī'ah*, all the dogmas, all the practices reside in the *dhikr*. One may be prevented by circumstances from fulfilling a particular prescription of the Law; one can never be prevented from remembering God.

The *sharī'ah* was revealed in time whereas the *haqīqah* has no beginning; it was before the creation of the world. The *sharī'ah* is bound to the *haqīqah*, but the *haqīqah* is not bound to the *sharī'ah*. *Spiritus autem ubi vult spirat.*

20

When the *faqīr* closes his eyes and pronounces the Name—in any circumstances, but before God and not before men—he manifests or realizes something very great; for these two actions or attitudes represent the whole Way.

To close the eyes is in fact to exclude the world, and to pronounce the Name is to affirm God. Excluding *Māyā* and affirming *Ātmā*.

Closing the eyes is the *Nafy* of the *Shahādah* (*lā ilāha*); pronouncing the Name is the *Ithbāt* (*illā 'Llāh*). Extinction of the accidents on the one hand; appearance of the Substance on the other. This is *Faqr* and *Dhikr*, and this is why these two elements contain the whole Way.

Nafy (or *Faqr*): "I am black . . ."; *Ithbāt* (or *Dhikr*): ". . . but beautiful". And likewise: "I sleep, but my heart waketh."

Referring to the quaternary *Haqq, Qalb, Faqr, Dhikr*, we shall say: *Faqr* combines *Haqq* and *Qalb*, for passive Perfection (*Faqr*) is realized as a result of Truth (*Haqq*) and through the Heart (*Qalb*); similarly, *Dhikr* combines *Haqq* and *Qalb* for the same reason, but applied to active Perfection (*Dhikr*).

And referring to the ternary *Makhāfah, Mahabbah, Ma'rifah*, we shall say: the operative coincidence *Faqr/Dhikr* may take place through Fear or Effort, through Love or Grace, or through Knowledge or Evidence, or again through all three at the same time and apart from any dimensional or modal intention.

In certain sacred images—notably those of the Buddha—the human Word or deified Man has the eyes closed and the breast naked: this is the non-manifestation of what is outward and the manifestation of what is inward; non-manifestation (or extinction) of the world and manifestation (or exteriorization) of the Heart or Self. To the interiorization of what is outward responds the exteriorization of what is inward; the first act corresponds to *Faqr*, and the second to *Dhikr*.

21

In the cases of T. and N. I did not pray just for a cure, because I foresaw all too clearly that the Will of God—for the good of these *fuqarā*—might be otherwise.

There cannot be a definitive, hence unvarying, equilibrium between God and man; God alone is immutable. Now He sometimes disrupts an equilibrium to replace it with a new equilibrium, which makes the *faqīr* undergo a kind of death: the *faqīr* still knows that *lā ilāha illā 'Llāh*, but he no longer knows who he himself is. He must therefore find a new identity on the basis of the single certitude that is left him, which is precisely that *lā ilāha illā 'Llāh*; in such nights nothing remains but the Truth and Faith and, conformably with these, Patience and Trust; they enable us to vanquish all the vertigos. One must realize a perfect equilibrium between the vertical and the horizontal; with most men, however, the horizontal takes precedence over the vertical, spiritual life becoming too human, too individual, too terrestrial; one must therefore start again more or less at zero and be born anew. All *Rahmah* lies in the supreme Name, and in *Rahmah*, which is inexhaustible, we cannot lose anything. Whoever dies for *Rahmah* is reborn in *Rahmah*.

22

The Name *Allāh* is the absolute Argument in the face of that cascade of absurdities which is the world. Therein lies an invincible axiom leaving no room for discussion; to ask "why" is already to disbelieve. The Name *Allāh* is our refuge from the din of earthly existence; the world, however it may rage, cannot possibly offer an argument stronger than this Name. We have no right to dash ourselves against the wall of the absurd, and we cannot put the blame on All-Possibility. The divine Name answers intellectually and existentially all problems, whether we are aware of this or not. To pronounce the divine Name is at once to die and be reborn.

"Blessed are they that have not seen, and yet have believed."

EDITOR'S NOTES

Numbers in bold indicate pages in the text for which the following citations and explanations are provided.

Preface

xiv: "There is no right superior to that of truth" is a saying of the Maharajas of Benares, frequently cited by the author.

Meister *Eckhart* (c. 1260-1327), a German Dominican theologian and mystic, was regarded by the author as the greatest of Christian metaphysicians and esoterists.

Ellipsis and Hyperbolism in Arab Rhetoric

2: *unconsidered oaths*: "God will not take you to task for that which is unintentional in your oaths" (*Sūrah* "The Cow" [2]:225; cf. 5:89).

"Give not that which is *holy unto* the *dogs*, neither *cast* ye your *pearls before swine*, lest they trample them under their feet, and turn again and rend you" (Matt. 7:6).

Note 1: In Greek mythology, the hero *Perseus*, son of Zeus and a mortal woman, is said to have killed the Gorgon *Medusa*, a cruel monster with so frightful a countenance that none could behold her without being turned to stone; returning from this victory, Perseus rescued the beautiful maiden *Andromeda*, who had been offered as a sacrifice to appease a giant sea monster, thus meriting her hand in marriage.

"*I am black, but beautiful*" (Song of Sol. 1:5).

3: "God createth what He will. If He decreeth a thing, He saith unto it only: *Be!* [*kun*] and it is" (*Sūrah* "The Family of Imran" [3]:47).

"*In the beginning was the Word*" (John 1:1).

4: Note 2: "*No soul shall bear the burden of another*" (*Sūrah* "The Children of Israel" [17]:15; cf. 6:165, 23:62, 35:18, 39:7, 53:38, 65:7).

5: Abu al-Qasim al-*Junayd* (d. 910), known for his insistence that Sufism should be firmly based on exoteric Muslim law and practice, taught that the ultimate return of all things into God is anticipated in the experience of *fanā*.

Shams al-Din al-*Samarqandi* (1250-1310), best known for his mathematics and astronomy, also wrote works of theology and philosophy.

6: "*Sin against the Holy Spirit*": "All manner of sin and blasphemy shall be forgiven unto men: but the blasphemy against the Holy Ghost shall not be forgiven unto men" (Matt. 12:31; cf. Mark 3:29, Luke 12:10).

9: Abu Hamid Muhammad *al-Ghazzali* (d. 1111) was an Islamic jurist and theologian, who later entered upon the Sufi path in search of a direct confirmation of God, which he described in his *Mishkāt al-Anwār*, "Niche of Lights", among other works.

Note 7: "They shall have fruits therein, and they *shall have what they desire*" (*Sūrah* "*Yā Sīn*" [36]:57).

11: *Thomas* Aquinas (c. 1225-74), a giant among the medieval scholastics and author of the monumental *Summa Theologica*, is considered by the Roman Catholic Church to be the greatest Christian theologian in history.

In the author's original French, the term rendered "self-evidence" in the phrase *metaphysical self-evidence of the Absolute* is *évidence*, which includes the idea of obviousness as well as that of corroboration or proof.

12: "*He punisheth whom He will, and He pardoneth whom He will*" (*Sūrah* "The Spider" [29]:21; cf. 48:14).

14: *The Prophet* "*seeks refuge in God from hunger and betrayal*": (*hadīth*).

The Exo-Esoteric Symbiosis

19: "*If thou wouldst reach the kernel, thou must break the shell*" is a traditional maxim that the author attributes to Meister Eckhart (see editor's note for Preface, p. 4).

The *Upanishads*, also referred to as the *Vedānta* since they were traditionally placed at the "end" of the *Vedas* (see below editor's note for this chapter, p. 21) and are seen by such authorities as Shankara as a synthesis of Vedic teaching, are Hindu scriptures containing metaphysical, mystical, and esoteric doctrine.

The *Brahmasūtra*, one of the chief sources of Vedantic wisdom, traditionally attributed to the sage *Badarayana* (first century B.C.), distills and systematizes the teachings of the *Upanishads* concerning *Brahma*, the Supreme Reality.

Ibn Ata Allah Iskandari (c. 1250-1309), an early master of the Shadhiliyyah *tarīqah* and an authority in both Islamic law and the Sufi path, was the author of a number of treatises, most notably the *Hikam* ("Book of Wisdom").

Note 3: *Shankarian* refers to the doctrine of Shankara (788-820), the pre-eminent proponent of *Advaita Vedānta*, whom the author considered the greatest of all Hindu metaphysicians.

Ramanujian refers to the doctrine of Ramanuja (1017-c. 1137), widely regarded as the classic exponent of *Vishishta Advaita*, the Hindu school of "qualified non-dualism", in which emphasis is placed on the personal nature of God.

Note 4: Umar al-Khayyam—*Omar Khayyam* (1048-1125)—was a Persian astronomer, mathematician, and poet, whose *Rubaiyat* ("quatrains") conceal a mystical apprehension of God under a veil of seeming skepticism and hedonism.

20: "Then spake Jesus to the multitude, and to his disciples, saying, The scribes and the Pharisees *sit in Moses' seat*. All therefore whatsoever they bid you observe, that observe and do" (Matt. 23:1-3).

He described many of their commandments as "*human*": "Then came together unto him the Pharisees, and certain of the scribes. . . . Then the Pharisees and scribes asked him, Why walk not thy disciples according to the tradition of the elders? . . . He answered and said unto them, Well hath Esaias prophesied of you hypocrites. . . . For laying aside the commandment of God, ye hold the tradition of men" (Mark 7:1, 5-6, 8; cf. Matt. 15:9).

21: In Hinduism, the *Veda* is a body of sacred knowledge revealed to ancient Indian seers and transmitted in the *Vedas*, sacred texts composed of hymns, ritual formulas, and metaphysical doctrines regarded as authoritative for both doctrine and practice.

Note 7: For *al-Ghazzali*, see editor's note for "Ellipsis and Hyperbolism in Arab Rhetoric", p. 9.

Shiite Muslims look to Ali and his descendents as the legitimate and authoritative representatives of the Prophet Muhammad, whereas *Sunni* Muslims accept the validity of the entire historical line of caliphs.

23: Note 8: *Abu Hurairah* (d. 678), a Companion of the Prophet Muhammad, was noted for his powerful memory and intelligence and for this reason was given permission by the Prophet to record and transmit *ahādīth.*

A completely analogous passage: "[Jesus] took [Thomas] and withdrew and told him three things. When Thomas returned to his companions, they asked him, What did Jesus say to you? Thomas said to them, If I were to tell you one of the things that he told me, you would pick up stones and throw them at me, and a fire would come out of the stones and burn you up" (Gospel of Thomas, 13).

Note 9: *Al-Khidr* is described in the Koran as "one of Our slaves, unto whom We had given mercy from Us, and had taught him knowledge from Our presence"; when *Moses* asks him, "May I follow thee, to the end that thou mayst teach me right conduct of that which thou has been taught?", he responds, "Lo! thou canst not bear with me. How canst thou bear with that whereof thou canst not compass any knowledge?" (*Sūrah* "The Cave" [18]:66-69).

"For this *Melchizedek*, king of Salem, priest of the most high God . . . to whom also Abraham gave a tenth part of all; first being by interpretation King of righteousness, and after that also King of Salem, which is, King of peace; without father, without mother, without descent, having neither beginning of days, nor end of life; but made like unto the Son of God; abideth a priest continually" (Heb. 7:1-3).

The "Krishnaite" aspect of the Prophet: Hindu tradition tells of the youthful dalliance of the *avatāra* Krishna with the adoring *gopīs* or cowherd girls of Vrindavan.

24: Note 10: Muhyi al-Din *Ibn Arabi* (1165-1240), author of numerous works including the *Futūhāt al-Makkiyah* or *Meccan Revelations*, was a prolific and profoundly influential Sufi mystic, known in tradition as the *Shaykh al-Akbar*, that is, the "greatest master".

"And when We said unto the angels: Prostrate yourselves before Adam, they fell prostrate, all save *Iblis*. He demurred through pride, and so became a disbeliever" (*Sūrah* "The Cow" [2]:34 *passim*).

25: Note 13: "*Sight cannot reach Him (Allāh), but He comprehendeth (all) vision. He is the Subtle, the Aware*" (*Sūrah* "Cattle" [6]:104).

26: "*There is no right superior to that of truth*" is a saying of the Maharajas of Benares, frequently cited by the author.

"*One thing is needful*" (Luke 10:42).

28: Attributed to the sage Valmiki, the *Yoga-Vasishtha* is an Advaitic dialogue between a human spiritual master, Vasishtha, and his divine disciple, Rama, concerning the relationship between consciousness and Reality and including the story of the realized Queen Chudala, *guru* to her husband, King Shikhidhwaja.

The *Bhagavad Gītā*, the best known and arguably the most important of all Hindu sacred texts and part of the much longer epic *Mahābhārata*, consists of a dialogue between the prince Arjuna and his charioteer, the *avatāra* Krishna, concerning the different paths to God.

30: In the author's original French, the term rendered "self-evidence" in the phrase *self-evidence of the divine Principle* is *évidence*, which includes the idea of obviousness as well as that of corroboration or proof.

31: *Asharism* is the doctrine of the Muslim theologian Abu al-Hasan al-Ashari (873-935), who taught that anthropomorphic descriptions of God in the Koran should not be interpreted as metaphors, but are to be accepted at face value "without asking any questions", and that God creates all human acts, thereby determining them, men nonetheless acquiring these acts and being thus responsible for them.

Plato (c. 427-c. 347 B.C.) was the greatest of the ancient Greek philosophers.

The works of *Plotinus* (c. 205-270), founder of the Neoplatonic school of philosophy, exerted a powerful influence on the mystical traditions of

Judaism, Christianity, and Islam (see also editor's note for "Tracing the Notion of Philosophy", p. 92).

The formula "in the Name of God, the Clement, the Merciful" is found at the beginning of all but one of the Koranic *sūrahs*.

For *Ashari*, see editor's note above.

32: *"God doeth what He will"* (*Sūrah* "The Family of Imran" [3]:40 *passim*).

34: Note 22: Jalal al-Din *Rumi* (1207-73), a Sufi mystic and poet and founder of the Mevlevi order, is well known for his insistence on spiritual love as the proper basis for the seeker's relation to God.

38: Note 26: *Chaitanya* (1486-1533), a Vaishnavite Hindu spiritual teacher and ecstatic devotee of Krishna, was regarded by his followers as an *avatāra* of both Krishna and his consort Radha.

Note 27: "And *David* danced before the Lord with all his might. . . . So David and all the house of Israel brought up the ark of the Lord with shouting, and with the sound of the trumpet" (2 Sam. 6:14-15).

"For the horse of Pharaoh went in with his chariots and with his horsemen into the sea, and the Lord brought again the waters of the sea upon them; but the children of Israel went on dry land in the midst of the sea. And *Miriam* the prophetess, the sister of Aaron, took a timbrel in her hand; and all the women went out after her with timbrels and with dances" (Exod. 15:19-20).

40: The *Fusūs al-Hikam*, or "Bezels of Wisdom", one of Ibn Arabi's most renowned works, consists of a series of mystical reflections on the wisdom embodied in the lives and characters of twenty-seven prophets.

Note 29: The *Tarjumān al-Ashwāq*, or "The Interpreter of Desires", is a collection of mystical love poems.

The de facto *existence of two esoterisms*: See the author's chapter "Two Esoterisms" in *Survey of Metaphysics and Esoterism* (Bloomington, Indiana: World Wisdom Books, 1986).

41: For *Junayd*, see editor's note for "Ellipsis and Hyperbolism in Arab Rhetoric", p. 5.

Paradoxes of an Esoterism

43: Note 1: According to *Augustine* (354-430), the most prolific and influential of the Western Church Fathers, "All things that are, are good, and as to that evil the origin of which I was seeking, it is not a substance, since, if it were, it would be good" (*Confessions*, 7:12).

44: *Joseph made himself known to his brothers*: "They said: Is it indeed thou who art Joseph? He said: I am Joseph" (*Sūrah* "Joseph" [12]:90).

Prophetic dream: "Joseph said unto his father: O my father! Lo! I saw in a dream eleven stars and the sun and the moon, I saw them prostrating themselves unto me" (*Sūrah* "Joseph" [12]:4).

"This is the interpretation of my dream of old that my Lord hath made real" (*Sūrah* "Joseph" [12]:100).

For the *Fusūs* of Ibn Arabi (see editor's note for "The Exo-Esoteric Symbiosis", p. 24, Note 10), see editor's note for "The Exo-Esoteric Symbiosis", p. 40; *Kalimah Yūsifiyah*, or "The Word of Joseph", is Ch. 9 of this treatise.

It is God Himself who taught Joseph: "We established Joseph in the land that We might teach him the interpretation of dreams" (*Sūrah* "Joseph" [12]:21).

Note 2: *The other dream*: "And Joseph dreamed a dream, and he told it to his brethren: and they hated him yet the more. And he said unto them, Hear, I pray you, this dream which I have dreamed. For, behold, we were binding *sheaves* in the field, and, lo, my sheaf arose, and also stood upright; and, behold, your sheaves stood round about, and made obeisance to my sheaf" (Gen. 37:5-7).

45: *Sadr al-Din Qunyawi* (d. 1274), Ibn Arabi's stepson and most prominent disciple and a close friend of Rumi's (see editor's note for "The Exo-Esoteric Symbiosis", p. 34, Note 22), was a Persian Sufi who wrote a highly esteemed commentary on his master's *Fusūs* as well as several works of his own.

Farid al-Din *Attar* (c. 1142-c. 1229), one of the most renowned of the Sufi poets and author of the *Elāhi Nāmeh* ("Divine Book"), is best known for his *Mantiq al-Tayr*, or "Language of the Birds", an allegory of the spiritual journey based on *Sūrah* "Sad" [38]:20: "And the birds assembled; all were turning unto Him."

Note 3: *He explained their dreams to his two companions in prison and then to the king: Sūrah* "Joseph" [12]:36-49.

46: *"Be cold"*: "We said: O fire, be coolness and peace for Abraham" (*Sūrah* "The Prophets" [21]:69).

Joseph sent his tunic to his father. "Take this my tunic; apply it to my father's face; he will recover his sight" (*Sūrah* "Joseph" [12]:93).

Throwing Joseph naked into the well: "So they did lead him [Joseph] off, and were of one mind to throw him to the bottom of the well" (*Sūrah* "Joseph" [12]:15).

"Take this my tunic; apply it to my father's face; he will recover his sight" (see editor's note above).

Note 7: Shihab al-Din Omar al-*Suhrawardi* (1145-1234), founder of the Suhrawardiyya *tarīqah* and well known for his theological learning, was author of the widely influential *'Awārif al-Ma'ārif*, or "The Gifts of Divine Knowledge".

47: Note 8: For *al-Ghazzali*, see editor's note for "Ellipsis and Hyperbolism in Arab Rhetoric", p. 9.

Aisha, the daughter of Abu Bakr and youngest of the wives of Muhammad, is quoted as the source for many *ahādīth*, especially those concerning the Prophet's personal life.

48: "Two (worldly) things have been made *lovable* to me, *women and perfumes*. But the light of my eye is in prayer" (*hadīth*).

A Church Father could refer, among others, to Irenaeus (c. 130-c. 200), who taught that "the Son of God became the Son of man that man, by entering into communion with the Word and thus receiving divine sonship, might become a son of God" (*Against Heresies*, 3:19); or to Athanasius (c. 296-373), who wrote, "The Son of God became man that we might become God" (*On the Incarnation*, 54:3); the essential teaching is common to many Patristic authorities.

Note 11: *"Opening of the breast"*: "Have We not opened for thee thy breast?" (*Sūrah* "Solace" [94]:1).

49: "*Average man*": The author has in mind the average man of a traditional civilization, not man diminished by the artificiality of the modern world; see the chapter entitled "Human Premises of a Religious Dilemma", p. 88, author's note 26.

For *Ashari*, see editor's note for "The Exo-Esoteric Symbiosis", p. 31.

"God *doeth what He will*" (*Sūrah* "The Family of Imran" [3]:40 *passim*).

Note 13: "With men this is impossible; but *with God all things are possible*" (Matt. 19:26).

50: "*In the image of God*": "God created man in His own image, in the image of God created He him; male and female created He them" (Gen. 1:27).

51: "*And the light shineth in darkness; and the darkness comprehended it not*" (John 1:5).

The *'Ihyā* of al-Ghazzali is his *'Ihyā 'ulūm al-dīn*, or "Revival of the Religious Sciences".

Abu Bakr (d. 634) was among the Prophet Muhammad's foremost Companions and served after the Prophet's death as the first caliph of Islam.

Omar Ibn al-Khattab (d. 644) was also a Companion of the Prophet and served as the second caliph of Islam.

Hasan al-Basri (642-728), one of the earliest and most influential Sufis, was noted for his insistence that the believer should always keep death and the final judgment foremost in his mind.

Note 16: Blaise *Pascal* (1623-62), a French mathematician, physicist, and Christian philosopher, was greatly influenced by the Jansenist belief that original sin is the defining feature of fallen man.

52: Note 17: Al-*Hasan* Ibn Ali (c. 624-669), the son of Ali and Fatima, daughter of the Prophet Muhammad, is said to have had nearly one hundred wives.

Ali Ibn Abi Talib (597-661) was the son-in-law of the Prophet Muhammad and the fourth caliph of Islam.

53: Note 19: For *Rumi*, see editor's note for "The Exo-Esoteric Symbiosis", p. 34, Note 22.

54: Note 20: *John of the Cross* (1542-91), whose mystical works include the *Ascent of Mount Carmel* and the *Dark Night of the Soul*, was a Spanish priest and co-founder, with Teresa of Avila, of the Discalced Carmelites.

Teresa of Avila (1515-82), whose most important work on the spiritual life is the *Interior Castle*, was a Carmelite nun and foundress, with John of the Cross, of the Discalced Carmelites.

56: Note 24: *Parvati* is the consort of the Hindu god Shiva; *Lakshmi*, regarded in most traditions as the consort of Vishnu, is the Hindu goddess of good fortune and the embodiment of beauty; in Kashmiri Shaivism *Tripurasundari* is the *shakti* or divine feminine energy shared by Parvati, Lakshmi, and Saras-vati; *Sharada* is a Hindu goddess of learning; *Sarasvati* is the consort of the Hindu god Brahmā.

57: *Rabiah Adawiyyah* (c. 713-801), one of the most renowned of Sufi saints, lived an extremely ascetical life, saying that there was no place in her heart for the desire of anything but God.

The *Rūh al-Quds*, or *"Sufis of Andalusia"*, is among the many works of Ibn Arabi (see editor's note for "The Exo-Esoteric Symbiosis", p. 24, Note 10).

59: Note 28: *Ibn al-Jawzi* (1126-1200) was a jurist, theologian, historian, and noted preacher and the author, among numerous works, of the *Kitāb al-Qussās*, "The Storytellers and Admonishers".

Note 30: *Thérèse of Lisieux* (1873-97), a Carmelite nun who was drawn to the monastic life as a very young child, is best known for her spiritual autobiography, *The Story of a Soul*, written at the command of her superiors shortly before her death at age twenty-four.

The *Immaculate Conception* is the Roman Catholic dogma that, from the first moment of her conception, the Blessed Virgin Mary was free from all stain of original sin.

The *Novissima Verba* ("newest words") of Thérèse include a record of her spiritual experiences and final conversations and counsels as collected by her fellow nun, Mother Agnes of Jesus, between May 1897 and her death on 30 September 1897.

61: Note 31: "Oriental Dialectic and Its Roots in Faith" is Ch. 7 of the author's book *Logic and Transcendence*, trans. Peter N. Townsend (London: Perennial Books, 1975).

62: Note 34: *Anne Catherine Emmerich* (1774-1824) was an Augustinian nun, stigmatic, and ecstatic visionary, whose revelations included detailed information concerning "The Dolorous Passion of Our Lord Jesus Christ" and "The Life of the Blessed Virgin Mary", both works dictated to Clemens Brentano and first published in 1833 and 1852, respectively.

63: Mansur al-*Hallaj* (858-922), the first Sufi martyr, was flayed and crucified by the exoteric authorities for his mystical pronouncement, *anā 'l-Haqq*, "I am the Truth."

Al-*Niffari* (d. c. 970), one of the earliest Sufi writers, was the author of "The Book of Spiritual Stations" and "The Book of Spiritual Addresses", works well known for the density and obscurity of their style.

Note 36: The Athanasian Creed, an early Christian statement of faith, says of Christ that he is both "God, of the essence of the Father, begotten before the worlds; and man, of the essence of his mother, born in the world: *true God and true man*, of a reasonable soul and human flesh subsisting".

64: *Hanbalite fideism* is the perspective of Ahmad Ibn Hanbal (d. 855), whose school of Islamic law accentuated a literal interpretation of the Koran, anthropomorphic descriptions of God not being interpreted as metaphors, but accepted *bi-lā kayf*, that is, "without asking any questions" or "*without asking how*" they apply to God.

Note 38: *Mutazilites* were members of an early Islamic theological school that insisted on the importance of reason in establishing a middle way between the extremes of unbelief and fideism.

65: Note 38: *Ibn Taimiyah* (1263-1328), a Muslim theologian whose literalistic views brought him into conflict not only with Sufis and philosophers but even his fellow Hanbalites, strongly opposed interpretations of the Koran that took refuge in the idea of *bi-lā kayf* (see editor's note, p. 64 above).

Note 39: For *Ibn Hanbal*, see editor's note, p. 64 above.

66: "*None knoweth its interpretation but God*" (*Sūrah* "The Family of Imran" [3]:7).

The Koran rejects the worship of idols: "Those who believe do battle for the cause of God; and those who disbelieve do battle for the cause of idols" (*Sūrah* "Women" [4]:76 *passim*).

Note 42: *An idol, which the Koran reproaches precisely for being deaf and dumb*: "Then turned he [Abraham] to their idols and said, Will ye not eat? What aileth you that ye speak not? Then he attacked them, striking with his right hand" (*Sūrah* "Those Who Set the Ranks" [37]:91-93 *passim*).

67: A *Cabalist* is a Jewish esoterist and mystic.

Note 43: *Imam Abu al-Hasan al-Shadhili* (1196-1258) was the founder of the Shadhiliyya *tarīqah*, an initiatic lineage from which are derived a number of other Sufi orders, including the Alawiyya and Darqawiyya.

69: "*The soul is all that it knows*" is the doctrine of the ancient Greek philosopher *Aristotle* (384-322 B.C.), for whom "the thinking part of the soul, while impassible, must be capable of receiving the form of an object; that is, it must be potentially identical in character with its object without being the object" (*On the Soul*, 3.4).

For *Veda*, see editor's note for "The Exo-Esoteric Symbiosis", p. 21.

The *Purānas* are Hindu sacred texts recounting events of ancient times and containing cosmologies, genealogies, descriptions of pilgrimages and rituals, and stories about the gods, demons, and ancestors.

70: For *Junayd*, see editor's note for "Ellipsis and Hyperbolism in Arab Rhetoric", p. 5.

"*Shining in the darkness*": "And the light shineth in darkness; and the darkness comprehended it not" (John 1:5).

"Jesus saith unto him, I am the way, the truth, and the life: *no man cometh unto the Father, but by me*" (John 14:6).

The *Mawlawiyah* (or Mevlevi) is a Sufi order popularly known as the "whirling dervishes" and deriving from Jalal al-Din Rumi (see editor's note for "The Exo-Esoteric Symbiosis", p. 34, Note 22), whom his disciples called *mawlānā*, "our master".

The *Shaykh al-Akbar* ("greatest master") is a traditional title of Ibn Arabi.

Gaudapada (sixth-seventh century A.D.), author of a commentary on the *Māndūkya Upanishad*, was the teacher of *Govindapada* (dates unknown), who in turn was the teacher of *Shankaracharya* (see editor's note for "The Exo-Esoteric Symbiosis", p. 19, Note 3).

71: "*Approach not prayer when ye are intoxicated*" (*Sūrah* "Women" [4]:43).

74: "*Against the Spirit*": "All manner of sin and blasphemy shall be forgiven unto men: but the blasphemy against the Holy Spirit shall not be forgiven unto men" (Matt. 12:31; cf. Mark 3:29, Luke 12:10).

Note 49: *Parable of the talents*: "For the kingdom of heaven is as a man travelling into a far country, who called his own servants, and delivered unto them his goods. And unto one he gave five talents, to another two, and to another one; to every man according to his several ability; and straightway took his journey. Then he that had received the five talents went and traded with the same, and made them other five talents. And likewise he that had received two, he also gained other two. But he that had received one went and digged in the earth, and hid his lord's money. After a long time the lord of those servants cometh, and reckoneth with them. And so he that had received five talents came and brought other five talents, saying, Lord, thou deliveredst unto me five talents: behold, I have gained beside them five talents more. His lord said unto him, Well done, thou good and faithful servant: thou hast been faithful over a few things, I will make thee ruler over many things: enter thou into the joy of thy lord. He also that had received two talents came and said, Lord, thou deliveredst unto me two talents: behold, I have gained two other talents beside them. His lord said unto him, Well done, good and faithful servant; thou hast been faithful over a few things, I will make thee ruler over many things: enter thou into the joy of thy lord. Then he which had received the one talent came and said, Lord, I knew thee that thou art an hard man, reaping where thou hast not sown, and gathering where thou hast not strawed: and I was afraid, and went and hid thy talent in the earth: lo, there thou hast that is thine. His lord answered and said unto him, Thou wicked and slothful servant, thou knewest that I reap where I sowed not, and gather where I have not strawed: thou oughtest therefore to have put my money to the exchangers, and then at my coming I should have received mine own with usury. Take therefore the talent from him, and give it unto him which hath ten talents. For unto every one that hath shall be given, and he shall have abundance: but from him that hath not shall be taken away even that which he hath. And cast ye the unprofitable servant into outer darkness: there shall be weeping and gnashing of teeth" (Matt. 25:14-30).

Human Premises of a Religious Dilemma

76: Note 3: For *Ashari*, see editor's note for "The Exo-Esoteric Symbiosis", p. 31.

For *Ghazzali*, see editor's note for "Ellipsis and Hyperbolism in Arab Rhetoric", p. 9.

Louis *Massignon* (1883-1962), a leading French Islamicist and Catholic priest, was best known for his magisterial study of the Sufi saint Mansur al-Hallaj (see editor's note for "Paradoxes of an Esoterism", p. 63), *The Passion of al-Hallaj: Mystic and Martyr of Islam.*

Abd al-Rahman Ibn Muhammad *Ibn Khaldun* (1332-1402), a Muslim historian and philosopher, called attention to the recurrent conflict between nomadic and sedentary peoples in his *Kitāb al-ʿIbar*, "The Book of Examples [from the History of the Arabs and the Berbers]".

78: Note 8: In traditional Western psychology, the *four temperaments* are the sanguine, phlegmatic, choleric, and melancholic.

79: Note 9: For *Omar Suhrawardi*, see editor's note for "Paradoxes of an Esoterism", p. 46, Note 7.

Ramakrishna (1834-86), a *bhakta* of the Hindu goddess Kali, was one of the greatest Hindu saints of modern times.

Shiva, the third god of the Hindu trinity—with Brahmā and Vishnu—is associated with the powers of generation and destruction.

"There is no lustral water like unto Knowledge" is a traditional Hindu teaching often quoted by the author, based in one of its formulations on the *Bhagavad Gītā*, 4:38.

82: "Behold, *the kingdom of God is within you*" (Luke 17:21).

Note 13: *"There are also many other things which Jesus did, the which, if they should be written every one, I suppose that even the world itself could not contain the books that should be written"* (John 21:25).

83: *"And the remembrance of God is greater"* (*Sūrah* "The Spider" [29]:45).

Note 15: Ahmad *al-Alawi* (1869-1934), a famous Algerian Sufi *shaykh*, was the author's spiritual master.

85: Note 18: "*Blessed are the peacemakers, for they shall be called the children of God*" (Matt. 5:9).

Note 19: *Dante* Alighieri (1265-1321), who in his *Divine Comedy* repeatedly condemned the popes for their involvement in politics, argued in his *De Monarchia*, or "Treatise on Monarchy", that the emperor should be the supreme temporal ruler, as in the time of Augustus.

Note 21: *Tiruvalluvar* (c. fifth century A.D.), a Tamil poet, ascetic, and saint, was a weaver by trade and author of a frequently translated work on the aims of human life, regarded by many Hindus as a sacred text.

87: Note 24: For *Ibn Arabi*, see editor's note for "The Exo-Esoteric Symbiosis", p. 24, Note 10.

Note 25: *Shankara* (see editor's note for "The Exo-Esoteric Symbiosis", p. 19, Note 3) set forth the fundamental principles of *Advaita Vedānta* in his *Ātmā-Bodhā*, a short treatise on "Knowledge of the Self".

88: Note 26: *Abdul Hadi*, "Universality in Islam", *The Veil of Isis*, January, 1934.

Tracing the Notion of Philosophy

89: For Muhyi al-Din *Ibn Arabi*, see editor's note for "The Exo-Esoteric Symbiosis", p. 24, Note 10.

Abd al-Karim al-*Jili* (c. 1365-c. 1412) systematized the teachings of Ibn Arabi, notably in his most important work, *The Universal Man*, which is concerned with both cosmological and metaphysical questions.

Pythagoras of Samos (c. 569-c. 475 B.C.), often credited with coining the word "philosophy", was one of the greatest of the pre-Socratic sages of ancient Greece, teaching a doctrine that was at once philosophical, mathematical, astronomical, and musical.

Another of the pre-Socratic philosophers, *Heraclitus* (fl. 500 B.C.), best known for his aphorism that "one cannot step twice into the same river", believed nonetheless that there is a single, underlying, and unchanging order in the cosmos, which he called the *Logos*.

Plato (see editor's note for "The Exo-Esoteric Symbiosis", p. 31) taught that the things of this physical and sensory world are subject to belief or opinion alone, true *knowledge* being reserved for the changeless world of the *Ideas* or Forms.

For *Aristotle* (see editor's note for "Paradoxes of an Esoterism", p. 69), to know a thing is to understand it in view of its *causes*: material, efficient, formal, and final (*Physics*, 194b).

According to *Solomon*, wisdom "is a treasure unto men that never faileth: which they that use become the friends of God, being commended for the gifts that come from learning" (Wisd. of Sol. 7:14).

"*Fear of God*": "The fear of the Lord is the beginning of knowledge" (Prov. 1:7).

90: *Thomas* Aquinas (see editor's note for "Ellipsis and Hyperbolism in Arab Rhetoric", p. 11) followed Aristotle in teaching that "the principle of knowledge is in the senses" (*Summa Theologica*, Part 1, Quest. 84, Art. 6).

Note 2: Hermann *Türck* (1856-1933) was the author of *Der geniale Mensch*, "The Man of Genius" (1903).

91: Abu Hamid Muhammad al-*Ghazzali* (see editor's note for "Ellipsis and Hyperbolism in Arab Rhetoric", p. 9) wrote *Tahāfut al-Falāsifah*, "The Incoherence of the Philosophers", a work accentuating the inadequacies of reason and the necessity of revelation and mystical knowledge.

Ibn al-Arif (1088-1141), an Andalusian Sufi master, was best known for his writings on the science of the virtues.

92: *Plotinus* (see editor's note for "The Exo-Esoteric Symbiosis", p. 31) endeavored to synthesize the teachings of *Plato* and *Aristotle* in his monumental *Enneads*, a collection of discourses compiled by his disciple Porphyry.

93: Note 4: For Ibn Arabi's *Fusūs al-Hikam*, or "Bezels of Wisdom", see editor's note for "The Exo-Esoteric Symbiosis", p. 40.

94: *One cannot testify to great truths except by the Holy Spirit*: "No man can say that Jesus is the Lord, but by the Holy Spirit" (1 Cor. 12:3).

In the cosmology of the pre-Socratic teacher *Empedocles* (c. 492-432 B.C.), the universe is a tapestry woven from four primary elements, fire, air, water, and earth (see the author's footnote 7), which are brought together and dispersed by two fundamental forces, love and strife.

Muhammad ibn Abd Allah *Ibn Masarrah* (883-931), an early Andalusian mystic and Neo-Platonic philosopher, taught that the visible world and its creatures result from the creative descent of the divine Will into primordial matter or "dust" (*al-habā'*).

95: Note 9: *Plato* wrote *in one of his letters*, "There does not exist, nor will there ever exist, any treatise of mine dealing [with "the subject I seriously study"]. For it does not at all admit of verbal expression like other studies, but as a result of continued application to the subject itself and communion therewith, it is brought to birth in the soul on a sudden, as light that is kindled by a leaping spark, and thereafter it nourishes itself" (*Letter VII*, 341d).

Synesius of Cyrene (c. 370-c. 414), who studied in Alexandria under the celebrated pagan Neo-Platonist Hypatia, was the Christian bishop of Ptolemais.

Note 10: The author introduced *The Transcendent Unity of Religions* (first published in French as *De l'unité transcendante des religions* in 1948) by explaining, "This book is founded on a doctrine that is metaphysical in the most precise meaning of the word and cannot by any means be described as philosophical. Such a distinction may appear unwarrantable to those who are accustomed to regarding metaphysics as a branch of philosophy, but the practice of linking the two together in this manner, although it can be traced back to Aristotle and the Scholastic writers who followed him, merely shows that all philosophy suffers from certain limitations which, even in the most favorable instances such as those just quoted, exclude a completely adequate appreciation of metaphysics. In reality the transcendent character of metaphysics makes it independent of any purely human mode of thought. In order to define clearly the difference between the two modes in question, it may be said that philosophy proceeds from reason, which is a purely individual faculty, whereas metaphysics proceeds exclusively from the Intellect" (trans. Peter Townsend [Wheaton, Illinois: The Theosophical Publishing House, 1993], p. xxix).

96: *Pyrrhonic logic*, that is, the logic of Pyrrho (c. 360-c. 270 B.C.), a Greek skeptic, who maintained that all knowledge, including the evidence of the senses, is uncertain.

97: *Koranic story of the initial pact between human souls and God*: "And (remember) when thy Lord brought forth from the Children of Adam, from their reins, their seed, and made them testify of themselves, (saying): Am I not your Lord? They said: Yea, verily. We testify. (That was) lest ye should say at the Day of Resurrection: Lo! of this we were unaware" (*Sūrah* "The Heights" [7]:172).

"Whoso knoweth his soul knoweth his Lord" (*hadīth*).

98: *"Beauty is the splendor of the true"* is a fundamental axiom of the author's perspective, an axiom he attributes to *Plato*.

René *Descartes* (1596-1650) propounded a philosophical method based upon the systematic doubting of everything except one's own self-consciousness, as summed up in the phrase *cogito ergo sum* ("I think; therefore I am").

For *Pyrrho*, see editor's note above, p. 96.

Note 11: *Ananda Coomaraswamy* (1877-1947), for many years curator of Indian art in the Boston Museum of Fine Arts and one of the founding figures of the perennialist school, was the author of numerous books and articles on art, religion, and metaphysics, written from the point of view of the primordial and universal tradition.

"Unto you your religion, and unto me mine" (*Sūrah* "The Disbelievers" [109]:6).

The Quintessential Esoterism of Islam

103: For *al-Khidr*, see editor's note for "The Exo-Esoteric Symbiosis", p. 23, Note 9.

106: Note 3: *Jacob's Ladder*. "And [Jacob] dreamed, and behold a ladder set up on the earth, and the top of it reached to heaven: and behold the angels of God ascending and descending on it" (Gen. 28:12).

107: Note 6: *Ramana Maharshi* (1879-1950), widely regarded as the greatest Hindu sage of the twentieth century, experienced the identity of *Ātmā* and *Brahma* while still in his teens, and the fruit of this experience remained with him as a permanent spiritual station throughout his life.

For *Ramakrishna*, see editor's note for "Human Premises of a Religious Dilemma", p. 79, Note 9.

108: Note 7: For *Ibn Arabi*, see editor's note for "The Exo-Esoteric Symbiosis", p. 24, Note 10.

110: *"Verily, my Mercy precedeth my Wrath"*: *hadīth qudsī.*

111: *"Lead us on the straight path"* (*Sūrah* "The Opening" [1]:5).

117: Note 18: *"Remember God at the Holy Monument"* (*Sūrah* "The Cow" [2]:198).

118: *The Koran enjoins the faithful to remember God*: "Therefore remember Me; I will remember you" (*Sūrah* "The Cow" [2]:152 *passim*).

Note 18: For *Ahmad al-Alawi*, see editor's note for "Human Premises of a Religious Dilemma", p. 83, Note 15.

Note 19: For *Shankaracharya*, see editor's note for "The Exo-Esoteric Symbiosis", p. 19, Note 3.

120: *"God became man that man might become God"*: see editor's note for "Paradoxes of an Esoterism", p. 48.

121: Note 21: Abu al-Qasim al-*Qushayri* (d. 1074), author of a commentary on the Koran, is best known for his *Risālah*, or "Epistle [to the Sufis]", a manual on the spiritual path.

The works of *Ibn al-Arif* (see editor's note for "Tracing the Notion of Philosophy", p. 91) included his *Mahāsin al-Majālis*, or "The Beauties of Spiritual Sessions".

122: *She* [Sayyidatna Maryam] *is mentioned in the* Sūrah *of "The Prophets"*: "And she who was chaste, therefor We breathed into her (something) of Our spirit and made her and her son a token for (all) peoples" (*Sūrah* "The Prophets" [21]:91).

Hypostatic Dimensions of Unity

128: "*Call upon* Allāh *or call upon* al-Rahmān; *to Him belong the most beautiful Names*" (*Sūrah* "The Cave" [18]:110).

Note 3: Origen (c. 185-c. 254), among a number of Church Fathers, speaks of Christ as the "*Wisdom of the Father*".

Note 5: *The Trinity that the Koran attributes to Christianity:* "They surely disbelieve who say: Lo! God is the third of three. . . . The Messiah, son of Mary, was no other than a messenger, messengers (the like of whom) had passed away before him. And his mother was a saintly woman. And they both used to eat (earthly) food" (*Sūrah* "The Table Spread" [5]:73, 75).

The Angelical Salutation—otherwise known as the *Ave Maria* or "Hail Mary"—describes the *Blessed Virgin* Mary as *gratia plena*, "full of grace", and says of her that *Dominus tecum*, "the Lord is with thee" (cf. Luke 1:28, 42).

Bernadette Soubirous (1844-79), to whom were granted several apparitions of the Blessed Virgin, asked "the beautiful Lady" who she was, and in her reply the Virgin applied the Catholic dogma (see editor's note for "Paradoxes of an Esoterism", p. 59, Note 30) to herself as a personal title, saying: "I am the *Immaculate Conception*."

129: "*I was a hidden treasure, and I wanted to be known*": hadīth qudsī.

Appendix

133: Selection 1: "The Book of Keys", No. 163, "*Hikmah, Dhikr, Jamāl*".

Selection 2: "The Book of Keys", No. 639, "The Gordian Knot".

"*Say:* Allāh! *then leave them to their vain discourse*" (*Sūrah* "Cattle" [6]:92).

134: Selection 3: Letter of 28 January 1956.

135: "*The world is false;* Brahma *is true; the soul is not other than* Brahma" is a summation of *Advaita Vedānta* traditionally ascribed to Shankara.

"An invisible and subtle essence is the Spirit of the whole universe. That is Reality. That is Truth. *You are That (Tat tvam asi)*" (*Chāndogya Upanishad*, 7.6).

"The Self was indeed *Brahma* in the beginning. It knew only that '*I am* Brahma' (*aham Brahmāsmi*). Therefore It became all. And whoever among the gods knew It also became That; and the same with sages and men. . . . And to this day whoever in like manner knows '*I am* Brahma' becomes all this universe. Even the gods cannot prevail against him, for he becomes their Self" (*Brihadāranyaka Upanishad*, 1.4.10).

Selection 4: Letter of 19 October 1974.

136: Selection 5: "The Book of Keys", No. 308, "Silence and Word".

The "lotus" (padma) *that contains the "jewel"* (mani): The author is alluding here to the Tibetan Buddhist formulation *Om mani padme hum*, a *mantra* meaning "O Thou Jewel in the Lotus, hail".

"*I am black, but beautiful*" (Song of Sol. 1:5).

Selection 6: Letter of 7 August 1979.

For *Shankara*, see editor's note for "The Exo-Esoteric Symbiosis", p. 19, Note 3.

For the *Veda*, see editor's note for "The Exo-Esoteric Symbiosis", p. 21.

137: Selection 7: "The Book of Keys", No. 1124, "*Faqr* Equals *Fitrah*".

"*O men, ye are the poor in relation to God, and God is the Rich, the universally Praised*" (*Sūrah* "The Angels" ["The Creator"] [35]:15).

138: "Thou shalt *love* the Lord thy God with all thy heart, and with all thy soul, and with all thy mind, and *with all thy strength*: this is the first commandment. And the second is like, namely this, Thou shalt *love thy neighbor as thyself*" (Mark 12:30-31; cf. Luke 10:27).

"Watch and pray, that ye enter not into temptation: *the spirit* indeed *is willing, but the flesh is weak*" (Matt. 26:41).

"*Hate our soul*": "If any man come to me, and hate not his father, and mother, and wife, and children, and brethren, and sisters, yea, and his own life also, he cannot be my disciple" (Luke 14:26).

Selection 8: Letter of 28 January 1956.

139: Selection 9: "The Book of Keys", No. 615, "The Alternative".

140: Selection 10: Letter of 3 February 1955.

Selection 11: "The Book of Keys", No. 1030, "Metaphysics of the Name".

141: "He that loveth not knoweth not God; for *God is love*" (1 John 4:8).

"And God said unto Moses, *I am that I am*: and He said, Thus shalt thou say unto the children of Israel, I AM hath sent me unto you" (Exod. 3:14).

Selection 12: Letter of 15 March 1974.

142: Selection 13: "The Book of Keys", No. 1008, "Islamic Esoterism and Esoteric Islam".

143: Selection 14: "The Book of Keys", No. 18, "The Divine Name as Answer".

Selection 15: Letter of 30 November 1978.

I am sending you here an article: The article is the sixth chapter of the present book, "The Quintessential Esoterism of Islam".

For *Ibn Arabi*, see editor's note for "The Exo-Esoteric Symbiosis", p. 24, Note 10.

144: *Ikhtilāf al-ʿulamāʾ rahmah*: "The divergence [of teaching] among the wise is a blessing" (*hadīth*).

Allāhu karīm: "God is most generous."

I wrote another [article] *on weaknesses found in "average Sufism"*: The article is the second chapter of the present book, "The Exo-Esoteric Symbiosis".

For *Asharite theology,* see editor's note for "The Exo-Esoteric Symbiosis", p. 31.

A third article, on the notion of "philosophy": The article is the fifth chapter of the present book, "Tracing the Notion of Philosophy".

Selection 16: Letter of 5 May 1945.

All the prophets are equal: "We make no distinction between any of His messengers" (*Sūrah* "The Cow" [2]:285).

Some are superior to others: "Lo! thou (Muhammad) art of the number of (Our) messengers . . . some of whom We have caused to excel others, and of whom there are some unto whom God spake, while some of them He exalted (above others) in degree" (*Sūrah* "The Cow" [2]:252-53); "These are they unto whom God showed favor from among the Prophets" (*Sūrah* "Mary" [19]:58).

The commentary by Ibn Arabi is his *Fusūs al-Hikam* (see editor's note for "The Exo-Esoteric Symbiosis", p. 40).

145: Selection 17: Letter of 17 January 1950.

146: The *Shaykh al-Akbar* ("greatest master") is a traditional title of Ibn Arabi.

Selection 18: Letter of 5 May 1945.

147: Selection 19: "The Book of Keys", No. 1155, "*Al-Khalwah*".

For the *Shaykh al-Alawi,* see editor's note for "Human Premises of a Religious Dilemma", p. 83, Note 15.

Spiritus autem ubi vult spirat is Latin for "the wind bloweth where it listeth" (John 3:8).

Selection 20: "The Book of Keys", No. 829, "Closing the Eyes and Pronouncing the Name".

148: Selection 21: Letter of 29 January 1975.

T. and N. were two friends of the author who had terminal illnesses.

Selection 22: "The Book of Keys", No. 1090, "The Absolute Argument".

149: "*Blessed are they that have not seen, and yet have believed*" (John 20:29).

GLOSSARY OF FOREIGN TERMS AND PHRASES

Ab alio (Latin): "from another"; originating from an extrinsic source.

Ad majorem Dei gloriam (Latin): "to the greater glory of God".

Advaita (Sanskrit): "non-dualist" interpretation of the *Vedānta*; Hindu doctrine according to which the seeming multiplicity of things is regarded as the product of ignorance, the only true reality being *Brahma*, the One, the Absolute, the Infinite, which is the unchanging ground of appearance.

Anamnesis (Greek): literally, a "lifting up of the mind"; recollection or remembrance, as in the Platonic doctrine that all knowledge is a recalling of truths latent in the soul.

Ānanda (Sanskrit): "bliss, beatitude, joy"; one of the three essential aspects of *Apara-Brahma*, together with *Sat*, "being", and *Chit*, "consciousness".

Ancilla theologiae (Latin): literally, "handmaiden of theology"; used among the medieval Scholastics in reference to the auxiliary role of philosophy or reason in the exposition of sacred doctrine.

Apara-Brahma (Sanskrit): the "non-supreme" or penultimate *Brahma*, also called *Brahma saguna*; in the author's teaching, the "relative Absolute"; see *Para-Brahma*.

Apocatastasis (Greek): "restitution, restoration"; among certain Christian theologians, including Clement of Alexandria, Origen, and Gregory of Nyssa, the doctrine that all creatures will finally be saved.

A se (Latin): "from itself"; self-originated.

'Asr (Arabic): in Islam, the afternoon prayer.

Ativarnāshrāmin (Sanskrit): in Hinduism, one who has entered a stage of life (*āshrama*) beyond all distinction of caste (*ativarna*); see *sannyāsin*.

Ātmā or *Ātman* (Sanskrit): the real or true "Self", underlying the ego and its manifestations; in the perspective of *Advaita Vedānta*, identical with *Brahma*.

Avatāra (Sanskrit): the earthly "descent", incarnation, or manifestation of God, especially of Vishnu in the Hindu tradition.

Barakah (Arabic): "blessing", grace; in Islam, a spiritual influence or energy emanating originally from God, but often attached to sacred objects and spiritual persons.

Barzakh (Arabic): as used in the Koran, a "barrier" or "separation" between paradise and hell, or this life and the next, or the two seas (fresh and salt); in the interpretation of Sufism, an "isthmus" connecting different planes of reality.

Basmalah (Arabic): traditional Muslim formula of blessing, found at the beginning of all but one of the *sūrah*s of the Koran, consisting of the words *Bismi 'Llāhi 'r-Rahmāni 'r-Rahīm*, "In the Name of God, the Clement (*Rahmān*), the Merciful (*Rahīm*)".

Bhakta (Sanskrit): a follower of the spiritual path of *bhakti*; a person whose relationship with God is based primarily on adoration and love.

Bhakti, bhakti-mārga (Sanskrit): the spiritual "path" (*mārga*) of "love" (*bhakti*) and devotion; see *jnāna* and *karma*.

Bodhisattva (Sanskrit, Pali): literally, "enlightenment-being"; in *Mahāyāna* Buddhism, one who postpones his own final enlightenment and entry into *Nirvāna* in order to aid all other sentient beings in their quest for Buddha-hood.

Brahma or *Brahman* (Sanskrit): the Supreme Reality, the Absolute.

Brāhmana (Sanskrit): a member of the highest of the four Hindu castes; a priest or teacher.

Chit (Sanskrit): "consciousness"; one of the three essential aspects of *Apara-Brahma*, together with *Sat*, "being", and *Ānanda*, "bliss, beatitude, joy".

Cum grano salis (Latin): "with a grain of salt".

Dharma (Sanskrit): in Hinduism, the underlying "law" or "order" of the cosmos as expressed in sacred rites and in actions appropriate to various social relationships and human vocations; in Buddhism, the practice and realization of Truth.

Dhākir (Arabic, plural *dhākirūn*): one who "remembers" God through invoking His Name; see *Dhikr.*

Dhikr (Arabic): "remembrance" of God, based upon the repeated invocation of His Name; central to Sufi practice, where the remembrance is often supported by the single word *Allāh.*

Distinguo (Latin): literally, "I mark or set off, differentiate", used in the dialectic of the medieval scholastics; any philosophical distinction.

Elohim (Hebrew): literally, "mighty ones, gods", but used in Judaism to refer to the one and only God.

Ex cathedra (Latin): literally, "from the throne"; in Roman Catholicism, authoritative teaching issued by the Pope and regarded as infallible.

Ex nihilo (Latin): "out of nothing".

Fanā' (Arabic): "extinction, annihilation, evanescence"; in Sufism, the spiritual station or degree of realization in which all individual attributes and limitations are extinguished in union with God; see *Nirvāna.*

Faqīr (Arabic, plural *fuqarā'*): literally, the "poor one"; in Sufism, a follower of the spiritual Path, whose "indigence" or "poverty" (*faqr*) testifies to complete dependence on God and a desire to be filled by Him alone.

Faqr (Arabic): "indigence, spiritual poverty"; see *faqīr.*

Fātihah (Arabic): the "opening" *sūrah*, or chapter, of the Koran, recited in the daily prayers of all Muslims and consisting of the words: "In the Name of God, the Beneficent, the Merciful. Praise to God, Lord of the Worlds, the Beneficent, the Merciful. Owner of the Day of Judgment, Thee (alone) we worship; Thee (alone) we ask for help. Show us the straight path, the path of those whom Thou hast favored, not (the path) of those who earn Thine anger, nor of those who go astray."

Fitrah (Arabic): in Islam, the natural predisposition of man, as created by God, to act in accordance with the will of Heaven; the original uprightness of humanity (cf. *Sūrah* "The Romans" [30]:30); in Schuon's usage, the primordial norm or "nature of things".

Fuqarā (Arabic): see *faqīr.*

Ghāfil (Arabic): one who is "forgetful" or "negligent" with regard to God and the spiritual life.

Gnosis (Greek): "knowledge"; spiritual insight, principial comprehension, divine wisdom.

Guru (Sanskrit): literally, "weighty", grave, venerable; in Hinduism, a spiritual master; one who gives initiation and instruction in the spiritual path and in whom is embodied the supreme goal of realization or perfection.

Hadīth (Arabic, plural *ahādīth*): "saying, narrative"; an account of the words or deeds of the Prophet Muhammad, transmitted through a traditional chain of known intermediaries.

Hadīth qudsī (Arabic): "divine, holy narrative"; a saying in which God Himself speaks through the mouth of the Prophet.

Hamdalah (Arabic): traditional Muslim formula of praise, a common form consisting of the words *al-hamdu lillāh*, "Praise to God".

Hamsa (Sanskrit): literally, "wild goose, swan", whose purity of color and gracefulness of flight make it a symbol in Hinduism of the renunciate, winging high above the mundane; see *sannyāsin.*

Haqīqah (Arabic): "truth, reality"; in Sufism, esoteric or metaphysical knowledge of the supremely Real; also the essential reality of a thing.

Haqq (Arabic): "the True, the Real"; in Islam, one of the Names of God, who alone is truly real.

Hylikos (Greek): a person in whom the material element (*hyle*) predominates over the spirit and the soul (cf. 1 Thess. 5:23; 1 Cor. 2:14-15).

Hypostasis (Greek, plural *hypostases*): literally, "substance"; the transcendent form of a metaphysical reality, understood to be eternally distinct from all other such forms; in Christian theology, a technical term for one of the three Persons of the Trinity.

Ijtihād (Arabic): literally, "exertion"; in Islamic law, an independent judgment concerning a legal or theological question, arrived at by those possessing the necessary qualifications through a reinterpretation of the Koran or *Sunnah*.

Imām (Arabic): in Islam in general, the "leader" of congregational prayer; in Shiite Islam, Ali or one of his descendents, considered to be the only legitimate successors of the Prophet Muhammad; in Sufism, a spiritual guide.

In divinis (Latin): literally, "in or among divine things"; within the divine Principle; the plural form is used insofar as the Principle comprises both *Para-Brahma*, Beyond-Being or the Absolute, and *Apara-Brahma*, Being or the relative Absolute.

Ithbāt (Arabic): literally, "affirmation"; in Islam, used in reference to the second part of the first *Shahādah*, consisting of the words *illā 'Llāh*, "but [except] God".

Japa-Yoga (Sanskrit): method of "union" or "unification" (*yoga*) based upon the "repetition" (*japa*) of a *mantra* or sacred formula, often containing one of the Names of God.

Jīvan-mukta (Sanskrit): one who is "liberated" while still in this "life"; a person who has attained a state of spiritual perfection or self-realization before death; in contrast to *videha-mukta*, one who is liberated at the moment of death.

Jnāna or *jnāna-mārga* (Sanskrit): the spiritual "path" (*mārga*) of "knowledge" (*jnāna*) and intellection; see *bhakti* and *karma*.

Jnānin (Sanskrit): a follower of the path of *jnāna*; a person whose relationship with God is based primarily on sapiential knowledge or *gnosis*.

Kāfir (Arabic): literally, one who "covers" or "conceals"; in Islam, the person who deliberately covers the truth and is thus in fundamental opposition to God and in danger of damnation.

Karma, *karma-mārga*, *karma-yoga* (Sanskrit): the spiritual "path" (*mārga*) or method of "union" (*yoga*) based upon right "action, work" (*karma*); see *bhakti* and *jnāna*.

Kshatriya (Sanskrit): a member of the second highest of the four Hindu castes; a warrior or prince.

Lā ilāha illā 'Llāh (Arabic): "There is no god but God"; see *Shahādah*.

Logos (Greek): "word, reason"; in Christian theology, the divine, uncreated Word of God (cf. John 1:1); the transcendent Principle of creation and revelation.

Mahabbah (Arabic): "love"; in Sufism, the spiritual way based upon love and devotion, analogous to the Hindu *bhakti mārga*; see *makhāfah* and *ma'rifah*.

Mahāyāna (Sanskrit): "great vehicle"; the form of Buddhism, including such traditions as Zen and *Jōdo-Shinshū*, which regards itself as the fullest or most adequate expression of the Buddha's teaching; distinguished by the idea that *Nirvāna* is not other than *samsāra* truly seen as it is.

Mahāyuga (Sanskrit): in Hindu tradition, a "great age", comprising four lesser ages (*yugas*) or periods of time, namely, *krita-yuga* (the "golden" age of Western tradition), *tretā-yuga* ("silver"), *dvāpara-yuga* ("bronze"), and *kali-yuga* ("iron").

Makhāfah (Arabic): "fear"; in Sufism, the spiritual way based upon the fear of God, analogous to the Hindu *karma mārga*; see *mahabbah* and *ma'rifah*.

Malāmatiyah (Arabic): literally, "the blameworthy"; a Sufi movement that accentuated self-reproach and endeavored to conceal virtue behind a façade of ignoble action.

Mantra (Sanskrit): "instrument of thought"; a word or phrase of divine origin, often including a Name of God, repeated by those initiated into its proper use as a means of salvation or liberation; see *japa-yoga*.

Ma'rifah (Arabic): "knowledge"; in Sufism, the spiritual way based upon knowledge or *gnosis*, analogous to the Hindu *jnāna-mārga*; see *mahabbah* and *makhāfah*.

Mater Dei (Latin): "mother of God"; a title of the Blessed Virgin Mary.

Materia prima (Latin): "first or prime matter"; in Platonic cosmology, the undifferentiated and primordial substance that serves as a "receptacle" for the shaping force of divine Forms or Ideas; universal potentiality.

Māyā (Sanskrit): "artifice, illusion"; in *Advaita Vedānta*, the beguiling concealment of *Brahma* in the form or under the appearance of a lower reality.

Nafy (Arabic): literally, "negation"; in Islam, used in reference to the first part of the first *Shahādah*, consisting of the words *Lā ilāha*, "there is no god".

Nāma (Sanskrit): a "name" of God.

Nembutsu (Japanese): "remembrance or mindfulness of the Buddha", based upon the repeated invocation of his Name; same as *buddhānusmriti* in Sanskrit and *nien-fo* in Chinese.

Nirvāna (Sanskrit): "blowing out, extinction"; in Indian traditions, especially Buddhism, the supremely blissful state of liberation resulting from the extinction of the fires of passion, egoism, and attachment; see *fanā*.

Para-Brahma (Sanskrit): the "supreme" or ultimate *Brahma*, also called *Brahma nirguna*; the Absolute as such; see *apara-Brahma*.

Philosophia (Greek): "love of wisdom, philosophy".

Pneumatikos (Greek): a person in whom the element spirit (*pneuma*) predominates over the soul and the body (cf. 1 Thess. 5:23; 1 Cor. 2:14-15).

Prakriti (Sanskrit): literally, "making first" (see *materia prima*); the fundamental, "feminine" substance or material cause of all things.

Primum mobile (Latin): literally, "the first moveable"; in Ptolemaic astronomy, the outermost sphere of the heavens bearing the fixed stars, moved by God, the "unmoved Mover", and in turn moving the lower spheres.

Pro domo (Latin): literally, "for (one's own) home or house"; serving the interests of a given perspective or for the benefit of a given group.
Psychikos (Greek): a person in whom the element soul (*psyche*) predominates over the spirit and the body (cf. 1 Thess. 5:23; 1 Cor. 2:14-15).

Qalb (Arabic): "heart"; in Sufism, the physical and spiritual center of man and seat of the uncreated Intellect; the place of intersection within the microcosm between the Divine and the human.

Qiyās (Arabic): literally, "measure, analogy"; analogical reasoning in Islamic logic and law; a method for applying the teachings of the Koran and *Sunnah* to issues and circumstances not explicitly dealt with in the traditional sources.

Quod absit (Latin): literally, "which is absent from, opposed to, or inconsistent with"; a phrase commonly used by the medieval Scholastics to call attention to an idea that is absurdly inconsistent with accepted principles.

Rahmah (Arabic): "compassion, mercy"; in Islam, one of the Names of God, who is supreme Compassion, Mercy, and Clemency; see *basmalah*.

Rajas (Sanskrit): in Hinduism, one of the three *guna*s, or qualities, of *Prakriti*, of which all things are woven; the quality of expansiveness, manifest in the material world as force or movement and in the soul as ambition, initiative, and restlessness.

Rak'ah (Arabic, plural *rak'āt*): literally, "bowing"; in Islamic prayer, one complete set of movements and postures comprising an upright stance, bowing at the waist, two prostrations, and sitting on the heels.

Risālat al-Ahadiyah (Arabic): "message of unity".

Sacratum (Latin): "consecrated"; a place or thing that has been consecrated or rendered holy.

Samsāra (Sanskrit): literally, "wandering"; in Hinduism and Buddhism, transmigration or the cycle of birth, death, and rebirth; also the world of apparent flux and change.

Sanātana Dharma (Sanskrit): "eternal law"; in Hinduism, the universal or absolute law or truth underlying specific and relative laws and truths.

Sannyāsin (Sanskrit): "renunciate"; in Hindu tradition, one who has renounced all formal ties to social life; see *ativarnāshrāmin*.

Sat (Sanskrit): "being"; one of the three essential aspects of *Apara-Brahma*, together with *Chit*, "consciousness", and *Ānanda*, "bliss, beatitude, joy".

Sattva (Sanskrit): in Hinduism, one of the three *guna*s, or qualities, of *Prakriti*, of which all things are woven; the quality of luminosity, manifest in the material world as buoyancy or lightness and in the soul as intelligence and virtue.

Sepher Torah (Hebrew): "Book of the Law"; in Judaism, the first five books of the Bible inscribed on scrolls and enshrined in the Ark of the Law in a synagogue.

Shahādah (Arabic): the fundamental "profession" or "testimony" of faith in Islam, consisting of the words *Lā ilāha illā 'Llāh, Muhammadan rasūlu 'Llāh*: "There is no god but God; Muhammad is the messenger of God."

Sharī'ah (Arabic): "path"; in Islam, the proper mode and norm of life, the path or way willed and marked out by God for man's return to Him; Muslim law or exoterism.

Sharīf (Arabic): literally, "noble"; used in Islam as a title of honor for those descended from the Prophet Muhammad.

Shekhinah (Hebrew): literally, "dwelling"; in Judaism, the dwelling-place, and thus presence, of God in the world.

Shūdra (Sanskrit): a member of the lowest of the four Hindu castes; a laborer.

Smriti (Sanskrit): literally, "that which is remembered"; in Hinduism, a category of sacred texts regarded as inspired but having less authority than the *Veda*, which is *shruti*, or "that which is heard".

Sophia (Greek): "wisdom"; in Jewish and Christian tradition, the Wisdom of God, often conceived as feminine (cf. Prov. 8).

Sophia Perennis (Greek): "Perennial Wisdom"; the eternal, non-formal Truth at the heart of all orthodox religious traditions.

Sunnah (Arabic): "custom, way of acting"; in Islam, the norm established by the Prophet Muhammad, including his actions and sayings (see *hadīth*) and serving as a precedent and standard for the behavior of Muslims.

Sūrah (Arabic): one of the one hundred fourteen divisions, or chapters, of the Koran.

Tamas (Sanskrit): in Hinduism, one of the three *guna*s, or qualities, of *Prakriti*, of which all things are woven; the quality of darkness or heaviness, manifest in the material world as inertia or rigidity and in the soul as sloth, stupidity, and vice.

Tarīqah (Arabic): "path"; in exoteric Islam, a virtual synonym for *sharīʿah*, equivalent to the "straight path" mentioned in the *Fātihah*; in Sufism, the mystical path leading from observance of the *sharīʿah* to self-realization in God; also a Sufi brotherhood.

Tasawwuf (Arabic): a term of disputed etymology, though perhaps from *sūf* for "wool", after the garment worn by many early Sufis; traditional Muslim word for Sufism.

Tawhīd (Arabic): "unification, union"; in Islam, the affirmation of divine unity as expressed in the first phrase of the *Shahādah*, "There is no god but God" (*lā ilāha illā 'Llāh*); in Sufism, the doctrine of mystical union; see *fanāʾ*.

ʿUlamāʾ (Arabic, singular *ʿalīm*): "those who know, scholars"; in Islam, those who are learned in matters of law and theology; traditional authorities for all aspects of Muslim life.

Upāya (Sanskrit): "means, expedient, method"; in Buddhist tradition, the adaptation of spiritual teaching to a form suited to the level of one's audience.

Wahdat al-wujūd (Arabic): "oneness of existence, unity of being"; in Sufism, the doctrine that all existence is the manifestation or outward radiation of the one and only true Being; associated above all with Ibn Arabi.

Vacare Deo (Latin): literally, "to be empty for God"; to be at leisure for or available to God; in the Christian monastic and contemplative tradition, to set aside time from work for meditation and prayer.

Vaishya (Sanskrit): a member of the third highest of the four Hindu castes; a craftsman, merchant, or farmer.

Vedānta (Sanskrit): "end or culmination of the Vedas"; one of the major schools of traditional Hindu philosophy, based in part on the *Upanishads*, esoteric treatises found at the conclusion of the Vedic scriptures; see *advaita*.

Virtus (Latin): "manly excellence, strength, valor".

Yā Maryamu ʿalayki 's-salām (Arabic): "O Mary, upon thee be peace."

Yā Rahmān yā Rahīm (Arabic): "O Clement, O Merciful"; see *basmalah*.

Yin-Yang (Chinese): in Chinese tradition, two opposite but complementary forces or qualities, from whose interpenetration the universe and all its diverse forms emerge; *yin* corresponds to the feminine, the yielding, the moon, liquidity; *yang* corresponds to the masculine, the resisting, the sun, solidity.

Yoga (Sanskrit): literally, "yoking, union"; in Indian traditions, any meditative and ascetic technique designed to bring the soul and body into a state of concentration.

Zuhr (Arabic): in Islam, the midday prayer.

INDEX

For a glossary of all key foreign words used in books published by
World Wisdom, including metaphysical terms in English, consult:
www.DictionaryofSpiritualTerms.org.
This on-line Dictionary of Spiritual Terms provides extensive
definitions, examples, and related terms in other languages.

BIOGRAPHICAL NOTES

FRITHJOF SCHUON

Born in Basle, Switzerland in 1907, Frithjof Schuon was the twentieth century's preeminent spokesman for the perennialist school of comparative religious thought.

The leitmotif of Schuon's work was foreshadowed in an encounter during his youth with a marabout who had accompanied some members of his Senegalese village to Basle for the purpose of demonstrating their African culture. When Schuon talked with him, the venerable old man drew a circle with radii on the ground and explained: "God is the center; all paths lead to Him." Until his later years Schuon traveled widely, from India and the Middle East to America, experiencing traditional cultures and establishing lifelong friendships with Hindu, Buddhist, Christian, Muslim, and American Indian spiritual leaders.

A philosopher in the tradition of Plato, Shankara, and Eckhart, Schuon was a gifted artist and poet as well as the author of over twenty books on religion, metaphysics, sacred art, and the spiritual path. Describing his first book, *The Transcendent Unity of Religions*, T. S. Eliot wrote, "I have met with no more impressive work in the comparative study of Oriental and Occidental religion", and world-renowned religion scholar Huston Smith said of Schuon, "The man is a living wonder; intellectually apropos religion, equally in depth and breadth, the paragon of our time". Schuon's books have been translated into over a dozen languages and are respected by academic and religious authorities alike.

More than a scholar and writer, Schuon was a spiritual guide for seekers from a wide variety of religions and backgrounds throughout the world. He died in 1998.

JAMES S. CUTSINGER (Ph.D., Harvard) is Professor of Theology and Religious Thought at the University of South Carolina.

A widely recognized writer on the *sophia perennis* and the perennialist school, Professor Cutsinger is also an authority on the theology and spirituality of the Christian East. His publications include *Advice to the Serious Seeker: Meditations on the Teaching of Frithjof Schuon, Not of This World: A Treasury of Christian Mysticism, Paths to the Heart: Sufism and the Christian East, The Fullness of God: Frithjof Schuon on Christianity,* and *Prayer Fashions Man: Frithjof Schuon on the Spiritual Life.*

SEYYED HOSSEIN NASR is University Professor of Islamic Studies at the George Washington University. The author of over fifty books and five hundred articles, he is one of the world's most respected writers and speakers on Islam, its arts and sciences, and its traditional mystical path, Sufism. His publications include *Sufi Essays, Knowledge and the Sacred, Religion and the Order of Nature, A Young Muslim's Guide to the Modern World, The Heart of Islam: Enduring Values for Humanity,* and *Islam: Religion, History, and Civilization.* A volume in the prestigious *Library of Living Philosophers* series has been dedicated to his thought. World Wisdom will be publishing *The Essential Seyyed Hossein Nasr* in 2007.